Three Days to Pearl

THREE DAYS

Peter J. Shepherd

TO PEARL

Incredible Encounter on the Eve of War

Naval Institute Press
Annapolis, Maryland

Naval Institute Press
291 Wood Road
Annapolis, MD 21402

Library of Congress Cataloging-in-Publication Data
Shepherd, Peter J., 1923-
    Three days to Pearl : incredible encounter on the eve of war / Peter J. Shepherd.
        p. cm.
    Includes bibliographical references and index.
    ISBN 1-55750-815-1 (alk. paper)
    1. Shepherd, Peter J., 1923- 2. World War, 1939-1945—Personal narratives, British. 3. Great Britain. Royal Air Force—Biography. 4. Pearl Harbor (Hawaii), Attack on, 1941. I. Title.

D811 .S4698 2000
940.54'4941'092—dc21
[B]

                                                                00-062467

Printed in the United States of America on acid-free paper ∞
07 06 05 04 03 02 01   9 8 7 6 5 4 3 2

I dedicate this book to the thirty or so unsuspecting souls, RAF personnel and civilians, whose lives were either abruptly extinguished or permanently blighted when, in a sneak air attack at dawn on 8 December 1941, Japanese bombs rained down on the RAF airfield at Sungei Patani in northern Malaya prior to Japan making any declaration of war against Great Britain.

Contents

Preface

For good reasons this book comes off the publisher's press almost sixty years after the events disclosed herein took place. At that time Great Britain and the British Commonwealth were already into the third year of World War II against Germany and Italy while the United States of America was—understandably—still trying hard to keep out of it. Germany had already marched into and occupied northern France and in June 1941 had turned its military machine against the Soviet Union.

Certain events revealed in this book were of the utmost significance and could have been heeded and acted upon to determine the course of World War II. Regrettably, this did not happen. It is around these hitherto-undisclosed events that this book has been written. Although totally unplanned and fortuitous, these most important happenings may well have gone down in history as being of immense significance.

The reader will ask, therefore, why events of such potential consequence have remained under wraps for so long. Simply, had the events come to light at a much earlier date the possibility of serious consequences would have been very real indeed and may have adversely and seriously affected certain political and military figures. Even more seriously, they may have stirred up enduring ill will between Great Britain and the United States of America. Furthermore, the consequences for me, the sole person able to relate the crucial events in their entirety, may not have proved to my advantage. Earlier disclosure could only have produced strife, possibly on a rather grand scale with no likelihood of benefit to anyone.

Wherein, then, does the difference now lie? I believe that the passage of time, well over half a century, has redefined official priorities, fogged memories, clouded judgments, mellowed views, and dulled interests. Many of those involved in the terrible events arising directly from Japan's attack on Pearl Harbor are no longer with us. However, still living are many individuals who were injured and permanently disabled in the attack, or who suffered in consequent events, whose enduring bitter memories may be stirred by the facts disclosed in this book. Those who were maimed or otherwise seriously injured at Pearl Harbor on 7 December 1941 will have been over the long years at a loss to comprehend why the manifestly unsuspecting defense authorities of the United States allowed Japan's huge task force to deliver its surprise attack after having steamed over 3,500 miles from Japan without detection. There are also those with considerable and specialized knowledge concerning the Pearl Harbor outrage and for those this book throws a startling new light on the matter, a light that will justify that which many have long said: "The full and true facts about Pearl Harbor will never be known." The author understands and sympathizes with the feelings of Pearl Harbor veterans for reasons made clear in the following pages.

To some, the facts disclosed herein will prove distinctly unpalatable, but I make no apology. Facts are facts, unchangeable and irrevocable, and, in almost all cases, are better faced than locked away for all time. This book imparts a pungent and sickening flavor to the Pearl Harbor affair that amounted to a near mortal blow to the U.S. Pacific Fleet—a staggering catastrophe that has proved to be a very special, indelible, poignantly evocative, and abiding landmark in the histories of the United States and World War II.

This introduction will serve to open the factual account that follows, an account that is sure, in varying degrees, to invoke astonishment, anger, and sadness. It begins in that part of 1941 Malaya now known as West Malaysia.

Three Days to Pearl

Prologue

Oahu, Pacific Hawaiian Islands, 7:45 A.M., Sunday, 7 December 1941 (Hawaii time)

In a bright early morning sky formations of rasping and roaring warplanes approached the island of Oahu at around ten thousand feet. A few miles out they took up meticulously rehearsed attacking positions; then, in exultation at the prospect of the destruction and carnage they were about to rain down on the barely awake and unsuspecting island, and in the realization that they had achieved total surprise, they set about their evil task. An hour later another wave of planes arrived to continue the murderous onslaught. By mid-morning it was all over.

In this inhuman criminal attack by Japan on the U.S. Naval Base at Pearl Harbor, Oahu, U.S. losses were horrendous: 2,403 killed, 1,178 wounded; eight battleships, three cruisers, three destroyers, all sunk, capsized, or badly damaged; 164 airplanes destroyed and many buildings and installations laid waste.

Thus it was that, without any declaration of war, ultimatum, or warning, and wholly without provocation or justification, Japan struck against the United States of America, thereby hurling that stunned neutral nation into the cauldron of horrors that was World War II.

Malaya 1941

The Malayan Peninsula runs almost directly north to south. It is some four hundred miles in length and around two hundred miles wide at the north and sixty miles at the south. At its southern extremity lies the island of Singapore, virtually on the equator. It is washed by the Straits of Malacca on its west and by the South China Sea on its east. Malaya (Malaysia, as it is now known) experiences a tropical climate with high temperatures and humidity throughout the year. Violent, prolonged thunderstorms occur almost daily in the two monsoon seasons. Malaya's terrain consists for the most part of mountainous primeval jungle, impenetrable swamps, rice (paddy) fields, and oil palm and rubber plantations.

By 1941 Malaya, including Singapore, had been part of the British empire for over one hundred years. It included a number of states that were, generally speaking, administered by Malay sultans under the guidance and direction of British advisors and residents. Though more or less independent of each other, they were, as a whole but in a confusingly complicated and cumbrous way, totally and effectively governed by the British.

The population of Malaya largely comprised the indigenous Malays, and together with some Chinese and Indians, amounted to around five million in total. Malaya was an extremely valuable asset to the British, owing to the fact that it produced and exported considerable amounts of rubber and tin. These two commodities contributed in a major way to the world's requirement for both. Commercially Malaya was prosperous. Generally speaking, the mixed races seemingly lived and worked in reasonable harmony in a happy and loyal way. Most Europeans who lived and worked in Malaya found life very pleasant, despite the decidedly enervating atmospheric conditions. Many compensations went with the colonial lifestyle, and these were enjoyed to the full by those who adapted and somehow managed to keep physically and mentally fit, notwithstanding the health hazards that abounded.

In view of Malaya's commercial importance and strategic position—it being a natural, desirable, and busy port of call for merchant shipping—the British had prudently created a sizable naval base on the north of Singapore Island to provide a secure and comprehensive facility for the handling and repair of naval vessels whose role it would be, if necessary, to deter and attend to any threat of hostile action from the surrounding seas. Additionally, to fight off any seaborne attack, a considerable number of fixed heavy-caliber naval guns had been sited at appropriate points to the south, west, and east of the island, and also at strategic positions close by on the mainland. A number of British defense officials believed that a military attack on Singapore could not be carried out by forces moving south down the peninsula owing to terrain and climatic difficulties. In addition, the sole road and single-line railway link between Singapore and Siam, both passing through the entire length of Malaya on its west side, could readily be made impassable to troops and support transport.

Some, however, thought differently. British RAF people argued that only complete mastery of the air could ensure the repulsion of any enemy attempting to advance from north to south throughout the length of the peninsula. They believed that the British could not possibly secure this crucial advantage with the meager quantity and type of aircraft presently at their disposal in Malaya. The RAF had pleaded for more airfields, aircraft, and personnel. To an extent these urgent requests had been met, several new airfields having been constructed and aircraft and personnel allocated. But the quantities and types of aircraft supplied were pitifully inadequate to do the job envisaged should it become necessary. Great Britain was already fighting for its life in Europe and North Africa and did not have the aircraft and men to send to the Far East where, at the moment, no war was being fought. Furthermore, the new airfields were hopelessly positioned in that they had been sited where their defense would be well nigh impossible. In effect they were little more than takeoff and landing strips for out-of-date aircraft where, with difficulty, a certain amount of maintenance work could be carried out.

During 1941 Japan continued its long-running military aggression against China and talked openly of its desire for the creation of a "Greater East Asia Co-Prosperity Sphere," with Japan as the driving influence and controlling member. Furthermore, Japan's imperialistic intentions and dreams of empire in the Far East had been made plain by the movement of Japanese troops and warplanes into Vichy French Indo-China with the consent of the Vichy French government under pressure from Germany and threats of direct military action by Japan. It seemed hardly likely, however, that Japan would go to war in an attempt to achieve total domination of East Asian countries. That would mean having to fight the British and also the Dutch who were the colonial masters of Java, Sumatra, and other territories collectively known as the Netherlands East Indies. It would also mean entertaining the very considerable risk of receiving swift and crushing retribution from the United States, for that country had an important interest in East Asia, namely the Philippines, and would not be overly delighted to have the Japanese seize territories by force from friendly nations in the general neighborhood.

But a grave crisis had developed for Japan. The Dutch, colonial masters of the oil-producing Java and Sumatra, had refused to continue to supply oil to Japan. Producing virtually no oil in its own islands, Japan needed supplies to support its domestic needs, continue its aggression in China, and build oil stockpiles once its military operations turned south to the East Indies region. Japan's warlike posturing and dark, ill-disguised pronouncements, its activities in China, and its entry into French Indo-China made the Dutch anxious; to continue to meet Japan's demand for oil would, therefore, be somewhat akin to supplying Japan with arms. The United States, also discomfited by Japan's creeping hostile activities and the fact that Japan was run by its military machine, also placed an embargo on the export of oil and other vital commodities to Japan. By late 1941 Japan had reserves of oil sufficient for barely three years of peace. Plainly something had to be done if Japan wished to continue its aggressive and imperialistic policies. Without oil Japan would have no option but to retreat back to its islands and be satisfied with an infinitely more humble and peaceable existence so that oil-exporting nations might, on sound commercial grounds, once more agree to meet its domestic oil requirements. Gone, then, would be Japan's cherished dreams of ultimately dominating Southeast Asia, Australia, New Zealand, and much of the southwest Pacific. But Japan was emboldened by the fact that Great Britain's attention was fully taken up by the war in the west. Japan was also a signatory to the so-called Tripartite Pact, whereby it recognized the leadership of Germany and Italy in the establishment of a new order in Europe, and those two powers in turn recognized Japan's leadership in the establishment of a new order in the Far East.

The three powers agreed to assist one another by political, economic, and military means should one of them be attacked by any power not involved either in the European war or in China. Even so, Japan had to face the stark and chilling fact that, if it were to continue with its policy of domination, chances were that the considerable wrath of the United States would be invoked, something that would mean, almost certainly, going to war against that powerful and hugely resourceful nation. If Japan were to be vanquished in such a war it would spell the end—total humiliation and ruin from which it would be well nigh impossible ever to recover. This presented Japan with a huge decision to make—whether to retreat humbly or, with the object of securing power and glory, fight and, if necessary, die. There was, however, just a chance that the United States might be persuaded, for the sake of peace, to close a blind eye to Japan occupying Java and Sumatra and possibly Malaya and Borneo. Japan no doubt considered this possibility but could have entertained little hope of such an arrangement ever being reached. The Japanese political and military minds were in a quandary. Would quiet reason prevail? Or would the fatal decision be made by the grim, fatalistic, and war-loving minds of Japan's warlords, who had ample arms and men at their disposal and who dreamed of achieving an even higher state of everlasting glory for their Divine Emperor—the so-called Prince of Enlightened Peace.

This, then, was the position confronting Malaya in the closing months of 1941. Would Japan move against the British? Would it attack the Netherlands East Indies? If it were to attack Malaya, would it be from the sea with Singapore as the first and principal objective? Would the attack be from the north, possibly through Siam? How real were these dangers and what should be done to deal with them?

Much discussion and deliberation went on among Malaya's defense chiefs. Much communicating went on between Malaya and London. The scourge of vacillation, bewilderment, and confusion became entrenched and, eventually, was overtaken by a curious kind of paralysis of purpose. Would anything happen? If so, what and where? How and when? Small wonder that the military lower orders, including quite senior officers, were told virtually nothing. The British administrators, tin-mine managers, rubber planters, banking executives, directors of commerce, and other more or less privileged individuals went on enjoying their sunny, comfortable ways of life and, on the whole, wasted little time pondering which way Japan would move and, subconsciously at least, continued to reject outright the notion that Malaya might be attacked by Japan. These people, their heads in the unique and cozy sand of colonial-style life, were too busy going about their normal business in a country where business was good, mostly pleasant, and rewarding.

Meanwhile, the United States was urgently trying to negotiate an agreement with Japan whereby, in effect, if Japan withdrew its troops from China and Vichy French Indo-China, the United States would lift its oil embargo. But Japan was dragging out the negotiations and—it was becoming clearer—was unwilling to agree to any forthright, unambiguous, and reasonable settlement. Nevertheless, Japanese political negotiators remained in Washington and continued to present themselves, bearing their very latest outrageous and unacceptable proposals with well-schooled dignity, gravity, and amicable inscrutability.

Throughout Singapore and Malaya desultory civilian administrative authorities as well as the military were preparing for possible war with Japan. Some progress had been made by way of local defense measures, such as air-raid precaution arrangements in Singapore and in the very few towns of any size on the peninsula. Food-storage arrangements to cope with a fairly prolonged siege of Singapore were also implemented. Little could be done about the provision of underground air-raid shelters on account of the island's high water level. Blackout arrangements were made, but this was to be effected by simply switching off the electricity to whole areas of the town, it being deemed impractical to insist on the use of blackout blinds and shutters in view of the high nighttime air temperature and humidity. These kinds of activity were, of course, quite new to the administrators and, in any case, it still seemed incredible and wholly unimaginable that anyone, even Japan, would venture to attack Singapore and Malaya. Things had been stable here for a very long time with Great Britain as powerful protector and controller. It was quite unthinkable, indeed almost laughable, to imagine the British being ousted by Japan who, to the average uninformed Briton, had done little for decades but grub around in China, bombing and shelling and skirmishing and generally behaving like inhuman savages, manufacturing inferior imitations of British products, its strange people bowing low to one another and gazing vacantly at the world through cheap spectacles with blank expressions remarkably suggestive of innocent surprise. This perception of Japan and the Japanese people bore little relation to reality and resulted from ignorance of the facts. Those who were in a position to know better did little to enlighten others less informed.

As for British military activity, troop reinforcements, including army and RAF personnel, continued to arrive throughout 1941. Very late in the year these forces were rightly brought to a so-called state of readiness. The only problem was that, within these forces and especially among the junior officers and lower ranks, hardly anyone understood what this "state of readiness" was all about, for the simple reason that they had not been adequately informed. The RAF continued as before, that is, doing precious little.

At some airfields a lot of time was spent in making mock airplanes out of bits of wood and canvas. These sham constructions were then positioned at various points on airfields with the object of deceiving chance or deliberate observers, whether from ground or air, into overestimating aircraft strengths. At least such was the general view, but those who put the sham constructions together were never fully enlightened on this point. This ploy went ahead notwithstanding the common knowledge that Singapore and Malaya both had a sizable Japanese population by way of business owners and their fellow-countrymen employees. Such businesses ranged from iron mine and shipping lines to barbershops and photography studios. In addition, it is beyond doubt that a multitude of indigenous individuals existed, each of whom would have gladly imparted information concerning such things as pretense aircraft to grateful paymasters themselves in the pay of Japan. Such real airplanes as there were spent little time in the air because there was no reason for them to do so apart from a little occasional practice flying and flight testing subsequent to maintenance work having been carried out. Ground staff, that is, the engine and airframe fitters, the armorers,

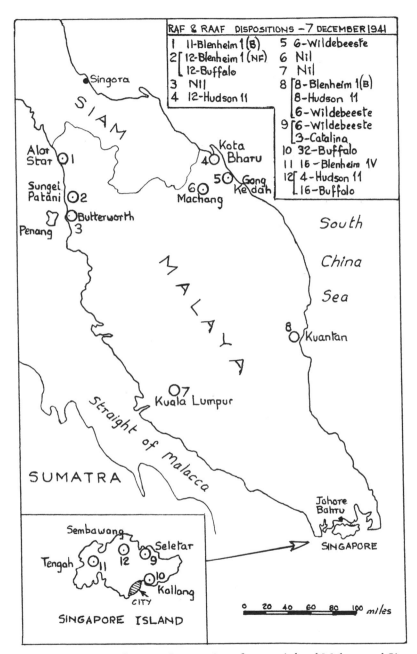

RAF & RAAF DISPOSITIONS – 7 DECEMBER 1941

1	11-Blenheim 1 (B)	5	6-Wildebeeste
2	12-Blenheim 1 (NF)	6	Nil
	12-Buffalo	7	Nil
3	Nil	8	8-Blenheim 1 (B)
4	12-Hudson 11		8-Hudson 11
			6-Wildebeeste
		9	6-Wildebeeste
			3-Catalina
		10	32-Buffalo
		11	16-Blenheim 1V
		12	4-Hudson 11
			16-Buffalo

Map 1. Disposition of RAF and RAAF aircraft on mainland Malaya and Singapore Island, 7 December 1941.

instrument fitters, and others, spent much of their time sitting around chatting, swimming, or sweating it out in the Navy, Army and Air Force Institute (NAAFI) canteen or on their beds. An insignificant amount of work was required to be done on aircraft after midday as the necessity for such rarely arose, and it had long been the practice for technical ground staff to knock off work for the day at lunchtime.

Life was easy, albeit at times considerably uncomfortable due to the tiring climate. Curiously enough, boredom was seldom a problem among the general rank and file, nor was there much complaining, even though pay in the lower ranks amounted to barely more than the cost of just one frugal night out every fortnight in Singapore or, if stationed in Malaya, some inferior place of entertainment.

The army and RAF higher-ups were kept busy devising and submitting defense plans—and, more often than not, having them rejected. Unlike the Japanese, whose overall military strategy was built on full liaison and cooperation between the army and navy, both of which had their own air forces, British defense strategy for Singapore and Malaya was critically hampered by the fact that the army, navy, and RAF largely worked independently, each having to seek and obtain approval from its top chiefs in London before daring to depart from already agreed procedure. This situation was in itself a recipe for major difficulty and dissension, especially in the face of the well-oiled and highly disciplined military machine Japan had painstakingly developed and currently had at its disposal. However, a plan was at last proposed that received the approval of the War Office in London. It related to the deployment of land troops designed to forestall a Japanese attack on northern Malaya through Siam, but which would mean British troops moving into Siamese territory without first obtaining the agreement of the Siamese authorities. The plan was code-named Matador but it was never implemented because, in the event, time was allowed to trickle out.[1] As things turned out, it became manifest that Matador would have failed anyway.

Then December arrived—December 1941, a landmark in time destined to be remembered and regretted by millions far into the future. No one could have believed or even dreamed that for Singapore and Malaya just a few short days of civilized normality remained, their long-established and pleasant colonial way of life almost at an end. For them, appallingly and sadly, things were about to change forever.

2 Arrival in the Far East

My ship, *Capetown Castle,* arrived in the Far East in early August 1941, accompanied by *Empress of Japan.* We had departed from war-torn Britain over nine weeks earlier and, having plowed through the seas in convoy with many other ships via Freetown, Capetown, Bombay, and Colombo, we finally reached Singapore, where it was still virtually peacetime.

Capetown Castle, a passenger ship of the Union Castle Line now being used as a troopship, had carried, on this occasion, RAF personnel. *Empress of Japan,* a somewhat larger, three-funneled vessel, carried army troops. The only two of the original convoy to proceed all the way to the Far East, the ships had sailed together since leaving Colombo a few days earlier. The last stretch of our journey from the United Kingdom had been uneventful and pleasant. As we throbbed ever eastwards through mostly calm, brightly sunlit seas, I at last experienced a sense of having left the war, its perils, and its many depressing restrictions, far behind.

On Singapore Island many of us were initially accommodated at a hutted transit camp tucked away in a rubber plantation. Personnel stayed at this camp until such time as they were post-ed to a more or less established station either on Singapore Island or on main-land Malaya. I remained at the transit camp for about six weeks and spent the mornings at nearby RAF Seletar, one of the oldest of the Far East stations, on the northern coast of the island and around four miles from the naval base. The station had a dual function. First, it was a maintenance unit, No. 151, where the inspection and overhaul of most types of aircraft then in serv-ice in the Far East were carried out. Second, it was the home base for two squadrons. No. 100 Squadron comprised six Wildebeest single-engine tor-pedo bombers while No. 205 Squadron boasted four Short Singapore four-engined flying boats. Shortly after my arrival at the transit camp these lat-ter obsolete machines were replaced by three hugely superior Consolidated Catalinas. The latter had been flown from the United States via Hawaii, Midway Island, and Manila by civilian crews. During the weeks of my stay at the transit camp I was assigned to No. 205 Squadron.

My RAF apprenticeship should have lasted three years, my having entered into a legally binding contract to this effect. However, when Great Britain declared war on Germany in September 1939 this contract was dishonored by the Air Ministry on the exceedingly dubious grounds that, under the pro-vision of the Emergency Powers Act (Defence) of 1939, the military author-ities were, in effect, empowered to change the terms and conditions of serving members of the armed forces at will. The fact that I was not yet a serving member of the RAF but was only someone training to *become* a serv-ing member when I reached the age of eighteen seemed to have been disre-garded. My service, as borne out by contract and records, actually com-menced some seven months after my apprenticeship had been prematurely terminated by flagrant breach of contract. Nevertheless, it had been decid-ed that my apprenticeship should be shortened from three years to two. I left the apprentice school at RAF Halton after only twenty months, still only sev-enteen years of age. I was then deemed to be a fully skilled aero-engine fitter capable of working, with minimum supervision, on any aero-engine then in use by the RAF. A few months later I was posted to the Far East where, for some weeks, I spent my time working on the twin Wright Cyclone engines of the Catalinas.

There was no talk of the war catching up with us in the Far East, at any rate as far as air raids and actual fighting were concerned. While it was known that Japan continued to look at Singapore and Malaya with covetous eyes, no one imagined that such ambitious longing would induce the Japanese to actually launch an attack on these British-controlled territories. No one in authority gave us any indication that there existed any potential and credible attacker who might be harboring the earnest intention to invade and throw the British out. Such newspapers as there were, notably the *Straits Times,* gave a good deal of space to articles concerning Japan's ever-lasting bickering and increasingly futile commercial negotiations with the Netherlands East Indies but never seemed to go as far as to warn that a Japanese attack on Singapore and Malaya should be considered a dire and real enough probability. I must admit to having given the matter much more than just the odd fleeting thought. I failed to understand why it was that life was going on exactly as usual, even though troops kept on arriving at the docks, dummy airplanes continued to be built, and so much appeared in the newspapers about the uneasy situation in relation to Japan. In retrospect, it was as though one was going through the motions of preparing for a cata-clysmic earthquake while remaining totally convinced that one would never happen. Just like the dummy airplanes, all the preparations and the half-hearted gossip seemed to be nothing but pretense. I well remember ponder-ing the prospect of Japanese troops suddenly overrunning Singapore and Malaya and, if such came about, what life would then be like. But insofar as no one else seemed to entertain the same worries, as far as I knew anyway, I simply accepted that everything was under control. After all, I was only eighteen.

Life in Singapore was, I strongly felt, rather like being back at the turn of the century, there being a distinctly old-fashioned colonial atmosphere about the place, as though things were some forty years behind the times. In a curi-ous way I began to develop a close affinity with this part of the world. As the weeks slipped by, this fascination grew.

One afternoon, when reading a magazine in one of the services clubs in Singapore town, I came across an article concerning Japan's aspirations for the commercial exploitation of resources in the Far East and the southwest Pacific. It made the point, quite unmistakably, that Japan saw itself as the future savior and grand developer of the many territories in the Eastern Hemisphere. As a starting point for this, Japan proposed that an arrange-ment of mutual cooperation should be created through which all major commercial and economic issues affecting the whole Far Eastern area would be discussed, agreed, and enforced for the benefit of all parties. Thus

Japan's conception of a Greater East Asia Co-Prosperity Sphere was established, but only in the minds of the Japanese.[1] It appeared that Japan, although ever ready to extol the potential virtues of such an organization, always failed to reply to the question as to which territories would be included. It was, of course, widely suspected that the actual territorial limits would be ever-expanding to match Japan's well-recognized imperialistic attitude and ambitions. This, together with the also well-known fact that Japan never hesitated to use sheer brute force when necessary to back up its inscrutable, dignified, yet usually wholly duplicitous negotiating acts, made other potential parties to the arrangement back off without interest. I wondered what all this was about because I had always understood that Japan had been on the side of Great Britain during the First World War. I had also been told that the Japanese were polite, humble, chivalrous, and honorable people who revered their ancestors, worshipped their emperor, and loved simple, exquisite things such as cherry blossoms and chrysanthemums. All this seemed, to me, to make them pretty reputable and perhaps even likable. "How come," I mused, "that Japan considered herself powerful enough and felt the need to start pushing the whole of East Asia around?" I just didn't get it.

Life in Singapore continued as it had for decades, but while I sensed a growing tension I was too immature to let it worry me unduly. From time to time I discussed my feelings with a few colleagues, but I was always met with a wall of disinterest and wariness. "What are you so anxious about?" and "Just relax and let the big chiefs do the worrying" were the kind of replies I got. Sometimes I raised the matter of the dummy airplanes. "Oh, that's just to kid people we've got more planes than we really have" was the standard reply, as if I hadn't known already. What, in fact, I wanted to know were answers to questions like, "Is it considered a matter of certainty that we shall be attacked by Japan?" "If so, when is this likely to happen?" "Are the defense forces fully prepared and are they deemed capable of repulsing an invasion?"

Toward the middle of September 1941 I began to feel that I was wasting my time in the Far East. One day it was announced that applications for pilot training were being invited. I seized this opportunity immediately, thinking that if I were to become a pilot I would stand a fair chance of becoming a commissioned officer, especially as I had been through RAF Halton, albeit rushed through with (as it eventually emerged) unlawful haste. I certainly didn't relish the thought of possibly having to stay in the Far East for five years in the position I was now in. In peacetime a posting to Singapore meant staying there for five years.

A week or so later I took the pilot medical examination, completed a written examination paper, and in a few days was informed that I had been put forward as being suitable for pilot training.

The days passed and I became increasingly excited at the prospect of being shipped away to a flying school, but three weeks later a number of us were told that we were to be posted to No. 27 Squadron at a place called Sungei Patani in northern Malaya, some four hundred miles away.

On or about 20 September 1941 the movement order for the transfer of twelve or so of us came through. We were ordered to pack our gear and be ready for transportation to Singapore railway station at 6:00 P.M. that evening. I spent the afternoon saying goodbye to a number of colleagues with whom I had traveled on *Capetown Castle* from the United Kingdom. After an early evening meal we boarded a lorry and were taken through Singapore town to the railway station. We arrived at 7:00 P.M. and were later told that our train would depart at midnight. We hung around the station until half past midnight and were then taken back to the transit camp that, of course, we had left over six hours earlier. No explanation for this pathetic fiasco was ever forthcoming. The following night, once again, we were carted off to the

The author at RAF Seletar, Singapore Island (September 1941), three months before Japan struck.

railway station at 6:00 P.M. At midnight we were allowed to enter the station proper to board our train, but it was not until an hour later that it set out on its journey to the north.

It was 8:00 A.M. before we pulled into Kuala Lumpur, having averaged less than thirty MPH throughout the night. Here we changed trains and at 10:00 A.M. set forth again behind a clapped-out steam locomotive that looked and sounded as though it had been in service since the turn of the century. The two quaint saloon coaches were each strongly reminiscent of a single-decker Victorian tramcar, and they furnished a matching level of comfort.

The day wore on and the terrain became substantially waterlogged, with paddy fields covering virtually the entire landscape, relieved here and there by rubber plantations. Vivid and impressive multicolored lightning, together with ear-splitting thunder, kept us company in the afternoon, but as darkness fell, the weary train crept into the miniature town of Sungei Patani. It had taken around eighteen hours for us to travel a little over four hundred miles, most of the time in considerable discomfort.

Once again, but now soaked, we were pushed into the back of a lorry and taken a mile or so to the RAF camp. The hitherto-deafening pyrotechnics of the prolonged thunderstorm had moved westward, out over the sea, by the time the lorry crawled through the camp's main gate. Inside, we traveled an additional quarter of a mile through utter darkness before fetching up outside a wooden hut that turned out to be the airmen's mess. The lorry drove off into the night, leaving us standing in inky blackness with the now-abating rain pattering dismally on indiscernible corrugated iron roofs and on the foliage of, I sensed, a thousand surrounding trees. There was no other sound except for the fading noise of the receding lorry, nor was there any movement around us. This, then, was our introduction to RAF Sungei Patani, a place of strange melancholy moods, something I was to quickly learn and be singularly affected by during the weeks that followed.

I was shown to a hut in a rubber plantation. I well remember the infinite darkness, the wetness and the heat, the silence and the feeling of isolation. A couple of hours later I got on to my bed, pulled the mosquito net down, tucked its bottom edge under the meager mattress, and lay down. The room had only two beds, the occupant of the other bed either asleep or unconscious; at any rate, he wasn't moving or making any noise and he had not bothered to lower his mosquito net. I considered doing that for him, but fatigue overcame my kindly thought. Then I had to get out again to switch off the light—a low-wattage bare bulb with a captive host of dancing and swirling insects. The rain continued now at something like a steady, almost comforting heavy drizzle. Thunder still rumbled and grumbled in the far distance, and every so often a silent flash of lightning half lit the room through the wide open door. Perspiring freely in the warm and clammy night air, I lay back with my eyes half closed, mulling over the events of the last twenty-four hours. Now the rain fell more gently on the corrugated iron roof, but somewhere a small stream was cascading down on to the saturated ground. In one of the nearby rooms a wind-up gramophone was playing, its muffled music just managing to reach my ears. Far from being intrusive, it had a quaint lulling quality; the tune, "Among My Souvenirs," was being plaintively sung by some chap whose voice was unfamiliar to me, the record sounding as though it might well have been made around a quarter of a century ago. A mosquito was striving to get at me through the net, its high-pitched whine just a few inches from my head. Presently the sounds faded and I fell asleep.

3 RAF Sungei Patani

My first impression of the camp at Sungei Patani was gained in darkness and rain. It had been an odd experience—a kind of scene-setting preview of what the place was like and the atmosphere that prevailed there. I was by no means alone in sensing something strange about this isolated outpost for in correspondence (conducted a great many years later) with chaps who had arrived there with me, it became clear that these now-aging men still well remembered our arrival, the pitch darkness, the rain, the lack of facilities, the endless lines of dripping trees, the utter quietness, and the absolute forlorn deadness of the place. They all retained vivid memories of our arrival there, our first meal, and the business of finding our sleeping quarters.

The following morning I found the atmosphere of the previous night replaced by a quite different ambience. Deep and forbidding darkness and dripping rain had given way to bright early morning sunshine that flashed in warm golden shafts through the foliage of line after line of rubber trees which came, all around, to within twenty or thirty feet of the hut in which I had slept. Red-tinted soil had already shed off or soaked up last night's rain and now, still thoroughly moist, began to cast off what dampness remained in slowly rising vapors that, a few feet above the ground, thinned, drifted, and then simply disappeared.

A pleasant aroma of damp vegetation filled the air, and the faint smell of woodsmoke, a smell that seemingly one encountered everywhere in Malaya in those distant days—and, oddly enough, in many places one still does.

One of the first things I noticed on walking around the clearing surrounding the hut was the presence of a number of oblong holes in the ground, about eighteen inches wide by eight feet long and four feet deep. Most of them contained a lot of rainwater, some pretty near full. We later gathered that they were slit trenches into which we should leap in the event of an air raid. It concerned no one in the slightest that a desperate dive into the nearest trench could easily have resulted in concussion, partial drowning, and possibly snakebite, for cobra were well-established residents over the entire region. The other thing about these trenches, and we were to learn this very quickly, was that airmen would fall into them on an almost nightly basis on their way back from the mess or the NAAFI, which was no laughing matter; they would then talk of making an official complaint to the station commander (in charge of the entire camp)—whoever he might have been. The fact was that to most airmen this officer remained totally unknown. We rarely saw him, and the vast majority never even bothered to find out his name or rank.

RAF Sungei Patani was an up-country airfield with little in the way of squadron backup facilities and virtually no social amenities. An exceedingly small grass airfield was surrounded mainly by rubber trees, though its northern perimeter was bordered by wild vegetation. There was a rudimentary control tower and a couple of enormous, amazingly conspicuous silver-colored aviation fuel tanks that, in a favorable light, an aviator with average vision could without any difficulty discern from twenty miles away. The combined capacity of these prominent ill-sited landmarks was—as it happened—no less than two hundred thousand gallons. A few wooden huts served as offices, stores, and minuscule workshops. A short distance away from the airfield, in the rubber plantation, more huts functioned as sleeping quarters, administrative offices, kitchens, messes, and a medical room-cum-sickbay. Adjacent to the airmen's mess was the NAAFI canteen, a source of cigarettes and beer.

There were no aircraft hangars on the camp; all work on the planes which by necessity had to be done under cover, being carried out in constructions known as pens. A pen, of which there were around half a dozen, was a makeshift affair made of wood with a corrugated iron roof; it had no doors, only a back and two sides. An aircraft would be pushed into a pen so that its front half, including engines, would be mostly under cover, leaving the rear section sticking out into the open air.

RAF Sungei Patani was the base for two squadrons of aircraft. The squadron to which I had been posted, No. 27 Squadron, was equipped with twelve twin-engined Bristol Blenheim light bombers with a top speed of only 265 MPH. The squadron, with older aircraft, had operated in the Northwest Frontier, India, for many years but in February 1941 had taken delivery of its new Blenheims and had then been relocated to Singapore. In May 1941 the squadron had moved to RAF Butterworth on mainland Malaya, and then in August 1941 had been sent even farther north to the new and unfinished forward camp at Sungei Patani. Hence, when I arrived at the camp, the Blenheims had been there just a few weeks.

The other squadron at the camp was No. 21 RAAF Squadron. This Australian fighter squadron was equipped with twelve Brewster Buffaloes. This plane—fat, squat, and blunt-nosed, thanks to its meaty unstreamlined radial engine—was hardly in the front rank of fighter aircraft as far as performance went. Its claimed maximum speed of 295 MPH was, according to those who flew one, a sick joke. Also the Buffalo had an unimpressive and frustrating rate of climb—not exactly what the doctor ordered for a front-line fighter. In 1939 this plane had been rejected for use as a fighter in Europe and a considerable number had been diverted to the Far East instead. At the time it had not been realized, though of course it should have been, that the Japanese Zero–type fighters were very far in advance of the Buffalo, whose niggardly maximum performance could be obtained only when the plane was in sound flying condition. This, unhappily, was frequently not the case. The whacking great engine proved to be very prone to failure in one way and another, and spares were virtually unobtainable in Malaya. On the whole the young Australian pilots thought little of the Buffalo, though no doubt a number of them experienced a thrill when barging through the air on a fine day at fifteen thousand feet with the huge engine sounding like a cross between an all-out racing car and a colliery winding engine on a busy shift.

Another thing about the Buffaloes that their pilots found a nuisance was the plane's armament, four .50-caliber guns, quite a lethal setup. The guns were found to be unreliable because they were chronically prone to jamming. So not only did the Buffaloes take forever to climb to a respectable height, but having done so, their guns could not be relied on to function. This situation was to prove not only daunting but also highly dangerous to those pilots who were eventually asked to take on Japan's vastly superior Zeros. So much for the Brewster Buffaloes of which, I learned, there were about sixty in service in Singapore and Malaya.

Sungei Patani airfield, a tiny affair, ran approximately west to east and was just long enough for the needs of the Blenheims and Buffaloes. There was no scope for anything other than short-field takeoff and landing procedures, especially as the air conditions considerably reduced available takeoff power and heavy rain increased the airfield rolling resistance. Sometimes, after a particularly violent and prolonged storm, the airfield would be simply closed to aircraft traffic for two or three days. An additional very real hazard to aircraft was the proximity of Kedah Peak, barely five miles to the northwest. At 3,500 feet this mountainous obstruction represented a big-time scourge to pilots when flying in minimum visibility conditions or at night.

A strange thing that nonplussed me at the time and has ever since is the fact that the Australians kept themselves totally apart from the personnel of No. 27 Squadron. It so happened that the station commander was also commander of No. 27 Squadron. This individual could, not only in theory but also in practice, tell the commander of No. 21 RAAF Squadron what to do in certain crucial matters. It is very likely that a certain disruptive top-level rivalry was at the root of the odd distancing of the two squadrons. Records and reports state that when the time finally came for vital cooperation, the station commander acted so slowly and reluctantly as to adversely and seriously affect the actions of the Australian squadron.

However, *that* was the situation that prevailed at RAF Sungei Patani at a time when its two squadrons should have been planning and working closely together in view of the fact that Japanese troops were now well established in French Indo-China, only five hundred miles away, and that Japan was continuing to behave as though it was planning to unseat the British in Singapore and Malaya at the first opportunity. But it must again be said that Japan's threatening behavior was lost on the vast majority of people, including military personnel. Not only did civilians—Europeans and locals alike—

find it impossible to believe that Japan would attack Singapore and Malaya, but so did the military high-ups, at least most of them. Such defense plans as were already being dreamed up were akin to half-hearted tongue-in-cheek solutions to a hypothetical situation, that is, they lacked genuine realism because of this all-pervading and virtually universal subconscious refusal to accept that Japan would strike; it was like preparing for something that one is convinced is not going to happen, and therefore one's heart is not in the task. It is only when it becomes clear that one has judged the situation wrongly, and that calamity is bearing down apace, that one starts to pay serious attention, typically by first becoming petrified and then implementing some hastily devised strategy that in itself, because of the last-minute rush and confusion, proves to be disastrous.

As the days passed, no special messages of warning concerning the Japanese issue found their way down to us in the lower ranks. If, in fact, such warnings *were* passed down at all, it is certain that they failed to reach our NCOs, that is, the flight sergeants, sergeants, and corporals. Most likely, warnings were not even given to officers, for, in that case, the essence of any important warnings would as a matter of routine have been conveyed to the NCOs. Hence our days were spent in an atmosphere of normality, or as near to normality as life at a place such as Sungei Patani could be. Taking into account all that was then known to the top defense chiefs, all manner of advisory cautions, warnings, instructions, and counsel ought to have been forthcoming from the station HQ. No such action was taken, however, due either to negligence and complacency on the part of the station commander or, possibly, to his not having been adequately informed of the stark danger that threatened Singapore and Malaya, his two squadrons, and the entire personnel at Sungei Patani.

It is safe to say that a good 80 percent of camp personnel were either naive young airmen or junior NCOs, all of whom assumed that all was well and that, if any major problem or threatening situation were to arise, they would be enlightened and instructed accordingly. I was young and immature. I was certainly one of those who automatically assumed that our officers knew all that was going on and that our safety and well-being were in capable hands. My own ingenuous assumption was the natural outcome of the brainwashing to which I had been subjected as an aircraft apprentice. Even so, I had not been at the camp more than a couple of weeks before I began to experience disturbing episodes of apprehension that seemed, on reflection, to spring from the fact that I already knew Japan to be adopting an increasingly threatening attitude—I

Table 1: Aircraft types used by the Royal Air Force in Malaya and Singapore, 1941–42

Aircraft	SpecificationsSpeed	Maximum (MPH)
Bristol Blenheim 1(B) bomber	Twin radial-engined monoplane	265
Bristol Blenheim 1(NF) night fighter	Twin radial-engined monoplane	265
Hawker Hurricane fighter	Single in-line engined monoplane	342
Lockheed Hudson 11 rec. bomber	Twin radial-engined monoplane	255
Brewster Buffalo fighter	Single radial-engined monoplane	295
Vickers Wildebeeste torpedo bomber	Single radial-engined biplane	137
Consolidated PBY Catalina rec. bomber	Twin radial-engined monoplane flying boat	177

Note: For disposition of squadrons, see Map 1, p. 9.

had read much about this while in Singapore. But there was also the fact that nothing substantial was being done or said about it. I was conscious that my airfield at Sungei Patani was no more than twenty miles from the Siamese border, which made the camp an easy target for Japanese planes if they chose to attack. If any RAF airfields were scheduled to be wiped out in an initial assault, it was certain that Sungei Patani would be high on Japan's list. Yet this fact, which was glaringly obvious to me, did not appear to have spurred the station commander or his close staff into action of any noticeable kind. Three other RAF stations in northern Malaya presumably operated under a more or less identical burden of administrative weakness. These were Alor Star, near the northwest border, with eleven Blenheims; Kota Bharu, close to the northeast border, with twelve Lockheed Hudsons and six Wildebeests; and Gong Kedah, some twenty miles south of Kota Bharu, with six Wildebeests (see table above).

I often pondered the Japanese question. From my lowly position, devoid of the benefit of official advice and guidance, I could not really see Japan attacking Singapore and Malaya—not in a month of Sundays. But I was basing my conclusion on a scrap of geography, a sprinkling of history, and an utterly misguided conception of Japanese morality, wisdom, and rationality. As it happened, millions of individuals worldwide were thinking the same way; included in this lot were a great many British political and armed forces' "big noises."

The twelve Blenheims of No. 27 Squadron were normally parked around the southwestern corner of the airfield near the pens, the control tower, and the two immense fuel tanks. Typically, at any time during daylight hours two or three of the Blenheims would be in the pens while one would be flying and the rest parked close to the control tower. The twelve Buffaloes occupied a dispersal area on the western end of the airfield and were always neatly lined up close together in a single row. It was an unusual thing indeed for more than one or two of them to be in the air at any one time for, normally, most were unserviceable for want of spares. So there it was; the Buffaloes with their business-like appearance and whacking great brute of an engine were just about impotent for want of spare parts.

Personnel in the camp probably totaled around three hundred, including the Australians and a fair number of Indian army personnel who assisted with guard duties. As far as my colleagues and I were concerned, we had very little to do once our morning work on the Blenheims was over.

Shortly after I arrived at Sungei Patani the season of the northeast monsoon commenced; in consequence, we spent a great many of our afternoons in the refuge of our huts, sheltered from the torrential rain. At such times we could do little in the way of serious reading due to the oppressive heat and humidity that enveloped us like a warm, wet blanket. When we moved it was like walking through an invisible cloud of steam. Nowhere on the camp was there any air conditioning or forced ventilation of any kind.

In the early afternoon the sky would start to darken. An intense gloominess would add to the already enervating conditions. The birds would gradually fall quiet, and an eerie silence would descend over the whole camp. Within the rubber plantation, where our huts were located, it would become particularly dark, the overhead dense foliage holding back any light that might remain in the cloud-obscured sky. Distant rumbling and muffled buffeting of thunder would follow a short time later. Rain would start to fall, first in large random drops and then, suddenly, in a deluging torrent that roared deafeningly on the corrugated iron roofs. Accompanying the rain would be lightning, often spectacular and unimaginable in its vividness and variety. Such lightning merited robust sound effects in no small measure, their seemingly endless variety in line with the complexity of the multi-colored lightning, ranging from simple and straightforward ear-splitting overhead detonations to ponderous, stretched-out, tentative crunching and grinding noises, followed by four or five seconds of suspicious stony silence, and then a brain-numbing barrage of explosions that tended to take one by surprise.

A well-orchestrated thunderstorm could be awesome, if not terrifying. There were a lot of them. Some days the show would go on and on well into the night, but usually the rain would move on and the sun would join us again briefly before beginning to sink, like a huge golden-red ball, below the trees. Night would swiftly fall, the trees would continue to drip slowly and steadily, and ground mists would start to form; yet the heat would continue unabated. Night was just an extended bore; dinner at 6:00 P.M. constituted a highlight, but one that was followed by hours of tedium.

Rationing of food such as existed back in the United Kingdom certainly did not apply here, and, what is more, the food dished up to us was virtually no different from that suitable for a much cooler climate. Thus it was by no means unusual to find ourselves eating lamb or beef stew with piping hot vegetables at midday—and that, very likely, after having already partaken of a bowl of steaming curried onion soup as a starter. Hot rice pudding or possibly some kind of suet pudding and custard would follow.

Evening meals were little different as far as quality and quantity were concerned. Bearing in mind that the outside air temperature rarely fell below 85°F (29°C) it will be appreciated that the tendency was to overfeed us. It was a diet that few could have sustained for more than a few months without becoming seriously clogged up in practically every department as well as putting on a dangerous amount of weight. The cooks, Chinese locals guided by RAF chaps, must have been working from some highly inappropriate cooking manual. Oddly enough, no one ever complained.

When the officers felt that we were not getting sufficient exercise, we were required to congregate at a certain place at 6:15 A.M. dressed in shorts and canvas working boots. A sergeant, mounted on a seriously corroded bicycle and wearing normal day clothing, would then set off into the trees with something like fifty airmen scampering after him. At this hour the plantation would still be quite gloomy, owing to the fact that full sunrise was not complete until around 7:15 A.M. After having loped through the semidarkness for a couple of hundred yards or so, the column of airmen would come to a gradual halt, like a slow goods train brought to a halt by buffers. At the head of the column would be the now-dismounted sergeant leaning against a tree and dragging out his cigarettes. "Time for a fag, lads," he would call out as though we had run at least five miles and were all gasping for a smoke. Within a few seconds a sizable cloud of tobacco smoke would rise up among the silent rubber trees. Even though I smoked cigarettes, as did the vast majority of my colleagues, I never bothered to take a supply with me on these pathetic jog trots. This halt for respiratory refreshment would be only a brief affair for, after five minutes or so, the sergeant would nip his fag, mount up, and push off back to his quarters. The rest of us would amble back to our huts to prepare for the day ahead. All told, the whole thing would take no more than fifteen minutes. Whoever dreamed that one up, and then never bothered to take any further interest in the matter, was very clearly one of Sungei Patani's incompetents.

Apart from the sheer novelty of it all and the extremely easygoing way of life, the camp had nothing whatsoever to offer either socially or culturally. I began to get the distinct feeling we had been dumped here, and it was not the kind of place to get my ideas for personal advancement off the ground. I wondered how long I was going to have to waste my time at the place. I felt so strongly about this that I decided to have a solemn, semiofficial word with my flight sergeant on the matter. I had seen him only a couple of times before and then only from a distance, for he rarely emerged from his wooden den of an office close to the control tower. I approached his hideaway one afternoon with some temerity because, of course, he was so much more mature and experienced than I. The door to his place stood ajar as I knocked. He looked up from his desk. My immediate perception was that he was around fifty, and not too well preserved at that. In reality, he could not possibly have been more than about thirty-seven. It turned out that he had just completed several years of service with the RAF on the northwest frontier of India. He was, in fact, an ex-apprentice, a product of RAF Halton, which meant that he had been knocking around various RAF stations, home and abroad, for some twenty years or more; it showed. He wore the wrinkled countenance of one who had spent too long attending to the interests of the British empire in some of its hotter and less salubrious RAF outposts. The man was obviously drained. Even the medal ribbons on his light-blue shirt looked drained, being noticeably faded and threadbare. The amazingly thick lenses of his free-issue steel-framed spectacles didn't do a lot to improve his appearance either. As I moved into the interior of his hothouse of an office, with its pungent smell of recently applied creosote, he peered at me in a melancholy sort of way. He rose from his chair and took a couple of steps backwards as though anticipating some kind of trouble. Immediately I noticed that his shorts extended to a remarkable distance below his knees, a sure sign that, sartorially, he was an old-timer and probably also one who had an aversion to the sun getting at his knees.

"What?" he asked abruptly.

I noticed that his teeth were in a poor state of repair. I moved a little closer to his desk. The air temperature in the hut must have been around 100°F (38°C), but at least he was sheltered from the sun—it was mid-afternoon, yet none of the customary storm clouds had so far gathered.

"Who're you?" he demanded before I had answered his first question.

"A.C.I. Shepherd, Flight Sergeant," I replied, then went on to explain to him that I would value his advice as to how I could advance my career prospects within the RAF. He seemed more interested to know what I could do now. I told him I was an ex-apprentice and an engine fitter.

"Engines, eh?" he said.

"Yes, Flight Sergeant," I continued.

"Any experience on Blenheims?"

"Yes, Flight Sergeant. I did a couple of months training on a Mk-1 at RAF Halton—Mercury engines."

"Splendid—splendid," he breathed, then, "Cylinder and piston changes?"

"Yes, Flight Sergeant, full major overhaul, including propellers."

"Splendid—I've got twelve of the buggers here and hardly anyone knows anything about them, including me."

"How old are you?" he asked. I caught a hint of suspicion in his expression.

"Eighteen, Flight Sergeant," I replied.

"Bit young for an ex-apprentice, aren't you?"

"Yes, Flight Sergeant. They shortened my apprenticeship to two years, on account of the war, but then terminated it after only twenty months. The Air Ministry said that the training facilities at Halton were needed for training flight mechanics who, as you know, receive only six months' training. In fact, it has been put to the Air Council that we apprentices should be simply sent home and discharged from the RAF. But it was pointed out that to do so would amount to a breach of faith with our parents and the education authorities who had specially prepared us for the RAF apprentice competitive entrance examination."

"How old were you when you left Halton then?"

"Seventeen, Flight Sergeant," I replied.

"But you weren't even old enough to commence service as a man with the RAF." He fired off three or four nervous grimaces in rapid succession and stood up, agitated, then sat down again straightaway as though having found the effort too much. "Stupid sods," he mouthed. "So instead of committing a breach of faith they committed a breach of contract instead—in their own interests, of course."

"That's correct, Flight Sergeant, but there's a war on."

He exploded, that is, as far as his rundown condition and the stifling heat in his office permitted. "Doesn't matter about the blasted war. They'll need fully trained ex-apprentices before long."

The flight sergeant closed his eyes and proceeded to fan himself with a sheaf of papers, but, even finding the effort of this too much, gave it up. He opened his eyes a fraction. "Anyway, what do you want?"

By this time I knew he wasn't going to bite my head off. Actually, I had begun to feel a bit sorry for the man. He had been too long in far-flung outposts of the empire, housed no doubt in drab and dreary RAF married quarters. "Well, Flight Sergeant," I began, "I realize it's a bit soon, but I was wondering what the chances are of my being regraded to leading aircraftsman in the near future."

I was about to add a little more in support of my case, but I missed the chance because he did his grimacing thing and dragged a perspiration-soaked packet of Pirate Brand cigarettes from one of his top pockets while saying, "We haven't got down to regrading and promotions up here yet. The squadron's only been established here since August." Then, to my surprise, he offered me a cigarette. I took one from the moist, grubby packet, and then he took up a box of matches from his desk and attempted to strike one. The matchhead was thoroughly damp due to the humidity and merely disintegrated without making even one spark.

"Got a light?" he asked defeatedly.

"No, Flight Sergeant."

"Well, go and get one then, there's a good lad."

I stepped out of his oven-like office and was able to return without delay with my cigarette lighted. Having got his own going from mine, he drew in deeply and gave me his attention.

"We'll have to see how you get on, but you'll get just the same chances as everybody else. I don't know how you got on at Halton in your final examinations, but I'm sure they won't have sent your records through yet. Did you get good results?"

He did not wait for my reply but instead groped around for a piece of paper and when he'd finished writing down something I noticed that he had used a laundry chit for the purpose. "Okay, lad, press on. I've made a note," he said, and closed our discussion with a gem of a grimace that looked as though it might have been triggered by a particularly sharp attack of wind in the bowel. I left him half-heartedly fanning himself and inhaling another cubic foot or so of cigarette smoke. I had no means of assessing how I had acquitted myself in my first encounter with this pleasant enough relic of a flight sergeant. Certainly he had been friendly, but it was plain that the poor man was all washed up, sick of the heat, and sick of life in the RAF.

Perhaps, I thought, I ought not to expect too much of him. Indeed, nothing ever came out of my discussion with him; in fact, we never met again—ever.

It was only a short walk back over the grass to the pen where I had been working on an engine of one of the Blenheims. The inside of the corrugated iron-roofed pen was like a furnace. No one was in there but me, and as I mounted an access ladder to get at the engine, I heard the first distant rumble of thunder.

I carried on working for the rest of the afternoon. It was unusual to have to work after midday, but this was one of those rush jobs—a modification involving fitting a special cooling duct to eliminate a problem hot spot on one of the engine's cylinders. All the Blenheims had to be modified in this way, and this was the last to be done. It was 5:30 P.M. or thereabouts by the time my task was finished and my tools tidied away. It had been a bit of a race against time for I wished to get back to my hut before the approaching storm broke. Looking out of the pen, however, I could see there was no way I was going to reach the hut without getting thoroughly wet. I could stay in the pen until the storm had passed, or I could set off and be caught by torrential rain. I started walking.

It will be understood that I am relating this part of my story as I saw, experienced, and interpreted things at the time, and that my perception, interest, and reasoning faculties were those of an eighteen-year-old. Naive and ingenuous I must certainly have been, due of course to nothing other than lack of experience. On occasions I quietly objected to annoying things that were of little consequence, but as for matters such as the camp administration and organization I simply assumed that all was well in these departments. Having said that, I should add that my concern and mystification continued to grow at the apparent lack of action by the camp administration in the face of the growing threat of Japanese hostility. With hindsight it is obvious that we lower orders were kept woefully in the dark as regards the knife-edge situation, and it is now clear that our masters were little better informed. By this I mean our masters at squadron level, and what applied at No. 27 Squadron, Sungei Patani, doubtless also applied at every squadron in Singapore and Malaya. Records show that such a plethora of uncertainty and confusion existed at the very highest level that there is little wonder that scant information and advice were passed down to squadron level. Even in *my* lowly position I could sense something ominous developing, and yet, in the absence of guidance or instruction from my superiors, I was unable to grasp exactly what it was that niggled away worrisomely in my mind at odd times of the day and night. I can only liken my disquiet and concern to that of certain animals which, at the distant approach of a thunderstorm, but well before the first noise of thunder is heard and even before the first drops of rain commence to fall, become restive and ill at ease, even to the extent of seeking some kind of protective shelter.

It was while trudging back to my hut through darkening rows of rubber trees with the thunder and lightning fast approaching that one of these episodes of dull and numbing apprehension fell upon me like a mantle. It was as though in a fraction of a second I had passed from one state of awareness to another—one that amounted to a forlorn and deep apprehension without apparent cause. The rain began its deluge long before I reached the hut where I showered and changed and joined in a bit of light banter with some of my colleagues before going to dinner.

Saturday, 29 November 1941

Around the third week in November some of us were given weekend passes to Penang, an island off the west coast of mainland Malaya some twenty-five miles to the south. At midday a few days later we were carted off in the back of an RAF truck along the tortuous, poorly maintained road to the ferry terminal where we eventually boarded an ancient vessel that transported us across the three-mile-wide Penang Strait. On getting off the ferry at Georgetown, the one and only town on the island, I teamed up with one of my colleagues, a chap named George as it happened, who like me was an aero-engine fitter. He was in his early twenties but looked much older, one reason being that he wore a more or less chronic hangdog expression that bestowed on him a rather miserable and brooding aspect. He also was somewhat bowlegged—not a lot, but a condition that one could hardly fail to notice. When he wore long trousers it wasn't too obvious, but in his regulation khaki shorts his legs really drew one's attention immediately. I had often wondered how he had managed to get into the RAF but had speculated that the condition must have progressed since his having entered the service around four years earlier.

We experienced no difficulty in finding a rickshaw since the ferry terminal was seething with them. The ride took no more than fifteen minutes, our painfully thin and scantily clad coolie trotting along in his bare feet and wide conical straw sun hat. He dropped us off outside a hotel, the Eastern and Oriental, at the northern end of Penang Road. We explored a little until we came to a services club, an old colonial building set back from the road. Inside, it was all lofty ceilings, overhead propeller fans, cane furniture, and high-shuttered windows. After the heat of the streets the place felt almost cool. There seemed to be no one in the club save we two and a handful of Chinese waiters. We lounged in cane armchairs and drank three or four bottles of Tiger and Anchor beer while listening to records that we played on a wind-up gramophone set in a tall, elegant rosewood cabinet inlaid with gilt flowers and leaves, no doubt gifted to the club by some retired civil servant or planter. We played, I particularly remember, "Singing in the Rain" and "Ramona," along with other tunes, though these two we played more or less repeatedly. The fans gently wafted air over us, delicately scented with the invisible fumes of smoldering joss sticks.

"Do you like the mysterious aroma of incense and sandalwood and all that stuff?" I asked George, knowing full well what his reply would be.

"No, I bloody don't," George confirmed. He did not go much on anything Eastern or Asiatic and tended to devote a lot of time to bleating on about wanting to get back to Cheshire, his hometown.

He grumbled on a bit more as the final few bars of "Ramona" oozed softly and plaintively from the gramophone. I rose from my chair, parked the pickup arm, stopped the turntable, and lowered the lid of the cabinet. Whether it was the beer, the joss sticks, or simply an instinctive thing, I could not say, but the funny thing was that, as I shut the lid of that gramophone, I had the sudden, crystal-clear feeling that my action marked the end of an era—as though I was conscious of having just closed the door on a part of my life. An explanation for this strange feeling does not come easily, but the fact remains that, just like an electric lamp that emits one sudden burst of bright light immediately before burning out, I can still plainly recall the almost rueful final moment when I closed that gramophone lid.

"Come along, George," I said. "Let's go and get something to eat."

By 7:30 P.M. day had ended and it was dark. There had been no afternoon storm. We ate in a cheap restaurant. The night was, as usual, hot and clammy, and the streets of Chinatown, just off Penang Road, were bustling and noisy with rickshaws, taxis, electric tram cars, radios, radiograms, and a multitude of miscellaneous discussions and arguments. The rich atmosphere was loaded with the smell of ripe fruit, perfume, joss sticks, cooking aromas, and the more or less ever-present nauseating emanations of raw sewage in various stages of biological decomposition.

"Bloody hell!" George shouted.

"What?" I called back.

"Stinks!"

"Too true—but interesting," I offered.

We continued to view the sights and presently came to a crossroad where an extra-loud blast of Chinese music hit us. Off to the right was an arched gateway festooned with brightly colored flashing lights. Over the archway, spelled out in even bolder and brighter lights, was "Elysee Cabaret." George, still wearing his sun-helmet, grabbed my arm and hauled me toward the brilliant portal. Once through the enticing barrage of Chinese music, amplified to pain-threshold level, we found ourselves in a smaller version of the New World and Great World centers back in Singapore. The latter two were well-known specialized attractions boasting a range of entertainment facilities that included bars, sideshows, dance floors, and the like; the principal supporting theme in both cases was that of a mind-blowing discordance of crashing music, both Asiatic and European.

This particular facility was first and foremost a kind of open-air dance hall with just a light sprinkling of peripheral sideshows as money-making diversions. The sizable dance floor was protected from the elements by a huge canvas canopy from which decorative lanterns were suspended. A mass of mock foliage festooned down toward the dancers. There were tables and chairs on three sides of the floor, bright lights, exotic decorations, and a well-stocked bar not much more than a hundred feet long. The Hawaiian-style band was doing fine, and the place was heaving with army and RAF personnel. Ranged up on one side of the dance floor were fifty or so Chinese girl taxi-dancers waiting to be asked to dance in exchange for tickets that one could purchase at conveniently sited kiosks.

George and I sat down at one of the tables. The band was playing a quickstep, and the dance floor was fairly busy. Once we were seated a pretty Chinese waitress came for our drinks order. "Hello, boys, what drinks you like?" The smile on her exquisitely overpainted face made thinking difficult.

I made a hurried decision. "Gin and tonic, please," I said. Then I looked at George, who for some reason was still wearing his sun-helmet. He was just sitting there gasping at the girl and looking stunned, his mouth open and saying nothing.

"I'm having gin and tonic," I said to him, "but what are *you* having?"

"Rum," said George.

"Bloody hell, you don't drink rum."

George gave a wry smile. "Well, I'm going to start," he said.

The girl understood. "One gin and tonic and one rum." She smiled and left us.

"Take your helmet off, George. It looks absurd in here." In point of fact it looked absurd on him at any time, being rather too large for him; it tended to bend the tops of his ears over. He removed it. A red mark showed across the full width of his forehead, and his hair was wet with perspiration.

Once our drinks arrived, we both ventured onto the floor. Fortunately the girls had been trained to follow every conceivable dance step that might come their way and even George's total lack of expertise failed to upset any of the long-suffering girls with whom he charged around the floor on his bent legs to the sometimes lilting, sometimes frenetic strains of the Hawaiian band. I managed to execute my own particular brand of ballroom dancing with the same girl each time. She resembled a delightful butterfly and exuded a fragrance like that of all the spring flowers one can possibly imagine. She had the neatest, whitest teeth I had perhaps ever seen. Her small lidless eyes shone brightly, but in them there was no obvious message or emotion, and, disappointingly, her breath smelled strongly of garlic. She was very young, maybe fourteen or so, and all a young lad could desire. George wasn't so fussy; he danced with any girl who appeared remotely female and who wore lashings of makeup.

Long before midnight the place was packed with British servicemen of one sort or another. The RAF figured prominently, more so than the army, although most of the latter were NCOs, owing, no doubt, to the fact that private soldiers did not have the money to spend on such relatively riotous living as this. By far the majority were Australians, both army and RAAF who, on the face of it, seemed to have far more money to spend than their UK counterparts. One consequence of this was that the Australians were much further into their drink than the rest. Every so often a violent skirmish would flare up, with tables and chairs viciously deployed in all directions; then, after a brief sorting out and settlement, someone would be helped out into the night to recover by the roadside or in the nearest monsoon drain.

Everyone was having a good time. There was no talk about the war currently being fought in faraway Europe and North Africa and on the high seas. Nor was there any talk of the defense of Singapore and Malaya against the Japanese threat, or of the defense of the Dutch East Indies against the same menace. The plain truth was that to 90 percent of those people cavorting that night in the Elysee Cabaret the Japanese threat simply didn't exist, no word of it ever having reached them. The prospect of a local war breaking out, involving Singapore and Malaya, just had not occurred to them; such a development was not even a remote possibility and therefore not worth devoting time to its consideration. Singapore and Malaya, to all intents and purposes, were British and would doubtless remain so. During all this light-hearted drinking, joking, and youthful scrimmaging there must have been few present who gave even a fleeting thought as to why they and their colleagues in arms were in Malaya anyway. Very few, if any, had yet pondered the thought as to why anyone would wish to commence hostilities against this happy, colorful, and delightfully old-fashioned corner of the empire.

After a few hours I noticed that George was evidently finding it restful and convenient to keep his eyes closed. "We'd better find somewhere to sleep," I shouted across the table to him.

I had had my fill of gin and tonic, which was just as well because I reckoned I had just enough cash left to pay for a bed somewhere and perhaps a bit of breakfast in the morning. George had given the rum a hammering and I was beginning to devise ways whereby I might get him into a rickshaw. As the evocative strains of half a dozen electric guitars echoed around the place I got up from my chair and struggled to get George to the nearest exit. The waitress who had looked after us was still hard at it, but now her painted mask looked dulled with fatigue and the smile she had given us earlier had faded.

It did not take much longer than fifteen minutes for me to get George outside with both army and RAF police types watching carefully, yet of course offering no help. A dozen rickshaws pounced on us despite George's by-now Quasimodo-style posture, sagging bent knees and his oversize sun-helmet. I pushed George aboard, then climbed in after him and instructed the coolie to take us to a place where we could sleep cheaply. He padded off along Penang Road, me counting my money and George looking as though at any moment he would fall overboard. His sole contribution to things at this stage occurred when he briefly came to his senses and vomited. He had enough sense to direct the stuff at ninety degrees to our line of progression. It shot out with a violent rush and an amazing strangled growl from George that sounded remarkably like a full-grown male tiger attempting to gargle with a couple of gallons of vegetable broth. The trajectory was exceptional and something that would have impressed even George himself had he not been feeling so indisposed. As it was, the descending crud cascaded down over the boots of a passing tough-looking Malay police sergeant. Our coolie, disturbed by the alien noise, glanced uneasily over his shoulder and, no doubt sensing a problem of some sort not necessarily to his ultimate advantage, put a spurt on, thereby avoiding any time-consuming involvement. We at once turned down a side street and in a few seconds were clean away from unwelcome complications. We spent what remained of the night in a moderate to poor but inexpensive Chinese hotel.

Sunday, 30 November

The following morning we took a tram car to a place named Springtide on the coast a couple of miles away, where one could sit on the beach under coconut palms. The tram-line terminated a good quarter of a mile from our destination, so once again we found ourselves sitting behind another hapless, half-starved, jog-trotting rickshaw coolie. The road, by some strange quirk of perspective, seemed to climb even though it stayed roughly level with the nearby sea, and our coolie began to gasp noticeably in the bright, fresh morning air. Springtide, we found, was a stretch of beach with a small hotel set by the side of the road that fronted on the broad sweep of sand. Around the hotel were a few small grassed lawns, flowerbeds, and palm trees. Naturally we avoided the actual hotel building and made straight for that part of the beach that was probably intended for the use of hotel guests only.

The water, almost dead calm, just washed unhurriedly up the beach now and again. It was clean and reasonably cool. We were virtually alone. I thought how strange it was to be here, paddling in the sea, away from the noise and bustle of Georgetown and away from the foreboding atmosphere of Sungei Patani. It was like being in a different world, distanced from the airplanes, the endless silent rows of rubber trees and the depressing gloom they inevitably threw over our accommodation huts. Over the water to the northwest about ten miles away I could see the Malayan coastline, and, farther into the distance, faint and hazy through the warm, humid air, I detected a clump of low mountains. From among these rose a peak much higher than the rest which, judging by its direction, was most probably Kedah Peak, the bane of pilots using the airfield at Sungei Patani. Many long years were to pass before I elicited confirmation of this, but, at the time, on that peaceful and memorable Sunday morning on Penang Island, I had the clear feeling that the mountain I could only just discern was Kedah Peak, or Gunung Jerai, as the Malays knew it. How different was the mood that its peculiarly forbidding proximity and influence brought to the camp compared with that of this deliciously restful haven, no more than twenty-five miles away.

Two Malay girls walked down from the hotel and onto the beach. Our eyes followed them as we made ourselves half presentable again. They began paddling in the sea about a hundred yards away whereupon George and I strolled in their direction. The girls merely put their heads down and kept on paddling in silence. With nothing better or more exciting to do we persisted with our pathetic overtures, but it must have been getting on for half an hour before we got anywhere. Even then they kept their distance, like around twenty yards or so, and cleverly contrived to put themselves between the two of us and the hotel.

They both spoke quite good English, but with strong Malay accents. They were on holiday with their parents. Both from Singapore, they were staying at the hotel. One of them was unusually tall for a Malay, and I guessed that she was of mixed race, as a great many of the peoples of Malaya were. She was beautiful, or at any rate appeared to be so from the distance that separated us. As they became more confident they allowed us to approach slowly to within a few feet. It was then that I noticed her bold slanting almond eyes, deep brown and glistening like glass. Her cheekbones were set high and her nose had only a suggestion of the general flattening and the flaring nostrils that is characteristic of most pure Malays. Her skin was quite dark and her hair long and shiny black under the wayward colorful silken covering she wore on her head. Whenever she spoke she addressed only me, her bright yet languid eyes holding mine with a kind of searching curiosity that I found disturbing yet exciting. I learned that her name was Wan. I knew that something had clicked between us, something that went well beyond the scope and intention of the trivial chatter that up to now had been going on among the four of us. How strange, I thought, how odd that in these unlikely surroundings and at this time on a November Sunday morning I should meet a girl so mysterious and enchanting as to fill me with an exquisite tenderness such as I had never before known; and I suspected, without having to be told, that she too had been affected in the same way. We had only just met for the very first time. An hour ago I had not even known of her existence, nor she mine, yet now we were being attracted and drawn together by an undeniable bond of nature. It was all so improbable, so unexpected, and so impossible. However the latter aspect of the matter never entered my mind even for an instant. I was sufficiently happy just to accept what had miraculously happened between us and had neither the time nor the composure of mind to consider the implications or the future beyond the next few minutes. What some would describe as being simply basic biological attraction, I instinctively felt to be a spiritually entrancing and wondrous thing, thrilling and precious. Though nothing was said between us my youthful mind saw the situation in this way and the possibility of complications arising never once occurred to me.

The four of us sat on the grass in the shade of a palm tree, and the scorching sun gradually climbed until almost directly overhead. The girls brought sandwiches and fruit juice from the hotel. I had already explained to them who we were, that we had come down from Sungei Patani for the weekend, and that we had little money left. A gin and tonic–type headache that I had been experiencing subsided so that I was able to enter into spirited conversation with Wan who, now close, looked even lovelier than she had looked when at a distance. George was clearly still suffering; his usual dejected expression had, if anything, intensified into one of pained melancholy. His breath still reeked of dark rum, and the fried tiger prawns, rich in garlic, that he had eaten at a hawker's stall had not improved matters for him. Fortunately, I noticed, too, that both girls had been at the garlic, and it did strike me that perhaps George's olfactory problem had therefore escaped their notice. Wan told me that her father was a doctor and that he worked in Singapore. She, a month younger than me, was in her first year of training as a nurse, also in Singapore. They were all returning to Singapore in a week's time, Sunday, 7 December.

I was already trying to work out in my mind how I could see Wan again. Then it struck me that it was virtually impossible because she was going back to Singapore, four hundred miles away, and I had absolutely no hope of going *there*. I felt myself becoming angry and determinedly desperate. Whatever the consequences, I had to see her again. "Wan," I said, "can I see you again next Saturday?"

Wan looked at me, surprised. She smiled, but on her forehead there was a frown. It was plain that she also wondered how another meeting would be possible. She spoke. "We be here next Saturday—last day for us. Why you want?"

I had no answer to her question that I could readily put into words. I struggled to reply. "Well, I just thought it would be nice if I could see you once more before you go home." She did not need to be told anything further. My reply had told her all she wished to know, and the way I had expressed myself had revealed my feelings toward her.

"Okay, Peter, if you be here, where we meet?" Wan glanced at her friend somewhat guiltily as though seeking tacit approval to her acquiescence.

My heart bounded. "I'll be here at around midday. If you come out onto the veranda you'll see me waiting," I breathed.

She stared into my eyes, gazing at me quietly as though trying to analyze my thoughts. Then she said, "That all right, Peter—I be here." Then again she repeated, "Don't worry—I be here." After her words had died away she continued to look into my eyes for some moments before lowering hers and smiling softly.

The girls went for more fruit juice, leaving George and me alone. He grabbed my arm.

"How the hell are you going to get another leave pass for next weekend?" he asked incredulously. He gave me the kind of guarded look that one gives to someone who has just uttered some bizarre remark such as those often made by unfortunates in the early stages of senile dementia.

"I don't know yet, George," I ventured. "All I know is that I must see her again. Once she returns to Singapore I'll probably never get the chance to see her again—ever."

George fell silent. He could see that I was determined and that he was wasting his time trying to reason with me. The two girls returned and we gratefully drank the juice they had brought with them.

Suddenly Wan said, with her quiet, enigmatic smile, "Peter, we go now. Our parents take us somewhere. I sorry we got to go. Hope see you next Saturday—okay?" Her brow creased as she spoke, as though she felt some doubt about my turning up as arranged.

George and I got the message, although I realized full well that we were not being given the push-off. "Don't worry, Wan," I said. "I'll be here— though I just might be alone."

"You can bet on that," George murmured so that only I could hear his words.

We all stood up because the magic occasion was at an end. We said our farewells, the girls drifted off, and we walked over to the rickshaws. The girls stood in the shade of palm trees and shyly waved as our rickshaw started off back to the tram-car terminus. After we had traveled about a hundred yards I turned my head to give a final wave. Wan, who had affected me so, was now standing alone, tall, slim, and forlorn. One of her hands was over her mouth as though in an involuntary gesture of worried concern and uncertainty, and she stared intently at our departing rickshaw. I lifted an arm and slowly waved it from side to side in a prolonged meaningful farewell. It was a gesture that was meant to be much more than just simply a courteous wave of goodbye. The meaning must have carried, for Wan's hand left her mouth and she began waving back at me. I lifted my helmet and waved with that until she disappeared from my line of sight, and suddenly a feeling of despair came over me. I sensed I had allowed something to slip away—something I might never get back.

The coolie jog-trotted us back to where the trams turned around for Georgetown. I was silent all the way. George fell asleep for a while, his helmet well down over his ears as usual. We passed through the kampung of Tanjong Tokong with its closely packed Malay wooden houses, where kids played in their singlets and sarongs and groups of mothers and grandmothers sat on verandas, gossiping and nursing innumerable infants.

Back in town all seemed to be different from the way it had been the previous day. There seemed to be more people about. It was hotter and even more clammy. Instead of feeling as yesterday, excited and exhilarated, we were now tired and dejected. We had had our bit of fun and had spent practically all our money. Our visit to Penang was virtually at an end.

A cinema, the Windsor, was showing a black-and-white Gary Cooper film. We went in, sat in the back row, and fell asleep. Now and again I woke up and watched five or ten minutes of the film. At the interval they came around with ice cream, but neither of us had sufficient money left to buy one. I spent the second half of the show worrying about how I was going to get back to see Wan on the following Saturday, and planning reasons why it was necessary that I should be given another leave pass—even devising ways of getting away from the camp without authority, and dreaming up schemes where I could raise the cash for the venture. The more I realized how impossible it was going to be, the more angry and desperate I became. I had smoked my last cigarette, George was fast asleep, Gary Cooper was binding on about something or other, and I was awash with perspiration.

The show ended, the lights came up, and everyone sang "God Save the King." We went out into the street where things had turned rather unpleasant. It was late afternoon, stiflingly hot and humid. The usual clamor of the streets seemed muted by the oppressive conditions. Dense clouds now hid the sun and, over in the east, the sky had darkened to a deep indigo. We dragged our heels to the ferry terminal, not even having enough cash left to hire a rickshaw. An unsettling stillness hung over the ferry as we shuffled aboard along with Chinese, Malays, and twenty or so British servicemen. The Penang of yesterday, and of only that morning, had somehow changed into a darkly disturbing place.

Bells rang, the ferry's engine sobbed into life, and black smoke broke from the funnel and was quickly carried away on a now-rising wind. The bow slowly turned toward the mainland, and the paddles began struggling with the dark, uninviting water. I felt sad that I was leaving the Malay girl behind forever, sad at leaving the island, and sad that our sunny uplifting break was over.

A sudden strong wind blew up, making the water choppy and causing the ferry to progress in uneasy jerking leaps over the water. It was almost pitch dark. Brilliant flashes of lightning gradually worked their way over to us from the east, although, so far, no noise of thunder reached our ears. We managed to find a spot of refuge behind a pile of life rafts and there George and I stayed for the rest of the half-hour journey. When the ferry tied up at the mainland we were both soaked to the skin, our elegant ceremonial sun-helmets all but ruined.

Halfway into the journey back to Sungei Patani thunder and lightning enveloped us and stayed with us until we entered the small town. Five minutes later the camp gates opened to let us through and then slammed behind us. Our lorry was immediately swallowed up by intense darkness. It proceeded to pick its way through the rubber plantation to a point where we alighted and then, like silent dejected shadows, drifted back to our various sleeping quarters.

Just as it had been when I had first arrived at the camp from Singapore, the rain now fell less vigorously but steadily enough to keep the trees dripping in a dismal and melancholy fashion. I began the uphill climb through the trees to my hut, the lights of which I was unable to see, though I knew it was impossible to get lost. All I had to do was to make sure I avoided the slit-trenches. It must have been my lucky night—I missed them all. I reached the hut at 9:00 P.M. I went to bed tired and ravenously hungry, but I knew that in the morning there would be bright sunshine and, after one of those ludicrous jog-trots through the trees, a good breakfast.

The following morning turned out as I expected, low mist over the airfield at first light, a spectacular sunrise, and, a little later on, bright sunshine with, here and there, wreathing vapors rising slowly from rain-sodden earth.

At work in one of the pens I spoke to one of my colleagues. "I'm hoping for another overnight pass for next Saturday," I said.

He glanced away from what he was doing. "You'll be lucky," he said sarcastically. "They grant passes only once a month."

"I realize that," I replied. "That's my problem and I've got to be in Penang by midday at the latest."

"A girl is it?" he asked, giving me a pitying look.

"Well . . ." I began.

He put his hand up in a gesture of mock horror. "It is, isn't it?" he exclaimed. Then his expression changed and he looked as though waiting to see if he had won a prize for guessing correctly.

"Yes," I agreed, "there *is* a girl."

"Chinese?"

"No . . ."

"Indian?"

"No, nothing like that." I felt myself becoming irritated.

"Well! What then?" he demanded. "She *must* be something."

"She could be English," I said musingly, "but she's not."

He returned to his work in that his hands resumed doing whatever they had been doing, though his eyes remained expectantly on me.

"Is it a case of your not knowing—or not being sure?"

"Of course not." Then I came out with it. "She's Malay with perhaps some other race mixed in."

Another chap came over and stood listening.

The first chap asked, "Well, didn't you find out for sure?"

I was now wishing I had not raised the subject. "There wasn't time," I said.

"What happened?" asked the newcomer.

"Nothing happened—it wasn't that kind of thing at all."

"What's all the fuss about then?"

I really did not feel disposed to continue what had become a major inquisition. "There's no fuss," I replied, again feeling that I had no control over things. It appeared that I couldn't even seek a bit of advice without getting bogged down in half-witted trivia.

They both went back to their work. A minute later one of them shouted over to me, "You'd better forget about trying for another weekend pass because there's no way you're going to get one." Then he added, "You'll just have to climb over the fence—that is, if you don't mind spending six months without pay in Changi jail."[1]

Now that I was broke there was little or no chance of my visiting the NAAFI after dinner for a bottle or two of beer. Instead I would go back to the hut to sweat and mope about the place, and try to scrounge a few cigarettes. If there was no thunder in the afternoon, it was pretty certain that such would descend on us during the night and probably before most of us had turned in. Conditions then would be even worse—darkness, everything saturated again, rain hammering on the corrugated iron roof, and thunder and lightning that shook the hut, interfered with conversation, and even drowned out the gramophone.

It was the time of the year when thunder was to be expected most days— the monsoon months of October through to the beginning of January. Sometimes I wondered which might be preferable, this time of the year or the months of summer when it would be dry but even hotter.

Oppressive boredom was the name of the game. No relief by either suggestion or action was forthcoming from our officers. Indeed, such officers as there were managed in some uncanny way to keep themselves well out of sight. I remember frequently thinking, and asking, "Where are they?" and "Where are their quarters and where is their mess hut?" and, again, "How many are there?" "Why don't they ever come out and be seen?" "Why don't they ever tell us anything?"

Neither was any useful guidance forthcoming from the NCOs, that is, the flight sergeants, sergeants, and corporals who were, in general, a morose and uninspiring lot whose personalities had been allowed to suffer and atrophy under the near-nonexistent direction of successive mediocre officers. It will be gathered that all this added up to management at a nonexistent level; in fact, in retrospect, I feel right in thinking that not one of the officers at Sungei Patani had ever received even a hint or suggestion of tuition in basic man-management.

At the time, I must admit, all this deficiency in the quality of our elusive leaders did not strike me as being too serious, although I was, of course, conscious that things were pretty slack and that the NCOs and airmen never received any enlightening information in regard to which way the situation was moving as regards Japan's grumbling hostility toward the East Asian nations. I just felt that all concerned had come to regard their presence here as a kind of an undisciplined, laid-back break from the normal service conditions that applied on well-established RAF stations such as at Seletar on Singapore Island. While I had a residual presumption that everything was all right and that the camp officers, under the direction of RAF High Command in Singapore, knew what they were about and would provide all necessary guidance should any emergency arise, all the same, my instincts were still telling me that something was brewing—that there was something we should know but were not being told.

I began to give really serious thought to how I was going to see Wan on the following weekend. I worked it out that I would need to be away from the camp for only around eleven hours, say, from 9:00 A.M. to 8:00 P.M. I could get to the Springtide Hotel by lunchtime, spend the afternoon with Wan and her friend, and then return to the camp. The difficulty was that passes were not given out for anything less than twenty-four hours, and *that* meant having to stay overnight, thereby incurring the expense of a bed and a meal or two. Since I had absolutely no money, not even enough for a packet of cheap cigarettes, it would clearly be impossible for me to stay overnight. Payday was not until two weeks hence and by then Wan would be back in Singapore.

The position seemed utterly hopeless. There would be no point in my groveling before some officer in the hopes of being granted compassionate leave because, without cash, I wouldn't be able to make use of it. Even if I

were successful in my quest to obtain a pass, I would then be reduced to cadg-
ing the necessary funds from my mates. It would mean having to borrow
twenty dollars or so, and I had as much chance of acquiring that much as I
had of finding buried treasure somewhere in the rubber plantation. My
dejection therefore deepened. Then on Tuesday evening, as a few of us were
walking down from the hut to the mess hut for dinner, my problem was
solved.

A scruffy, little, bedraggled orderly-room corporal walked toward us and,
when about twenty feet away, shouted out, "All leave passes are canceled!"
He then proceeded past us, head down, his rubberized cape shedding rainwater.

I turned after him. "Sorry, Corporal," I said, "what was that?"

He stopped and blinked at me through eyes wet with rain. "Leave passes
stopped. No more leave passes," he said.

"Why?" I called after him because he had already resumed his miserable
way.

"How should I know?" came the grudging reply over his shoulder.

My usual pleasurable anticipation of the meal to come had now well and
truly departed. Leave passes had been canceled. Evidently everyone was now
confined to camp. Going over the fence, which I had considered a possibility, was now out of the question. A few hours absence without leave would
have been a serious enough offense, but the act of quitting camp during a
period of apparent and specifically notified emergency, as this no doubt was,
would more than likely amount to desertion and the penalty attaching to this,
along with all the shame and everlasting self-reproach, made the whole thing
a nonstarter in my books. Any hope of my seeing Wan again completely vanished in the instant the corporal's words, "No more leave passes," registered
in my mind. By the time we reached the hut that served as the dining hall I
had already stopped worrying about the matter; Wan had slipped from my
grasp just as I had feared she might, and *that* was an end to it.

The dining hall was full. I joined the queue, got my food, sat down at one
of the long tables, and began eating. I had the distinct feeling, even though
I knew it not to be the case, that I had been plonked down in the middle of
a stage among all these actors, all amateurs whose varying degrees of talent
were being adversely affected by nervous tension. I could almost imagine a
voice suddenly shouting, "Cut!" or perhaps, "No, no, no—not like that!"
whereupon everyone would fall quiet and wait for corrective guidance. I

tried to close my mind to such meaningless thoughts, thoughts that I knew to be nonsensical and silly but at the same time seemed to have a frightening relevance. It was as though reality was being swamped by an unpleasant and burgeoning unreality. I deliberately began to eat more quickly, so as to give myself an immediate purpose and thereby take my mind away from such disconcerting thoughts. But the more quickly I ate, the more discomposed I became. I was glad to finish eating and step out into the darkness where the only sounds were the dripping of rain and the muffled throbbing of a diesel generator down on the airfield.

Lights in the close-by NAAFI hut beckoned, but being entirely without funds and hardly in the mood to try pitting my wits against potential lenders of the price of a bottle of beer and a few cigarettes, I veered away and began the climb back up through the trees. Once in the hut someone would help me out with a smoke. All the slit-trenches kept out of my way. I was getting good at avoiding them in that I had not stepped into one for a week or more; in this respect, however, I reckoned I must now be well into borrowed time.

4

Tension and a Surprise Summons

Morning, Wednesday, 3 December

I joined the dawn jog-trot as usual and then had breakfast. No reason had yet been given as to why all leave passes had been stopped, beyond that an emergency situation had arisen. Some of the airmen had heard on the wireless that the whole of Singapore and Malaya had been brought to a "state of readiness" and that certain troop movements were now taking place. Much official information could, in fact, have been conveyed to we lower orders at Sungei Patani, for matters were fast developing in certain quarters—matters which, though unknown to service personnel generally throughout the country, were the cause of a great deal of fluster and confusion among the military and political high-ups both at High Command in Singapore and at the War Office in London. In the meantime, we at the camp were allowed to plod on in ignorance, although no doubt the station commander and his close associates had been informed as to what was going on.

In the total absence of any official guidance it was impossible for us to understand what all the fuss was about. Those among us who had more than an average interest in the latest state of affairs listened avidly to news reports on the wireless. The communal wireless was in the NAAFI hut and therefore, owing to the row that generally went on in that facility, it was more often than not impossible to catch all that issued from the set.

After breakfast I tried to hear what was said on the early morning news report but failed to glean anything other than that a lot of troop movements were taking place consequent to certain intelligence concerning the latest positioning of Japanese naval and merchant ships off Southeast Indo-China. There was no mention of any recent diplomatic negotiations between Japan and Great Britain or of any statement made by Japan concerning Singapore or Malaya. Whatever was going on, if in fact anything, the wireless news people either did not know or had been restrained from broadcasting it.

On the way to the airfield one chap said, "Relax. If the Japs were about to attack us we'd have been told as much by now. The powers that be wouldn't keep us in the dark if things were that serious. In any case there'd be all kinds of arrangements to make and precautions to take—and we've heard absolutely nothing."

The airfield was very quiet. A glance at the parked Buffaloes, and a quick count, told me they were all there and that very little activity was taking place around them. Anyone casually gazing out across the airfield at the verdant green vista on its far side and up at Kedah Peak, which seemed today to be even closer than usual, would have taken a lot of convincing that Malaya was under any kind of threat. Everything looked so normal and undisturbed, quiet and peaceful. The sky was bright blue and such clouds as there were were floating very high up as little snow-white wisps. The early morning mist had disappeared, and already a heat haze was shimmering over the grass at the distant end of the airfield. There was absolutely nothing this morning to give the impression that imminent danger loomed. The air was warm and fresh and clean, with only the faintest hint of aromatic woodsmoke to give it that special Malay character.

As I became involved in my work, my thoughts and feelings were greatly detached from those I had recently been having. Completely gone were the strange misgivings, the pressing sense of foreboding, and the odd fleeting spells of inexplicable depression.

At ten o'clock Myers appeared on his bicycle. Notionally, he spent all his official time cleaning and reconditioning sparking plugs. He even had a small hut-cum-workshop exclusively allocated for this purpose. On the side, however, he operated a tea-swindle (unofficially selling tea at a high price), and it was reckoned that this activity not only took up a good percentage of his time but also made him a fair bit of money. On this bright morning Myers's battered tea urn was, as usual, strapped to a kind of metal platform he had rigged up over the back wheel. Across the handlebars were the two wooden trays in which he carted his sparking plugs around.

Myers also specialized in handing out crap advice, his opinions being often ludicrous and preposterous. "What'cher you idle bastards!" he called out in one of his more sociable forms of greeting. "Get your mugs ready. This lot's been specially made for you."

We knew that the tea had not been specially made for us; in fact, it had in all probability been hawked around the entire squadron for at least half an hour and by now would be stewed to a deep orangey-brown color and be imbued with a suitably matching taste.

As he dispensed his brew into our mugs Myers kept his rubbishy banter going. He was sweating furiously and had to break off every two or three minutes to wipe his spectacles. "You lot *do* realize that the Japs are on the move, don't you? Well I can tell you this much—they won't get very bloody far. They wouldn't dare start anything against the British out here; we'd slam them back to Tokyo in five minutes. Who the hell are they anyway? Just a tribe of vacant faced bastards. Plus they all wear glasses. Cheeky sods!"

There was no stopping him. He had evidently been honing his patriotic dissertation while on his morning round. "No," he almost shouted, "forget the Japs. If they start anything funny in Malaya they'll be on their way back to the Land of the Rising Sun in one bloody big jump."

"Push off," someone at last growled.

"Sod you then," Myers retorted. "Glad enough of the tea though, aren't you?" He extricated his bicycle from the legs of the Blenheim's left undercarriage; he always propped the thing up against one or another of the wheels despite frequently being rebuked for doing so.

George, the chap with whom I had palled up on the Penang jaunt, stepped toward Myers. "I'll give him a push off," he said.

"Me, too," another fitter volunteered.

Myers, discerning some kind of threat in the making, stood on his pedals hoping to achieve a swift departure, but the two caught up with him and, one on either side of the saddle, gave a concerted push, then proceeded to shake the whole contraption from side to side, much as kids are inclined to do.

Myers yelled out all kinds of inventive foul-mouthed expressions at his two tormentors before they finally let him go. By now he was traveling at a fair pace, and it was unwise of him to turn his head so as to further berate the two. "Stupid prats—make your own bloody tea in future I should," he shouted, having momentarily lost interest in navigating his bike. The machine wobbled dramatically; to steady it Myers lowered his feet to the ground and sort of ran with the bike as it careened off the perimeter track and onto the airfield. He then did another unwise thing by jamming the brakes on, whereupon the bike stopped dead. Myers shot clean over the handlebars and finished up sitting in a pool of lukewarm tea, his precious sparking plugs now scattered in the grass around him. He was furious. "You cross-eyed bastards!" he shrieked at the two who had been the cause of his mishap.

A grass mower that looked as though it had been constructed from scrap motorbikes was working its way across the airfield. It came close to the pen, spraying a fountain of sweet-smelling grass cuttings into the air, its Malay operator hunched dejectedly over the wheel. He was vibrating in rhythm with his charge and manifestly hating every minute of it. The sun climbed higher. The delightful morning wore on and, apart from the occasional racket of the mower, the airfield remained tranquil.

At noon most of us knocked off work for the day. The usual gang was at my table at lunchtime. Conversation, if one could call it that, was mainly centered on the "state of readiness." Rumors naturally abounded and were being passed from one table to the next, with nothing remotely credible being imparted in any direction. One of the camp telephone operators, a general duties airman who had received two days' instruction on the camp's primitive facility that had just two outside lines and about a dozen internal extensions, was sitting at our table. We pumped him for information, but he claimed not to be able to throw any light on the matter. In fact, many rumors, ultimately proven to be accurate or otherwise, originated in those days in telephone switchrooms by courtesy of nosy and inventive telephone operators who were not averse to putting their own bizarre interpretations on what they had heard. But this particular operator had nothing to say; we gained absolutely nothing from him.

On leaving the mess hut, feeling uncomfortably distended, I walked over to the NAAFI canteen to find out if anyone there had heard anything new and also to find someone in a sympathetic mood from whom to borrow a few dollars. It turned out that I was lucky, getting my hands on enough to buy a packet of Pirate cigarettes and a dozen bananas. My benefactor was a leading aircraftsman whom I had helped out with a small loan a few weeks earlier. He was in his late twenties and fed up to the back teeth with life on the camp. He had another chronic worry in that he had a girlfriend back in England who was, as he put it, "a real raver." His problem, of course, was that several hundred young chaps in her town doubtless saw her in the same way. Having listened to him banging on about his absent girlfriend for five or ten minutes, and having nodded my head solicitously now and again, and tutted when I considered it to be appropriate, I had made my move by asking him for the small loan.

"What's your view on this latest scare?" I asked, having heard more than enough about his girl.

He pulled himself out of his lovelorn misery and looked at me through eyes dulled with chronic heartache. "What? You mean this 'state of readiness' thing?"

"Yes."

"I can't understand it," he said. "It makes no sense to me. Who would venture to attack Malaya? At the same time, who could our boys be preparing to attack?" He was puffing on a Burmese cheroot, a useful-looking thing about an inch in diameter and probably four inches long. When he blew out, the smoke enveloped us both.

"It's got to be the Japanese," I replied. "They're doing all this occupation stuff in French Indo-China and negotiating some kind of military deal with Siam. If the Siamese government gives them the all-clear to move their troops into Siam it means they could be on the Malayan border within forty-eight hours."

"What's going on in French Indo-China then?" he inquired. It was pretty clear that he had been taking little or no interest in such developments.

"Don't you ever listen to the news on the wireless?" I put to him. "The Japs have been allowed by the Vichy French administration in Indo-China to position their military planes in that country, and, what's more, to move their troops through there without restriction or opposition of any kind. You do know, don't you, that the Vichy French are completely in the hands of the Germans and therefore do everything the Germans direct them to do—well, *almost* everything. There are, of course, many French people in Indo-China, as in France, who would disobey the Germans if it were half safe to do so, but the fact remains that for all practical purposes the French administration in Indo-China complies with the dictates of Germany. The Japs and the Germans have agreed by pact to help one another militarily so that French Indo-China is in no position to attempt to keep the Japs out. If you take a good look at the map you'll see that the Japanese now control a hell of a lot of territory north of Malaya, and even if they're not given permission to move into Siam, there's no doubt they would do so anyway if it suited them."

He put his cheroot down in a rusty ashtray and helped himself to one of my bananas, obviously feeling himself entitled. "But why should all *that* bother us here in Malaya?" he asked as he began munching.

I was amazed he knew so little. "Because Japan is not greatly interested in Indo-China apart from that it presents itself as an ideal launching pad for military operations against those territories in South-East Asia that have plentiful supplies of oil," I explained, calling on the scanty knowledge I had gained from old newspapers I had seen lying around and from reports on the wireless. "Japan would love to get its hands on Java and Sumatra—and then there's Borneo."

"What about Java and Sumatra and Borneo? I thought those places were nothing but jungle."

"Hell no," I replied. "They all have lots of oil and rubber."

"But Java and Sumatra are Dutch, aren't they?" he asked.

"Yes—well, the Dutch *control* both places."

"And Borneo is British?"

"No. The British control only part of Borneo. A large part of the country is controlled by the Dutch."

He discarded the banana skin and took up his cheroot, looked at it, then discarded that also. His face had an expression of deep distaste, which did not surprise me for the chewed end of the thing was in a disgusting state.

"Why doesn't Japan get the oil it needs from Java and Sumatra—come to that, why not also from Borneo?"

"Because the Dutch and the British and the Americans have all placed an embargo on oil supplies to Japan," I told him.

"Beats me," he grunted. "I just don't understand it."

"Well, it's simple, really. Japan has no oil of her own and has been refused supplies until such time as Japan withdraws her troops from China and French Indo-China. Apparently the Japs are not willing to do that, therefore it's at least a possibility that they'll try to get oil by force. In any case, it is well known that Japan would like to play the role of leading nation in the Far East—I mean financially and commercially as well as militarily. They've made this more and more evident over the past two years or so. But the point is that the Japs would have little chance of invading Java and Sumatra successfully without first subduing Singapore and Malaya. The Dutch, don't forget, are our allies and we wouldn't just stand idly by whilst Japan seized Dutch territories."

He began to slope off in the direction of his hut.

I called out after him. "The United States wouldn't like it if the Japs started anything this close to the Philippines. So if they don't want America after them, they'd better not do anything stupid. They'd be totally mad to risk going to war against America."

I rather think my last words fell on deaf ears because my departing friend gave no indication that he had heard. Perhaps, I thought, he was already compiling, in his troubled mind, a suitably worded letter to his girl. He would have to go easy on the pathos lest the censor burst into tears.

Already the sun's hitherto-dazzling brightness had started to subside and there was the kind of silence that falls over everything when thunder is in the offing. I could see that the blueness of the sky was being obliterated by a widespread darkening translucent veil.

Back in my room I sat on the edge of my bed, wondering what I should do to pass the time. Just when I thought how quiet everything had become, the gramophone started up and once again the melancholy strains of "Among My Souvenirs" drifted plaintively into my room. It was not that I disliked the song but rather that everything about the way it was played—from the poor condition of the record and the haunting voice of the male singer to the way the turntable kept running down—I found disturbing. The poignant, strangely brooding, and more or less constantly waxing and waning music imparted to the atmosphere an almost palpable quality of cheerless foreboding.

Feeling restive, I wandered around other rooms in the hut hoping to find something to snap me out of my dismal mood. In the room where the gramophone was being played I found three airmen in the extreme depths of boredom. They wore identical expressions that spoke of low spirits and discomfort, each sweating profusely, which wasn't surprising as the room was a malodorous oven and the air thick with cigarette smoke. As I entered all three turned to look at me but not one spoke. I stood in the doorway, having no desire to breathe the heavy fumes that enshrouded the three. Then the turntable began to slow, as it was wont to do, being gummed up inside no doubt with tobacco-smoke precipitates and a variety of vintage insect remains.

"Sod the thing!" one chap spat out vehemently. He got up from the bed on which he was sitting to crank the handle.

"Just wind the bloody thing up," one of the other two said, "and stop moaning."

"What the hell do you think I'm going to do?" asked the first chap viciously. "I notice *you* don't bloody strain yourself."

"Oh, just do it—and do it properly this time. You can chuck the damn thing away as far as I'm concerned."

The third occupant stood up and ground out his cigarette butt on the concrete floor with his shoe. "Oh dry up, you two. Take it in turns to wind the bloody thing, then there'll be no argument. I'm fed up anyway listening to that blasted record." He pushed past me and left the room, muttering under his breath.

The turntable gathered speed and "Among My Souvenirs" once more regained an acceptable pace for its closing bars:

I count them all apart
and, as the tear drops start,
I find a broken heart
among my souvenirs.

The final notes of the melancholy coda faded and I turned away, leaving the remaining two to sweat it out with nothing to relieve their suffering but the dodgy gramophone and a couple of records from a bygone age.

I moved on to another room and found six airmen playing cards, sitting on the floor squeezed in between the two beds that were the room's sole items of equipment apart from a couple of ramshackle bedside lockers unworthy of being described as furniture. The room was like the inside of a pressure cooker even though its shutters and door were wide open.

"Want to join in?" someone asked. "I'm about cleaned out. You can take my place." I noted his expression of financial defeat and physical distress.

"No, thank you," I replied. "I'm totally broke."

The banker gave a mirthless chuckle. "Most of these sods are nearly that, too," he said unkindly and proceeded to scoop up yet more cash to add to his pile.

In a way I was glad to have been able to give the best possible reason for not joining in. Since I had just showered and changed into clean things, the idea of sitting all afternoon in the steam and smoke of that dump failed to excite me.

I watched their hectic goings-on for probably half a minute longer before wandering off to George's room. He was not there. His roommate told me he was at work on the airfield.

"Doing what?" I asked. I was a bit surprised because it was unusual to be required to work in the afternoons.

"He was called back after lunch—an urgent engine overhaul job apparently."

"Poor old George," I said. "He won't go a bundle on that. It's bad enough in the mornings but in the afternoons the heat's absolutely terrible."

I returned to my room and put on a shirt, then walked down toward the pens where I understood George to be working. It took me no more than five minutes to reach that part of the airfield where I knew I would find George. I found his Blenheim parked in front of the pens, each of which housed a plane. Four aircraftsman fitters were working with George as I approached. He saw me as I walked toward him and called down to me from the access platform on which he was standing in his one-piece khaki overall. "What the hell do you want?"

"I don't want anything," I said. "Just thought I'd come down to break the bloody boredom."

George stared down at me for a few seconds, then gasped, "God! You must be desperate, Peter."

He wiped his hands. His face was flushed and perspiration was running from his brow and dripping from his nose and chin. From under his pith helmet a straggly stray lock of his brown-going-grey hair dangled over one of his eyes.

He wiped his face. Then, "Still worrying about that Malay girl?" he shot at me.

I would have preferred it had he not raised this particular matter, but as he had done so I was obliged to give some sort of reply.

"Not really," I said, dodging giving a direct answer. "No point. There's no way now I'm going to see her in Penang on Saturday. The only thing is that I'd have liked to let her know why."

"Yeah, there's that to it," agreed George, "but why worry? It's all beyond your control now."

"I can't even write to her—or telephone," I added. "God knows how long the post takes up here. In any case I don't even know her full name so I wouldn't know how to address a letter to her at that Springtide Hotel—she'd never get it. I can't telephone the hotel because I don't know the number in the first place, and, in the second place, there's no public telephone on the camp. Add to that the fact that I've no money for the telephone even if there was one, and if I got through to the hotel I wouldn't know who to ask for— and even if I did know who to ask for she might not be around to take my call. It's utterly hopeless, George."

"Put like that, I should say you're right. Just forget it," George replied, not very sympathetically or helpfully.

"What are you doing anyway?" I asked.

"Engine top-overhaul," George replied. "Rush job for some reason. It's not really due yet—must be on account of the scare."

"I wouldn't mind as long as I knew what the devil's going on. Have you heard anything?" I asked.

"Not a bloody thing. No one knows anything, but it's obvious that something's coming up to the boil. But the bastards never tell us anything, and it's no good expecting them to."

"What time are you knocking off?" I asked. He had started work again.

"Six o'clock—dinner time," he replied. "But it looks as though we'll be rained off long before then."

The sky grew even darker and the heat now bored up from the ground and remained trapped under the overcast. The stillness was uncanny, as though everything had succumbed to the terrible heat and humidity. Whenever the sound of metal on metal reached my ears it sounded sharp and unnaturally intrusive, as though in some perverse way it deliberately contrived to break through the hushed silence that prevailed.

On looking across toward the west boundary of the airfield I could see the twelve Buffaloes lined up as though ready for action. I had not seen any of them flying for some days, and even now nothing was going on around them. It was difficult to think that these perky and seemingly business-like planes were next to useless due to chronic engine and gun problems. Behind the Buffaloes loomed Kedah Peak like some watching, brooding entity.

Suddenly and sharply rain began to fall. I ran to the shelter of the nearest pen from where I watched George and his mates shut up shop on the Blenheim. They were all thoroughly drenched by the time they joined me, irritated at having to break off so suddenly but relieved in the sense that they had now probably finished work for the day.

George joined me and morosely examined his gently steaming overalls and his squelching work shoes. The other fitters stood a little apart from us, staring disconsolately out of the pen. Heavy rain pelted down on the concrete perimeter track and bounced up in a multitude of miniature fountains. The concrete was awash, water pouring off it and onto adjacent stretches of the grassed airfield. Such grass as could be seen from the pen, through the descending torrent of rain, now appeared to be flooded. The Blenheim on which George and his colleagues had been working was just a dark shape that now and again could be faintly discerned through the deluge. Kedah Peak was totally obscured.

There was no talk on account of the terrible din of rain on the roof of the pen, inside which it had grown very dark indeed. There seemed to be no letup in the ferocity of the storm though, surprisingly, there had as yet been no sign of thunder. Nevertheless something about this particular deluge made me uneasy. Somehow it was different in character from the customary onslaughts. George, I noticed, looked a bit fidgety as though bracing himself in anticipation of something unpleasant.

A sudden, near-deafening increase in the volume of noise announced that the rain had changed to hail. We saw that the ground was being quickly covered by huge hailstones. George stumbled over to the lighting switch and switched on the four low-wattage bulbs. No sooner had he done this than a monumental flash of blue-white lightning exploded immediately in front of the pen, accompanied by an ear-splitting detonation of thunder. The lights went out and several well-above-average obscenities were shouted out in automatic reaction. We remained for a few seconds crouched in our various instinctive positions of self-protection. For a further ten seconds or so we remained stunned, no one saying anything. Then, as it dawned on us that the strike had missed the pen and that none of us had been hurt, there was a bit of tentative laughter.

I had never experienced any fear of lightning, having never directly observed at close quarters its colossal damaging power. I had never, even in the slightest way, been adversely affected by lightning, yet I had been through a lot of quite violent thunderstorms, many of them since arriving in the Far East. This particular strike had been close and in fact had scorched a patch, some ten feet across, in the hailstone-covered grass immediately in front of the pen. But, more to the point as far as I was concerned, was the fact that the flash had jolted me. I felt a numbing tingle through my right side from shoulder to foot, and my arm and leg continued to quiver as though with diffuse minor cramps. My future attitude to lightning was to prove very different from that which it had been prior to this event.

When I brought to the attention of all present in the pen that I had received a slight shock from the lightning discharge, they were all solicitous and concerned, but I assured them that, as far as I could tell, I had suffered no serious harm. Within a few minutes the tingling and numbness disappeared, though my arm and leg continued to tremble very slightly.

A light drizzle continued just to ensure that things stayed reasonably moist, but for George and his colleagues work was over for the day. They had a brief discussion whether or not to resume work and by unanimous decision packed away their tools. After waiting for the rain to stop, they pushed off to their quarters.

Because my clothing was dry I saw no point in going back to the hut and thereby getting wet. I decided to stay in the pen in the hopes that the rain would, before long, stop completely. Already the sky was clearing from the east. On looking at my watch I was surprised to see that it was only 3:45 P.M. It had been so dark for the past forty minutes that I had come to feel that it was late evening. Then something came to my notice—something that marked the very beginning of an episode in my life that has, over long years, remained vividly and hauntingly in my mind.

Over the past fifteen minutes the rain had ceased completely. It was now much lighter with even a few pale shafts of sunlight breaking through untidy clouds in the southwest. The hailstones on the airfield had melted and vanished. In the air hung the smell of warm wet and fresh vegetation, a wonderfully clean smell like that of an English woodland in the warmth of August after a light evening shower. Imposing on this delightful smell were the background smells of rubber and engine oil and all the other not-unpleasant odors that inevitably emanate from the complicated workings of airplanes and which, to young and enthusiastic aero-fitters, is pure meat and drink.

What had come to my notice was the faint sound of an approaching aircraft. I walked out of the pen to the edge of the airfield and searched the sky for the source of the engine noise. The sound grew rapidly louder—a rich, fruity sound with plenty of power to it. Then, from my right, the aircraft roared across my line of vision and rushed at low level over the western half of the airfield, banked hard to the left, and, climbing slightly, turned about and disappeared behind the trees.

I immediately recognized the plane as a Lockheed Hudson, a twin-engined, twin-finned, American-built aircraft used mainly for maritime reconnaissance work and, from time to time, for the clandestine nocturnal delivery of agents and supplies to resistance workers in hostile areas. We had never seen a Hudson at Sungei Patani, although there were two squadrons of them in Malaya, No. 1 at Kota Bharu and No. 8 partly at Kuantan and partly at Sembawang on Singapore Island, both being RAAF squadrons.

It seemed to me that the Hudson had been inspecting the airfield in preparation for a landing, and that it had perhaps been holding off for some time until visibility improved. I scanned the eastern sky, as it would be from this direction that its landing approach would be made. Sure enough I almost immediately caught sight of the plane, very low down, making its turn onto its final approach run. It could not have been any more than a couple of hundred feet above the tops of the rubber trees as it came in, nose and flaps down and engines revving furiously. Clearly the pilot had correctly gauged the length of the airfield and was about to execute the shortest of short-field landings. Its engines cut as it cleared the eastern boundary of the airfield and the plane sank promptly to within a few feet of the grass, held off for a few seconds, and then touched down, sending back a huge spray of water from the collection of miniature lakes the storm had created. The plane came to a stop barely a couple hundred feet from the western perimeter, between the line of Buffaloes and the pens where I was standing. It was now only about a hundred yards from me.

An RAF van came along the perimeter track and, when just outside the pen, turned onto the airfield and splashed across to the Hudson. I noticed the plane bore no identification markings on its unusual camouflage livery, which consisted of random splashes of dark grey, reddish ochre, and bright green. Normal camouflage colors for British aircraft at the time were beige and drab green; therefore, the Hudson looked most unusual and even somewhat fancy when viewed at close quarters.

The van stopped in front of the Hudson but well to one side of it. Someone got out of the passenger side of the vehicle, walked as close to the nose of the plane as was advisable, in that the propellers were still idling, and looked up at the pilot, who by now had slid open the side shield of the cockpit. Some kind of shouted exchange ensued, the details of which were drowned to me by engine noise. The person on the ground, whom I did not recognize, pointed back toward the eastern end of the airfield, the end at which the Hudson had touched down. He then climbed back into the van, which splashed back to the perimeter track and proceeded to depart in the direction of the control tower.

My curiosity was by now thoroughly aroused. This was something that by no means happened every day. The strange camouflage, the absence of identification markings, and the landing on an airfield so waterlogged that it would normally have been closed for at least twenty-four hours rendered the event something rather special. I imagined that the Hudson must be carrying some VIP in connection with the "state of readiness" scare—perhaps someone wishing to see for himself the actual level of readiness we had so far managed to achieve here at Sungei Patani.

Directly after the van left the scene the Hudson's engines revved up and the plane turned and trundled past the line of Buffaloes and over to the far side of the airfield. Once there its engines broke into a throaty roar and it virtually raced back to the eastern end of the field where it turned and stopped. Its two engines cut out and once again the airfield fell silent.

At this point, because the Hudson was a little too far away for me to see what might come next, I moved away from the pen. I had seen all I was likely to see and, as it had ceased raining, I walked into the plantation and made for my hut.

The sun's rays pierced through the foliage of the rubber trees and shone through the shutters of my room in blinding daggers of brightness. This sharp intrusion of light dispelled the earlier gloom, but the sun was rapidly sinking down to the western slopes of Kedah Peak and in another hour or so the clearing around the hut would begin to darken. Once more an eerie silence would clamp down over everything.

Evening, 3 December

I lay on my bed and slept. When I awoke I felt stupefied, as though a vampire bat had been getting at me. It was well past the time for dinner. I got up from the bed, grabbed my knife, fork, and spoon, and hurried off to the mess hut. The sun had disappeared with only a glorious low-down orange glow in the sky to show where it had been. In the hushed quietness of the plantation a multitude of long shadows blended into the darkening earth from which thin early vapors of night rose.

I ate very little dinner. Nothing special was talked about during the meal except that word was passed around that two British naval ships, *Prince of Wales* and *Repulse,* had arrived in Singapore.[1] Some of us had vaguely heard of these vessels, *Prince of Wales* being a battleship and *Repulse* a battlecruiser. The wireless, it seemed, had not stated why these two powerful capital ships had been sent out to the Far East; therefore, the general assumption was that they were here to confirm that the British were ready and fully capable of repelling any attack on either Singapore or Malaya. No one expressed any particular surprise or delight at this item of news for the simple reason that naval ships had frequently been used in various parts of the world as a deterrent to would-be attackers. Their presence struck none of us as an indication that something big might be about to transpire.

Most of us had finished eating when a loud voice shouted, "575176 Shepherd!"—my number and name.

In an instant a profound hush fell on the proceedings. To a man, the gathered airmen looked around to see who had barked those words out so authoritatively. The source of the almost-chilling shout was a sergeant whom I had never before seen. I stood up and raised my hand, thus causing all present, including three or four Chinese servers, to eyeball me with surprise and sympathy.

"Come here, lad!" the sergeant called out, beckoning me to join him.

I negotiated the tables and chairs and stood before him. "Yes, Sergeant?" I inquired. He was surprisingly well groomed and turned out, considering the time of day, looking as though he had washed and changed into clean clothes just a few moments ago. Of medium height and probably twenty-six or twenty-seven years of age, he looked as though an intensive slimming course would benefit him. He was obviously a nontechnical type—I would have known him had he been otherwise. It seemed possible that he might be attached to the orderly room organization, which was a closed book to the majority of fitters and flight mechanics. His well-rounded shape suggested that here was a chap who spent a good deal of his time on his backside, typing, sorting, stamping, and filing. However, despite his apparent lack of physical fitness, he had at least contrived to discharge his clerical duties well enough to have achieved the rank of sergeant while still relatively young.

"Aircraftsman Shepherd?" he asked imperiously.

"Yes, Sergeant."

"You're wanted in the orderly room—straight away."

"What for, Sergeant?" I inquired, for this was a most unusual summons: the last time I had received such a summons I had been informed that I was to be posted overseas.

"There's a squadron leader who wants to see you about something," the sergeant replied.

"Squadron Leader who?" I asked, by this stage becoming not only increasingly curious but also a little uneasy.

"Palliser, or Balliser—or something. None of us have seen him around before today. He's not on the strength at Sungei Patani. We think he must have flown in first thing this morning."

"Okay. I'll just get my things from the table."

I turned to go back to the table at which I had been sitting to collect my knife, fork, and spoon. "Look sharp, lad," the sergeant called out after me.

How ridiculous, I thought, that I had to be pushed around like this by someone who spent his days shoveling papers about and growing fat due to a disinclination to exercise, or to overeating, or both. He was no doubt the type who did everything by the book—punctiliously referring to the manual on each occasion he transferred any particular document from one tray to another, having of course rubberstamped it en route, and then making and initialing a suitable note on the appropriate record form.

At the table I swigged the last of my tea and grabbed my utensils. I then went over to the wash-up sink, but the sergeant shouted to me, "Never mind that. Do it later!" He evidently was used to giving orders and having them obeyed, within the bounds of the orderly room anyway, but it was plain that he had had little to do with technical personnel who, generally speaking, received reasonably courteous treatment from their NCOs. I had by now decided I did not much care for him.

In answer to my casual questioning as we walked, he told me that he had arrived at Sungei Patani only a few days before and, curiously, I thought, that before coming to the camp he had been stationed "here and there." On the way to the orderly room I wondered why I had been summoned and could envisage only two things—my pilot training posting had come through, or I had been reported for hanging around on the airfield while off duty. It was likely to be bad news if it was not the pilot training thing.

The orderly room, simply another hut, consisted of a couple of rooms for the duty NCOs and clerks, another for the telephone exchange operator, and, along a corridor, three or four more rooms used by the station commander, his adjutant, and such other officers as he had to help him run the camp.

The sergeant told me to wait, then passed through a doorway and along the corridor. From where I was standing I saw him stop at an office door and give a discreet, almost timid knock. I heard the door open and saw the sergeant step into the office. I strained my ears to pick up what was being said, but the only sound I could hear came from the telephone exchange room—very low muffled speech—perhaps the operator engaged in a sneaky conversation with one of his fellow sufferers at some other RAF camp.

The sergeant returned. "Right, follow me," he mumbled, now not nearly so bumptious and full of himself.

I suddenly thought of something. "I'm not wearing any head-dress," I pointed out. "I can't salute as I am."

"Oh, never mind that. Just follow me," he said with noticeable irritation.

Then I saw a pith-helmet hanging on a peg. I grabbed hold of it and put it on. I had to ram it on because the thing was at least two sizes too small.

The sergeant went first. He still seemed cowed and not at all the man he had hitherto been. The office door stood slightly ajar. He knocked rather timidly again and bent an ear for the invitation to enter.

"Yes," spoke a voice from within.

The sergeant looked uncertain as to what to say or do. He just stood there, waiting.

"Yes, come in!" the voice called out.

With this the sergeant leapt into action. He pushed open the door and walked quickly into the office. He then stood with his back to the door and nodded to me to go in.

I went in and the sergeant closed the door behind us. The office was dimly lit. A figure sat at a desk. That was all I had the time to take in before the voice at the desk said, "All right, Sergeant, thank you. You can leave us now."

The sergeant said, "Yes, sir," and pushed off. He closed the door meekly and quietly behind him.

I was left standing facing the person behind the desk. I had been in the office a matter of ten seconds and thought it the right time to salute. I therefore drew myself to attention and saluted the officer. His eyes, I imagined anyway, were on me; I must have been right because he saluted in return, something that immediately struck me as odd because he was not wearing a cap. Furthermore, his salute was like something out of a Hollywood movie.

My eyes became somewhat adjusted to the miserable lighting level, and I was able to see things in a bit more detail. The officer, squadron-leader stripes on his epaulettes, was a slight figure of a man. His hair was fair and very much thinning, so much so that it had not only receded at the temples but had also quit an appreciable area at the front of his head. He was, I judged, around thirty-five. His complexion was smooth and pale, with no sign of sunburn or prolonged exposure to a tropical climate. He was clean-shaven and had eyes that might have been described as light blue, or grey— nondescript eyes that, despite the absence of any strong color, were nevertheless striking in a peculiar way. His shirt, blue, with perspiration patches around the armpits, displayed little to indicate anything of his personal history or prowess. Thus there were no medal stripes, no pilot's wings—nothing apart from the squadron-leader stripes.

I remained standing to attention before him. He scanned a couple of papers that lay on the desk. Then he raised his head and our eyes met for the briefest instant. After that, even though we continued to look one another in the face, I felt strangely aware that his eyes were looking straight through me. It was the kind of expressionless stare into which one can read absolutely nothing. His face was the face of someone who is daydreaming and yet, though his eyes seemed not to be focused on mine, I caught in them the almost imperceptible responses revealed in eyes that are closely following some movement or are concentrating on something.

He spoke. "I see that you have applied for pilot training, Shepherd." His voice was ill-suited to his face. I had expected a fairly high-pitched voice— probably a bit fussy with a bit of genuine or assumed class about it. Instead, it turned out to be rather deep, measured, cautious, and softly spoken. In it I detected a slight accent that could have been Australian or South African. It struck me as the voice of a man who, by nature, or under the present circumstances, was being extremely careful about what he said. I instinctively felt that he was very probably already gauging how gullible I was and how much he could slip past me. What with the way he was regarding me, and his style of vocal delivery, I began to feel uneasy but at the same time was heartened to learn that the summons was connected with my pilot training application rather than some misdemeanor I had perpetrated.

"Yes, sir," I replied.

"Done any flying at all?" The blank gaze stared straight through me again.

"Only a couple of pleasure flights as a schoolboy and a few flights in Harvard trainers at RAF Kidlington, sir."

"Any problems with those?" he asked. "I mean—any sickness or dizziness or anything like that?"

"No, sir."

"Do you know anything about American planes?"

His question surprised me because the Harvard trainer, which I had mentioned a few moments ago, *was* an American plane.

"Just the Harvard, sir. I worked on them at Kidlington."

He appeared, for a moment, to be somewhat taken aback, but he quickly recovered his composure. Not once did his eyes cease boring through mine.

"Ah, yes, of course," he breathed, and then he looked down at his papers.

Then I suddenly remembered having undertaken two weeks of training on Lockheed Hudsons when invitations had been put out for engine fitters to volunteer to act as flight engineers on the type. It had been in late 1940 when Hudsons were about to be flown directly to the United Kingdom from America instead of being transported by sea. Due to very heavy shipping losses in the north Atlantic it had been deemed safer to get them to the United Kingdom in this way even though it entailed a nonstop flight of almost eleven hours. Although many Hudsons had been brought over in this way I had, as it turned out, not been called for this duty despite having volunteered and despite having received intensive technical instruction on the aircraft. I remembered thinking at the time that perhaps someone had at last taken notice of the fact that I was still only seventeen and that, under the terms of my apprenticeship contract, my service with the RAF had not yet even commenced.

"Then there's the Lockheed Hudson," I added. "I did a two-week intensive course on them in late 1940."

At this the squadron leader became noticeably interested. He stared through me even more piercingly and sat motionless as though suddenly ossified. "Oh," he breathed gruffly. "So you know something about Hudsons then?"

"Very little, really, sir."

"Well, how much do you know? Tell me about them. There's no need for you to stand to attention by the way."

I stood easy and racked my brains. I was able to remember a number of technical points.

"Sir, the Lockheed Hudson is a twin-engined aircraft having Wright Cyclone radial air-cooled engines. It has Scintilla magnetos and three bladed variable pitch propellers—er," I hesitated, wondering how much he wanted from me.

"Yes. Carry on, please."

"Twin fins. Retractable undercarriage. Fuel pumps on both engines and an electrically driven pump for take off, landing, and emergencies. Four fuel tanks—total capacity, I think, of around five hundred gallons with provision for added long-range tanks. Two thirty-volt generators of fifty amps output. Sperry automatic pilot, Fowler flaps. Stalling speed around 90 MPH. Cruising speed 140 MPH. Maximum speed 240 MPH." I paused for breath.

He had now relaxed a little and had picked up his two papers and was straightening them by tapping them on the desktop. "That's fine," he said.

If I had pleased him with my little homily, the fact did not reveal itself on his wan countenance. A transient lifting of the corners of his mouth, more a fleeting wry smirk than a smile, was the only indication he gave to indicate how well I had acquitted myself.

"Shepherd, if you had the necessary spares and equipment," he said, "do you think you could carry out some maintenance work on a Hudson?" The question sounded easy, or at least might have sounded that way to someone having little understanding of aircraft. To the squadron leader it was a question that was as straightforward to answer as, say, "Are you able to tell me how many feet there are in a mile?" Therefore, he, for one, had scant knowledge of aircraft or of engineering matters.

"It would all depend on the work that needed doing, sir," I replied. "Even routine maintenance can be extremely complicated and almost always calls for at least two fitters. A basic inspection and perhaps a few external adjustments would really be the limit of my capabilities—and of course I would need to have an engine maintenance manual available for reference."

"Quite," he replied. "I do understand. But what about the odd repair—like some kind of work to repair minor damage to the aircraft itself. Could you cope with something like that?"

He clearly had not a clue about airplanes and no doubt thought that keeping a plane flying was no more difficult than building a model plane out of balsa wood.

I did not much care for the direction the discussion was going, and furthermore I was baffled as to what it was all about. However, I was reluctant to talk myself out of something that might ultimately prove to my benefit. Therefore I put on my most confident expression in an effort not to put him off at this early stage.

"Oh yes, sir," I assured him, "providing I had the parts. I wouldn't envisage any difficulty with that." If he noticed me gulp, he said nothing.

The borrowed helmet had started pinching. I pushed it back a little to ease my discomfort. He watched as I did this and I felt it prudent to explain the situation to him. "The helmet's not mine, sir—borrowed it from a peg in the orderly room—it's rather too small for me."

He laughed—at least I think he did. He made a noise that might well have been a laugh, although he might just as well have been experiencing difficulty in clearing his throat. His mouth went through none of the grimacing contortions that accompany a laugh. "Take the damn thing off then," he instructed.

"Thank you, sir," I said, doffing the thing.

He rose from behind the desk. "Look here, Shepherd," he said. Then he sat down again.

Outside, the light had now all but gone. In ten minutes time it would be quite dark, but there would be a fair-sized moon if the sky stayed clear. Inside the room the only illumination was a solitary shaded bulb around which danced an excited troupe of mosquitoes and a medley of other insects. The whirling gathering was swelling by the minute. Through a half-opened window came the muted sound of wireless music, but hardly the kind of music that would be deemed appropriate to the present circumstances. The tune was a song called "Caravan"—a quickstep I had often heard played during Saturday night dances at Woodstock back in England. Woodstock had been the first village along the Oxford road out of RAF Kidlington where I had worked on Harvards earlier in the year.

It was not a large office. There was no carpet on the floor. In it stood just the writing desk, a few utility chairs, and a table, the last set against a wall. There were half a dozen coat pegs screwed to a wall adjacent to the door. It was dim and hot.

Having sat down again, he resumed speaking. "There's something you may like to do. It presents an opportunity for you to expand your experience."

An older hand than I would most likely have sensed red lights flashing and danger bells clanging at this, but not me. I was still too young and trusting to perceive a really oily "con" heading in my direction. His eyes were gazing through me again. The faint shadows of flying insects were cast on his shining pate like a moving lacework pattern.

"What would that be, sir?" I inquired enthusiastically—all ears.

He carried on. "It will be entirely on a voluntary basis, of course."

"Yes, sir?" I inquired again, wishing he would get on with it.

He leaned back in his chair, expressionless. "Are you interested?" By all means I was interested. What little he had so far told me, although it amounted to next to nothing, could hardly have failed to interest me. The words "Hudson" and "voluntary" indicated a change of aircraft and suggested a bit of excitement with, perhaps, recognition of some sort at the end.

"Very interested, sir," I replied. "Could I ask what the job is, sir?"

He got up again and shut out the drifting dance music by closing the window. I immediately imagined I could feel the air in the room becoming warmer. Perhaps his slimness, I thought, had the effect of making him appear taller than he in fact was, as he lounged back against the window, hands in the pockets of his khaki slacks. I had not seen many officers at Sungei Patani, apart from a few commissioned pilots, but the squadron leader struck me as being the poorest specimen of the lot. He lacked both the bearing and the manner of an officer, and his lack of sundry decorations and pilot's wings gave him a sartorially impoverished appearance.

He was nevertheless a squadron leader and therefore on the fourth rung up the commissioned rank ladder. To me he was very much one of that class of elevated beings whom I was expected to admire and respect. I consequently paid close attention to what might come next.

He leaned forward and, holding me with those eyes, started up. "A Lockheed Hudson landed on the airfield this afternoon. It's not an RAF plane, but we've agreed to provide it with assistance. I believe that you'd be the ideal chap for the job—all on a voluntary basis, of course."

This was the second time he had mentioned the voluntary angle, and once again I translated the word into excitement and recognition. I would here add that at no time did he go to the trouble of pointing out that voluntary assignments almost always seem to terminate rather unpleasantly for the volunteer. I was ripe for getting myself involved in anything exciting and rewarding—but, as will be appreciated, I was considerably wet behind the ears.

"I understand, sir," I said, with what I thought to be appropriate gravity. "I'm willing to give any help I can." My words clinched the deal and by uttering them I unwittingly became involved in an intrigue that was to prove not only utterly baffling but, also, forever disturbing.

"Well, Shepherd, this is what you could do to help us. Please listen carefully. Commit everything I say to memory. Write nothing at all down and speak to absolutely no one about any part of it, either before or after your job is completed. Don't worry about your supervising NCO because all that will be taken care of. Just regard the whole affair as a spot of special leave. All you'll be required to do will be to go along with the suggestions I'll now make to you. Drag up a chair and sit down."

I did as he asked. He resumed his seat. I could feel my heart beating faster with excited curiosity. He continued speaking for quite some time, and as he did so I was only vaguely aware of the myriad mosquitoes that darted around the light bulb, of the stifling heat of the dimly lit room, of the outside silence broken only now and again by low passing voices that came and went no more intrusively than the momentary sighing of a light wind. Nor was I any longer aware of the odor of creosote and stale perspiration.

5 Night Flight to the North

"The Hudson is en route to the North. Apart from the pilot there's only one other person in the crew—let's call him 'the observer,' although he's a little more than that. Anyway, it happens that this second chap has been taken ill and has had to be withdrawn from the flight. This means that the pilot cannot continue unless he gets a replacement observer."

The squadron leader fell silent for a few seconds, giving me time to digest what he had said. Then he carried on. "This is where you come in, Shepherd. I think you're just the lad for the job—young, keen, fit, and technically qualified."

At this almost matter-of-fact revelation my mouth dried up. A quiver of excitement rippled through me. Instinctively I drew a deep breath to get more oxygen into my system. It was not the time for me to say anything— I would have found it well nigh impossible to do so anyway.

But my mind was racing. He had said nothing about flying being part of the job. There had, of course, been the pilot training thing, and he had asked me if I had done any flying. I had said nothing that could possibly have given him the impression that I could climb into a Hudson and become a competent observer in about two minutes flat. And what good was my smattering of technical knowledge about the Hudson going to be if I was flying in the thing? I worked my brain hard and took several more deep breaths, yet I still could not see why I should have been singled out for the task. I had never even worked on a Hudson and certainly had never flown in one. I thought I should put him right on a thing or two before he became too carried away. It meant butting in, so I did.

"Excuse me, sir," I said. "I must make it clear that I've had absolutely no experience as a member of a flight crew and that my knowledge of Hudsons is only theoretical."

He gave a quick dismissive wave of his hand. "That's okay, Shepherd—you'll cope, I'm sure. Actually it's unlikely that you'll be called upon to do anything much—perhaps a spot of very minor work on the engines or something when the Hudson lands at the other end. You'll be returning to Sungei Patani well within twenty-four hours—in the same aircraft, of course. That's all there'll be to it, except perhaps for a bit of lifting and loading. I must mention that the flight will be quite a long one—probably around four hours duration—so prepare yourself for some boredom. Everything will be taken care of for you—flying overalls, parachute, food and drink, etc. The pilot will give you all you need and answer your questions. He's a very experienced chap—been flying for years, I understand."

I had stopped hyperventilating even though the room's atmosphere had become something like that of a horse box stuck in a traffic jam on a hot midsummer day. He continued, but only after he had opened the window a little and let in a few breaths of warm night air together with another dozen or so mosquitoes. He closed it again. "This is not an RAF flight, but you shouldn't let that bother you. I should tell you that you won't lose anything by it—in fact, quite the reverse may turn out to be the case."

A lot of questions were queuing up in my head—basic questions to which I needed answers. He seemed, now, to be the sort of person who would not mind responding to a few fundamentally reasonable queries—despite the eyes which, it seemed, had still not yet managed to get me into focus.

"Where will the Hudson be going?" I asked.

"You'll be flying to the north, Shepherd. However, it needn't concern you at the moment."

I turned a few facts over in my mind and came up with something that raised another question. "But four hours flying north would mean Burma or perhaps Siam, sir," I ventured. "Am I close to the mark?"

His movement in his chair might have been him easing a back strain or sorting out his trouser gusset, but it struck me as being a lot more like an embarrassed squirm.

"I'm afraid we can't go into that just now," he said, a bit pained. "The pilot will tell you in good time."

I was swiftly getting the hang of the rules applying to voluntary assignments—basically one is given minimum information and asks no questions. The arrangement seemed very much balanced in favor of all parties except the actual volunteer. Should I make myself a nuisance by insisting on answers to my questions? Or should I go along with it in the interests of excitement and the lure of recognition? Then I remembered that he had told me the pilot would tell me all I needed to know. I could always pull out if I were still unhappy after speaking to him. I relaxed and listened.

"Look, Shepherd," the squadron leader breathed quietly, beginning to tidy up his two pieces of paper again. "I must get on now. What you must do is talk to the pilot. The only thing is that he'll be unable to see you for another hour or so." He folded the papers and stuck them in his trouser pocket. This seemed an abrupt end to the discussion; after all, I had learned very little beyond that I had been sought out to go on a four-hour flight to a place as yet unidentified to me but somewhere outside Malaya. I had not yet been told the purpose of the flight, nor with whom I was going. The whole thing seemed very odd. The fact that I knew not who the squadron leader was did not in itself worry me unduly, and I would stress, yet again, that I was just a youth of eighteen who had been trained to comply with orders and follow instructions given by officers and NCOs without question. It is now amazing to think that, at the time, I was so unworldly and meekly compliant that if a pilot officer, which was the lowest commissioned rank in the RAF, had ordered me to climb to the top of the nearest tree and there sing the national anthem, I would almost certainly have obliged. Unusual things happen in the armed forces simply by courtesy of discipline, unswerving compliance with orders, and a convenient and expected willingness on the part of the rank and file not to think too much. Hence it is that the most remarkable and also the most pathetic, dreadful, and catastrophic events take place in the military from time to time.

"When will the flight be carried out, sir?"

"Ah—speak to the pilot about that, Shepherd. He'll give you all the details." He was now yanking open the door. "Anything more?" he asked.

"Yes, sir. When will I meet the pilot?"

He stepped out into the corridor. "If you follow me I'll show you where he'll be a little later on."

I closed the office door behind me. A low, murmuring voice drifted toward us from the direction of the telephone exchange; the guy in there, apparently, was not yet through bending the ear of some kindred spirit perhaps two or three hundred miles away. I could not hear the wireless music I had heard some time ago. We reached the orderly room office where I returned the bantam pith-helmet to its peg.

Outside, the air was a smothering damp blanket. A low half moon hung in the trees like a bright golden lantern. We walked the length of a pathway to another hut about a hundred feet away. A door stood open. Inside, a few niggardly lamps burned as in the hut we had just left. If there was one thing they specialized in at Sungei Patani it was dim electric lamps—doubtless a necessary measure to minimize the load on the electricity generator. The squadron leader led me along a short corridor to a door. It was locked. He turned to me. "There you are, Shepherd. This is where you'll find him, say, in an hour or so. Be careful to listen to all he says and I urge you to do exactly what he says—that's very important. Are you quite clear on that?"

I was still enthusiastic, and still deferential. "What is his name, sir?" I asked, being interested to know whom I would be meeting.

He gave me one of his stares, that is, as though I were not there. His balding head, glistening with perspiration, caught a bit of grudging light from a lonely overhead bulb. It gave the top of his head an uncanny, incandescent appearance, as though it had suddenly assumed an orange-red temperature.

"His name? Ah, just refer to him as the Hudson pilot for now. He'll let you know how to address him."

"There's another thing, sir," I said.

"What's that?"

"I have no money, sir. I may need some." I stood there, feeling like an inconsequential pauper, which in a way I was. He merely stared back at me, his head still glistening.

"I shouldn't think you'll need any," he replied. Thus dashed was my foolish hope that he might fish fifty dollars or so from his trouser pocket by way of advance expenses. "The pilot will see you all right, I'm sure," he added.

He was obviously anxious to be off. I could tell that because he pushed past me and strode down the corridor toward the outside door. But he suddenly stopped, causing me to bump gently into him.

"I'm sorry, sir," I said.

"That's okay," he replied. "My fault." He said all this without bothering to turn around to face me.

Then, still without turning, he added, "Shepherd—just remember. Don't say a word to anyone about this. Absolutely no one. Don't say anything about any part of it either before you fly or when you get back. If anyone in authority wants to know anything, just refer them to me. But I stress again—don't discuss any of it with a soul. Do you understand that?"

"Yes, sir—I understand—thank you, sir," I said.

We had almost reached the door and I expected him to turn to dismiss me formally. He did not do so, however, but simply walked off into the darkness. I stood in the doorway, watching as he went. But then he must have realized he had forgotten something for he half turned and over his shoulder said, "Have a good flight, Shepherd—but I may see you again before you go." With that he gave a wave that looked like a back-handed salute or something. Whatever it was, it in no way resembled the approved salute as shown in the manual. I did nothing in return. He would not have seen anyway. The darkness swallowed him up.

I wandered off toward my hut. It was a little after 8:00 P.M. Both excitement and uncertainty occupied me as I walked through the trees. I could have dealt with my excitement better had I known exactly when the Hudson would be taking off and who the pilot was. I had been told nothing about him. Would he be the quiet fatherly type or young and bumptious? What was it he was expecting me to contribute to the flight?

I decided not to go to my room but instead to go down to the NAAFI hut where I might be able to borrow a few cents with which to buy a beer. I found the air in there heavy with cigarette smoke. A dozen or more airmen were sitting at tables, chatting and sipping beer and squash. Banana skins, beer bottles, cigarette tins and packets littered the tables. Ashtrays were overflowing. To a man these young people looked as though they had recently emerged from a Turkish bathhouse. All were flushed with the heat and perspiring freely. Most, against regulations, had removed their shirts despite the sly and silent attentions of mosquitoes. It was not the mosquitoes that flitted around the lightbulbs that presented the difficulty but rather the loners that, virtually invisible, lurked and planned and probed where to alight for the undisturbed meal that might, after just a few minutes, very well leave the unsuspecting donor with considerable ongoing health problems.

A few heads lifted when I entered and I stood motionless for a few seconds, scanning the tables for a potential benefactor. Someone succumbed to my cringing and very soon I was sitting at a table and swigging from a bottle of Tiger beer. One of the young Chinese boys behind the bar, who had latched on to me some weeks earlier and who had persuaded me to help improve his English, slipped me a handful of bananas.

The talk was about the latest news report on the wireless, the general gist being that a state of emergency had been proclaimed by the governor of Singapore, Sir Shenton Thomas, two days earlier, that is, on 1 December. Apparently many of Singapore's residents were at last waking up to the fact that Japan might just be idiotic enough to go on the rampage against Far Eastern territories, including Singapore and Malaya. It had been reported that the atmosphere in Singapore was a confusing mixture of bewilderment, anxiety, near panic, and downright indifference. It seemed that up and down Malaya troops were being strategically deployed and the whole of the armed forces defense organization was now at a high state of readiness. Strangely enough, Sungei Patani appeared to have missed all this, at least for all we airmen knew. In northern Malaya substantial troop movements were being effected in the light of the possibility that Japan might decide to march into Siam and then cross the border into Malaya. The wireless had assured us that the commander in chief was keeping his finger on the pulse of developments. This character, Air Chief Marshall Sir Robert Brooke-Popham,[1] had control of both the RAF and army forces but not those of the navy. He had served many years with the RAF, had retired in 1937 but had been recalled for service with the outbreak of World War II. He had a reputation as an exceedingly pleasant and sociable chap but one who was much inclined to be hesitant and muddle-headed. His voice, it was said, was remarkably high pitched and jerky in delivery—in fact, a voice that in itself inspired no one. He sported a large RAF-type moustache, wore shorts that completely covered his knees, and used his hands as temporary filing cabinets, being rarely seen without an untidy bunch of documents in each hand. He was balding; moreover, he was too long in the tooth for the job he had been handed. The general verdict among those who knew him, and even among those who had met him for just a brief period, was that this amiable curiosity of an officer was, sadly, very much past his best. However, it should be remembered that the war in Europe and North Africa and other places had, and still was, making deep inroads into the reserves of those of acceptable "social class" possessing top leadership qualities.

For Sir Robert Brooke-Popham, as with Singapore and Malaya, time was fast running out. It would have taken a far more competent person than this incumbent commander, and a vastly superior force of aircraft, to repel the thunderous tide that was peaking up and about to overwhelm the Malayan peninsula.

On the wireless there had also been reports concerning sightings of an unusual number of Japanese naval vessels off the southeast coast of French Indo-China. To counterbalance this ominous news it had been confirmed that the two British naval ships, *Prince of Wales* and *Repulse,* had arrived in Singapore, both of which had made a slow close in-shore trip around to the naval base. Receptions had been held on *Prince of Wales* for local VIPs. It was even thought certain that the Japanese consul general had been entertained aboard the battleship.[2]

The members of the group into which I had insinuated myself seemed to be making scant sense of this wireless news. The general opinion was that it was still all a "storm in a teacup." That was as far as it went for them—and who could be surprised at this, for, despite the state of emergency proclamation, we airmen on the camp had been told precisely nothing.

No warning had been conveyed to the airmen by any officer or NCO. So at Sungei Patani it was "business as usual," that is, no change, just silence.

One wonders if this lack of communication between the camp senior officers and the other ranks in regard to matters of potentially grave significance such as the Japanese threat was in accordance with policy and standing orders. If so, in this case it amounted to downright criminal disregard for the safety of personnel and equipment. At the least unfavorable judgment it demonstrated incompetence and dereliction of duty on a condemning scale.

The air in the canteen had become well nigh unbearable, there being an all-pervading smell of bananas, beer, cigarette smoke, and perspiration. Because of the dim-out regulations the window shutters were supposed to be kept closed during hours of darkness, but, despite this, many were fully open, thus allowing the light to get out and the mosquitoes in.

Time was moving on. Very shortly I would have to begin making my way to the hut where I hoped I would find the Hudson's pilot waiting to see me.

"You're quiet, Peter," said one of the group.

"Tired," I replied, "and hot."

I knew that this was the time for me to be on my way before I became drawn into some probing chatter that might give rise to suspicion concerning my reticence. I remembered a joke I had heard a few days earlier and reeled it off as well as I could, reckoning that on reaching the punchline I could remove myself from their company while they were cracking their sides. Under the pressure of the circumstances, the joke turned out to be a bit of a flop. It went off like a thunderflash in a wet sandbag, but produced a weak laugh here and there—not quite of the quality I had intended but enough to present me with the opportunity to make myself scarce. I rose from my chair and made for the door, nodding on my way to a couple of the Chinese bar boys who seemed to have overheard my joke and enjoyed it rather more than my friends had done. They were both grinning from ear to ear and showing rows of faultless white teeth. Out of the corner of my eye I briefly glimpsed one of the warning posters. I had read it many times. Under a sketch of a shrewd looking owl was the exhortation,

A wise old owl sat in an oak
and the more he saw
the less he spoke;
And the less he spoke
the more he heard.
Why don't YOU be like
this wise bird?

Now a thick layer of mist lay over the ground. As my feet moved through it I sensed the smell of dampness, but it was a warm dampness that made breathing seem difficult. I walked slowly toward the hut where the pilot would be waiting and did not see a soul on the way. The covering of ground mist thinned as I climbed the incline. I was glad of that because it marginally lessened the risk of my stepping into a slit-trench.

I passed the orderly room. It was in near darkness, although I noticed a few horizontal shafts of light coming from closed shutters. Then I reached the hut where I would be meeting the pilot. The outside door stood ajar as before. I stepped inside into air filled with the pleasing fragrance of cigar smoke. One or two of those grudging lamps enabled me to find my way along the corridor to the office. I could hear no sound.

With some nervousness I squared myself up to the door and raised my hand to knock. I need not have bothered, for the door suddenly flew open. My first impression of the man was a little disappointing. I had been fully expecting to see someone a little bit special in some way—probably a tall, thin, and darkly sunburnt ice-cool type, or at any rate someone who looked as though he would feel quite at home when flying an airplane through a severe thunderstorm at twenty thousand feet—whatever such a person might look like. Instead, the person who had yanked the door open appeared to be quite ordinary, medium height and weight with, at first sight, unremarkable features. His hair, or what there was of it, consisted of a covering that was probably black. However, it was so short, having been trimmed in "convict cut" style, that to make an accurate assessment of its shade presented some difficulty. His eyes were dark and his cheeks and chin were dark. Altogether he was quite a dark person. He might have needed a shave, though I suspected that even if he had had one there and then he would still have been dark. It was an unremarkable face—and a face that would leave even the most perceptive judges of men guessing as to the type of man who possessed it.

He stood with his back toward the office lamp; consequently his face was in shadow. The corridor light, what little there was, managed to highlight a number of gold fillings in his teeth which otherwise seemed to be in very satisfactory condition. He stretched out his hand. I had not done a lot of handshaking during my time with the RAF. Officers never shook hands with airmen—neither did NCOs, nor the airmen between themselves. It was a fair handshake as handshakes go—no hearty but false knuckle-crunching performance. But neither was his hand weakly limp and clammy. In fact, I found it a pretty genuine, not too brief kind of handshake.

It had taken not much more than five seconds for him to open the door, shake my hand, and gently pull me into the office. Then he said, "Hello. I imagine that you must be Peter Shepherd. You were asked to come here to see me for a chat. Is that so?" He had retreated with his back up against a desk, half sitting on it, his hands on his hips.

"Yes, sir," I replied. "The squadron leader said I would find you here."

He was, I estimated, in his late twenties or early thirties. His height was probably an inch or so less than mine, which made him a little over five-nine. He was in khaki trousers, unusually narrow from the knee down and tucked into his boots. His silk shirt appeared to be of a dark burgundy shade, though it was difficult to judge under the meager bulb. The boots, I noticed, were of calf leather and a variation of ones worn in places like New Mexico, but somehow were far more stylish. Altogether they were simple clothes, quite ordinary, but someone would have had to be on close terms with the night security guard at some top-flight outfitters to have procured them at anywhere near a reasonable price; it was the right kind of gear.

He pushed a chair toward me with a foot and indicated to me to be seated. "Make yourself comfortable," he said. "Do you smoke?"

"Yes, I do, as a matter of fact," I replied. It mattered not to me that the air was already fully laden with cigar smoke—one cigarette could hardly ruin its quality any further.

He handed me a tin of Guinea Gold cigarettes. A fifty tin, already opened with maybe half a dozen missing. "Keep them," he said, as though giving away a few strips of chewing gum. Then he lit me up with a silver lighter. I guessed it was silver and not plated nickle or something because it had an adornment that looked suspiciously like gold.

Though the window and its shutters were wide open, his cigar, a classy panatela-type job, had filled the room with its fragrant aroma. The fumes were curling slowly and gracefully around the lightbulb, but the mosquitoes and their friends seemed not to notice.

His clothing gave away nothing about him except that here was a man who liked wearing distinctive and expensive gear and presumably had the money with which to make it possible. He was not in uniform of any description, so he was almost certainly a civilian. He moved to the back of the desk and sat down. There was no twinkle in his eye, but there might just as well have been because when he spoke I had the clear impression that it was with some amusement. "I understand you're coming with me on the flight," he said. His words were spoken with some kind of accent—slight but definite and one I could not place. They constituted a statement rather than a question.

"Yes," I said. "I'd very much like to go along with you, that is, if you agree."

Then he smiled. "I have to agree, Peter. I have no choice. You've been selected and offered as being suitable for the job. I'm without my second man. He's been taken ill and it's important that I have with me someone who's able to do certain things if the need should arise. You appear to have the requisite qualifications, Peter. You've been recommended to me on this basis, but of course I must ask you a few questions before we go too far. Is that okay by you?"

"It's fine by me," I agreed.

His few questions turned out to be quite a tough grilling, lasting half an hour or more. His initial inquiries probed into my background, education, RAF apprenticeship, and what I had learned as an apprentice. He asked how much flying I had done but did not appear too surprised or disturbed when I explained that I had done very little. He had already been informed that I was currently waiting to be posted to a flying training school, having been found suitable in all respects for training as a pilot. He was, of course, particularly interested to hear what I knew about the Hudson and questioned me on matters concerning the Cyclone engine. I told him of the short theoretical course I had undergone and the reason for this.

His accent, I decided, was probably that of a Dutchman who had lived all his life in the Far East and had therefore picked up more than a little of the Anglo-Indian and Eurasian ways of pronunciation. Then it became obvious to me that his features spoke of mixed blood and I guessed him to be, most likely, the product of a Dutch father and a Eurasian mother. His eyes without doubt gave away his Asiatic connection as also did his high cheekbones and the very slightly flattened bridge of his nose. Not at all a badlooking chap, bright, quick on the uptake, and with the personality to match. Whoever he was he gave the impression of one who was doing well and enjoying it.

He said, "You are rather young to be out here with the RAF, aren't you?"

"Yes," I replied, thinking that this was where he would say, "Well, it's been nice talking to you, but I'm afraid I must turn you down." I continued. "My apprenticeship was unusually short owing to the war. They sent me out here long before they should have done. Anyway, as you already know, I'm still only eighteen, but I feel myself capable of doing what might be necessary to help you."

He gave a little dismissive wave with his hand. "That's okay, Peter. I wasn't meaning to say that you're too young to come along with me. Just remarking on the fact of your youth. You've been thrown in the deep end at a very early age, that's clear."

I did not reply to his observation but just sat waiting for what might come next. He stood up and closed the window. The steamy warmth of the office did not appear to be affecting him. His cigar was now a dead butt in an ashtray. He came around to my side of the desk, sat down on one corner of it, and looked at me carefully as though finally deciding the time had arrived for him to tell me something. I sensed that the decision was not coming that easily. In fact, quite a few seconds went by before he stirred and said, "No doubt you're waiting for me to tell you something about the flight."

"Yes, sir," I said. "I'd really like to know where we would be going—and when, of course."

"We'll be flying to the north—and quite a distance."

"The squadron leader told me it might take four hours."

"About that I should think."

"And would that be to Burma or Siam?" I asked.

"Maybe. It's too early for me to say. I'll know a short time before we take off."

"Are you saying that you're in agreement with my going with you?"

He smiled and showed his gold fillings. "Sure. I'm happy if you are."

"Oh," I said, but it was really more of a gasp of excitement than surprise. At last things were moving for me. I experienced an amazing relief—a relief of mind in that at last I was conversing with individuals well above my station. They were people who, I assumed, knew a lot more about life than the NCOs, which was the highest echelon with whom I currently managed to converse.

He returned to the back of the desk and stooped to pick something up from the floor. It was a brown leather grip of larger than usual proportions—old-looking with plenty of straps and locks. A casual thief would have needed half a day to open the thing, assuming he had been able to lift it. I could tell it was heavy by the way it clunked on the tabletop when he set it down.

"When will we be going?" I asked.

His eyes regarded me steadily, his face frozen into an expression that was neither hard nor sympathetic. It was simply a cool face devoid of anything I could interpret as being an indication of any particular emotion or unspoken message.

"Early tomorrow morning," he said abruptly.

"As soon as that," I blurted out. I had imagined the flight being carried out some time within the next twenty-four hours but hardly as soon as that.

"Yes," he said. "In fact, providing the weather's reasonable I hope to take off at 3:00 A.M." Then his face broke into a smile.

I remember expressing surprise at this last revelation. Then he continued. "I know it's all rather a rush for you, but it's quite essential I'm afraid. I take it that there's nothing to prevent you turning out at, say, 2:00 A.M.?"

"Oh, no—nothing. It's just a question of getting myself organized in the meantime," I replied hastily, not wishing to give the impression that I was having second thoughts in the matter. "But there are a few points I'd like to discuss."

He glanced at his watch. I had already noticed it. It was a wristwatch and a half, in line with the rest of his gear—a really useful-looking, impressive timepiece that gave off expensive golden reflections even under the poor lighting. The bracelet it was on must have cost as much as I earned in six months.

"Okay, fire away," he said. "But be as brief as you can because we must get some sleep."

"When shall we be returning to Sungei Patani?"

"Early the following morning—the fifth. All being well it will be a 4 A.M. takeoff."

"So we'll have an overnight stay wherever we finish up?" I ventured.

"Yes—well, a few hours anyway," he replied.

"What about flying clothes?" I asked. "I have nothing of that sort."

He assured me that he had in the Hudson everything I would need, including a parachute and an inflatable life jacket.

"Of course it's most unlikely that you'll need to use a chute, but I'll give you some instruction once we're in the plane. Do you know anything about them?"

"I know how they're constructed and how to pack them and, in theory anyway, how to use them. We did all of that at the apprentices school," I replied.

"No need to bother about that then. Anything else?"

"About the work I may have to do on the Hudson. Are you carrying any spares?"

He had begun to make it clear he was anxious to be on his way. He tried the grip for weight but immediately set it back down.

"I've got quite a lot of stuff—plugs, oil, tools, and a range of useful spares in the Hudson. Don't worry yourself on that score, Peter. There are also a number of maintenance manuals."

"Where have you flown from?"

He ignored my innocent question as though it had never escaped my lips. I knew when to shut up, and I did so. I wanted to ask him if he was a private pilot, why his plane was done out in peculiar camouflage colors, and why the plane had no identification markings, but somehow it did not seem to be the right moment. My questions would have to be raised at another time.

"Look, Peter," he said, "we'll need to be at the Hudson by 2:15 A.M. I suggest that you report here at 2:00 A.M. I'll arrange for some sandwiches and coffee to be brought here for us. You'll need a call so I'll organize that with the duty officer for 1:30 A.M. Does all that sound reasonable?"

It made sense to me, but then I was still juggling a hundred thoughts and my mind was not yet exactly cool and clear.

"Yes, it sounds good to me, sir. By the way, where will you be sleeping?" I asked. Then it struck me as an impertinent question to ask. However, he was in no way upset by it.

"In the next room," he replied, quite affably. "They've put a bed in there for me—and a net."

"Could I ask you to let me know the purpose of the flight?"

He turned his head and looked at his leather grip in a way that seemed to indicate a connection between it and my question. It was one of those subconscious body movements that occasionally half tells one something.

"I can't really give you that information yet. I'm only halfway into the picture myself. It's one of those things you don't need to bother about," he said.

His words came right off the cuff as though he had been waiting for my question and had his reply pat and ready. It was then that I experienced my very first misgiving about the matter. It was not that it occurred to me something underhanded was going on, but simply that, once again, I was not being told the facts. At the same time I instinctively felt it unwise to upset the apple cart by demanding to know all the details; therefore, I just kept my mouth shut and acted like the trusting innocent I suppose I really was.

"I understand, sir," I said politely, though not understanding at all.

"Okay then," he replied, and the way he said it left me in no doubt that our discussion was at an end. I opened the door for him because he had taken his grip from the table and had already moved to leave the office. "I'll expect you here at 2:00 A.M. Get some sleep now—and, remember, no drinking. Well, no more than a couple anyway."

He did not see my rueful smile. "No chance of that," I said. "I couldn't afford a beer even if I wished for one."

He stopped, halfway into the corridor. "Broke?" he inquired.

"Cleaned out, sir. Haven't a cent," I replied frankly.

His smile was good-natured and agreeable. "Ah, perhaps I'll be able to do something about that tomorrow," he murmured quietly. Then he walked off down the corridor to the next room.

I watched him as he went. When he reached the door of the adjacent room, he turned and said, "Oh, by the way, you don't have to address me as Sir—just call me Jan." He was gone before I could reply.

Before switching off the light I looked quickly around the office. Apart from the desk with its cheap, brass-plated regulation ashtray, two chairs, and an empty waste-paper bin, the room was pretty bare. A horde of insects was still furiously active around that lonely lightbulb. There are times when, in a mood of dejection or gripped by nostalgia, I think of that office and how it was there that I started on a course the memories of which, being quite irradicable, continue to lurk uneasily in my mind to this very day.

The time was now coming up to 10:30 P.M. Ground vapors still hung around in patches here and there. Bullfrogs were in full voice. The moon, a few days from full, was even brighter. It shone down through the trees and had around it a curious halo—something that, for some reason, occurs frequently with the full moon in Malaya. On the way to my hut I saw a few airmen making for their sleeping quarters.

By 10:45 P.M. I was back in my room where I found my roommate hidden away under his mosquito net trying to read. I went out to the washroom, cleaned myself up for the early morning start, then collected together the few things I would need to take with me. I pushed them all into my canvas haversack. Then I told the other chap that it was time to kill the light. He bleated about this, but before he could argue his case persuasively enough I switched it off. I got under my mosquito net, closed my eyes, and spent the next two hours sweating like hell and turning over in my mind all that had been said to me since being unceremoniously whisked away from the mess hut.

Thursday, 4 December 1941

An airman from the guard room woke me at 1:30 A.M., having apparently first roused the occupants of two adjacent rooms and, as he went to pains to tell me, having been told to "get to hell" in decidedly unfriendly terms. He had been apologetic to all concerned and pleaded a certain confusion of mind owing to having propelled his bicycle headlong into one of the near-by trenches.

But I was unworried by this trivial disaster. I switched on the room light so as to see what I was about. The other occupant stirred, sat bolt upright, and proceeded to study me through the gauze of his net for a full ten seconds, then, clearly failing to grasp what was going on, he laid his head down again and resumed his sleep.

It took a little longer than I had planned to get to the hut where earlier I had discussed the flight with the pilot, Jan. He was waiting for me, dressed in a khaki flying suit. The same insects, or those of the current shift, were cavorting around the glimmering lightbulb. He had one of his trim cigars going. On the table stood two enormous thermos flasks and a cardboard ration box containing sandwiches. Incredible as it may seem, I also remember there being four huge green apples.

We settled a few minor points, meanwhile gulping down cheese sand-wiches and coffee. Jan was anxious to get cracking. He had not shaved and his face looked even darker than it had just a few hours ago.

"I understand it's all right out there, Peter," he remarked.

"Pitch dark. No rain, but a lot of low mist," I replied.

"Yes, that's what the duty pilot told me half an hour ago. The airfield's a bit swampy, but it can't be any worse than it was yesterday—although they've shut up shop to RAF aircraft."

"Shall we be able to get off then?" I inquired, suddenly alert to the fact that he was proposing to take off when RAF planes were being denied the privilege on safety grounds.

"I don't think there'll be any problem. In a case like this, it's up to me. I take off at my discretion."

It did not seem to have occurred to him that I might have cared to express an opinion in the matter. I had the clear feeling I had been rushed into the business, and had not been allowed the opportunity to weigh things up suf-ficiently. My mouth was as dry as the Sahara, my heart was dancing the light-fantastic, and my knees had begun to feel a bit useless. It was not down to excitement. I was scared. Had Jan suddenly announced that he was going to call the flight off, would I have been bitterly disappointed? Like hell I would! In less than five minutes I would have been back in bed thanking my lucky stars. My common sense was trying to tell me something, and I knew it.

But Jan did not call the flight off. Instead he hurried things along. We left the hut—me with my haversack, the two thermos flasks, and the ration box, and Jan with his leather grip and a valise of sorts. I had to lead him down to the airfield—only a matter of five hundred yards or so and a relatively easy walk once we reached the road that ran through the camp from the main gate to the airfield.

"How come they haven't supplied any transport for us?" I asked Jan.

"Don't know really," he replied. Then he went quiet in a way that politely told me to belt up. He must, mentally anyway, have been doing his pre-flight checks.

At the control tower, such as it was, we walked around to the duty pilot's office. The whole place seemed to be deserted. I could barely discern Jan in the near total darkness. I heard him mouth something. It sounded like some kind of muffled curse—in Dutch.

"This is not what was agreed," he growled. "They said that someone would meet me here at 2:45 A.M."

Then, as though by magic, two figures loomed silently out of the darkness about ten feet away.

"Halt! Who goes there?" a voice shouted querulously.

"Friend!" I called back quickly and somewhat anxiously. "In fact, there are two of us!" I called out again.

"Advance and be recognized," came the response, and a beam of light from a hand torch shot out at us. The beam was about as bright as the general run of lights on the camp. Another minute and it would give up the ghost for sure.

What with the utter darkness, the niggardly illumination afforded by the torch, the encumbrance of the things Jan and I were carrying, and the fact that the latter seemed to have no form of identification about his person, the encounter degenerated into a fiasco. It struck me that the two interrogators could be anyone, perhaps even saboteurs—a notion of very short duration, however, because I reckoned that no two enemy infiltrators could have been schooled to act so convincingly pathetic as these two. One of them was a Sikh corporal, the other an airman of crass demeanor and a dimwit to boot.

Jan, I could tell, was becoming irritated—so much so that he produced a string of words in Dutch. The Sikh could not have noticed, as it had become obvious that he barely understood English, let alone Dutch. But the lame-brained airman froze, then, after a delay of some seconds, he got the message. "You're not English!" he bawled, panic stricken.

Before Jan was able to get an explanation off the ground, the sound of a motor vehicle being started up reached our ears. A hundred yards or so away its headlights stabbed into the night, then it turned in our direction and proceeded toward us. It quickly reached us, then stopped. I recognized it as an RAF utility van.

The two guards turned away from us as the van drew near, thus clearly demonstrating their perilous lack of training. The vehicle's headlamps were then dipped, but its engine remained ticking over. Out of it climbed the squadron leader who had interviewed me the previous evening. He was dressed as before, khaki trousers and blue shirt with squadron-leader stripes. He was without any form of head-dress. After sending the guards on their miserable way, he took Jan to one side—about twenty feet to one side, in fact. They conversed for a while in hushed tones. I was left standing beside the van. In the driving seat sat an airman who looked half asleep. He paid me no attention. In the back of the van sat another airman, wearing spectacles and dangling his legs out over the lowered tailboard. When I walked toward him he gave a kind of grunt of embarrassment, then got up and retired into the dark interior. It seemed to me that he had taken me for someone with whom, for some reason, he should not converse.

Then the squadron leader came over to me, leaving Jan lugging his two bags to the van.

"Hello, Shepherd," he said. "All right?"

"Yes, thank you, sir."

He produced a torchlight and put a hand on my arm. "Just step over to the van, Shepherd," he said. There he relieved me of my identification papers, including my Sungei Patani camp gate pass, signed, I recall, by the camp adjutant.

"Any more documents or papers?" he asked.

"No, sir."

Then he asked me to empty out my canvas bag and proceeded to rummage through my things. He carefully examined the bag for markings and, finding none other than my service number, gestured to me to put my things back. Following this he ran his flashlight over my clothing.

"You'd better not wear this," he said, indicating the jacket I had on. "You've got a shirt in your bag—put that on instead."

The shirt carried no markings or labels to show that it was in any way connected with the RAF, whereas the jacket had RAF wings at the top of the sleeves. Although the squadron leader had said nothing about recognition markings, I was not so dumb as not to comprehend the purpose of his scrutiny. If I had been somewhat excited and wary up to now, it was nothing compared with the apprehension and uncertainty I now began to experience. I was already being carried away by events and, also, in the back of my mind the thought of adventure and possible recognition continued to spur me on, albeit at an increasingly diminishing rate.

The van then took us via the southern perimeter of the airfield to the Hudson, which was precisely where I had seen it come to rest the previous afternoon.

A few stars glittered in a cloud-flecked sky. The Hudson stood silent, close to the boundary of the airfield, its shape and strange camouflage colors revealed in the beams of the van's headlights, its wheels half immersed in a blanket of ground mist.

"Right then," said the squadron leader from the passenger seat, "I'll go across the airfield in the van and help these two airmen put down the paraffin flares. They'll give you a green light from the other side—then you can take off when you're ready." Jan and I had ridden in the back of the van with the second airman along with various items, including a dozen or more paraffin flares, as yet unlit.

As the squadron leader finished speaking, Jan stuck his head through the opening between the back and front of the van. "No! I want to check the field first. It may be like a swamp."

The outcome of this minor altercation was that Jan and I rode in the back of the van while it was driven across the airfield and back. There were no flooded patches to speak of and Jan declined the use of paraffin flares. "Just keep the green Aldis lamp on me as I do my takeoff run," he said crisply. I detected a note of irritation and tension in his voice.

Back at the Hudson Jan did a quick walk-around inspection with the aid of a battery lantern. The van then withdrew to the opposite side of the airfield. There had been no further discussion between Jan and the squadron leader; in fact, I could not help noticing that a certain last-minute coolness between the two had developed.

Jan had intended to be away by 3:00 A.M., but it was ten minutes past the hour before the Hudson was ready for takeoff. In the meantime I donned a flying suit Jan had found for me—a lightweight job, crumpled and smelling strongly of damp and mildew. There was also a canvas flying helmet with built-in earphones. "You won't need boots," he said. "We won't be flying high enough for you to need them." We each struggled into an inflatable life jacket.

While I donned my malodorous flying suit, Jan was up front in the cockpit carrying out essential checks and whatever else needed doing.

He called back to me, "Your parachute is up here. There's no need to wear it, but I'll show you how to strap it on when you come forward." Then when he came back into the cabin, he pointed out the storage position of the inflatable dinghy—actually in a locker forming part of the fuselage hatch through which we had climbed to get into the plane. He also pointed out the emergency exits and the WC can.

When at last I found myself sitting buckled up in the right-hand seat next to Jan, I felt I really should have been having a good shower and a change of clothing instead of venturing out on a four-hour flight into the unknown. The lighting in the Hudson was a shade less than minimal. The cockpit was warm and stuffy. Through the windshield there was a wide view of absolutely nothing except darkness. Then suddenly, to the far right, I caught sight of a green light—the far end of our takeoff run. In between us and that solitary guiding light there was nothing but two thousand feet of rain-soaked grass and pitch darkness.

Jan was busy. I tried to follow his actions, but my heart was doing a rush job again, my chest tingling with a discomforting warmth. I could have downed half a pint of water in a few quick gulps on account of my mouth feeling as dry as dust. "Have you got enough fuel?" I asked.

"Yes, Peter," he replied, still peering at his gauges and checking various switches and control levers. "I took the opportunity to fill up after I landed yesterday."

I glanced at my watch. It was now 3:15 A.M. "Okay," said Jan. "Ready, Peter?"

"Yes," I replied, just sitting there and hoping he was as good a pilot as my judgment had already persuaded me he probably was.

I watched with utmost attentiveness as Jan set the throttle and mixture levers, flicked two or three switches, then engaged the left-hand engine starter. A sharp click was immediately followed by protesting noises from the engine, as though in a mechanical sense it was objecting to being wakened at this early hour. Through the side screen I could vaguely make out the tips of the propeller blades turning sluggishly and jerkily into and then out of my field of view. A muffled metallic cough then followed, then silence but for the rhythmic cranking noise of the engine. Then came another, more boisterous cough. The Hudson juddered as though shaken by a miniature explosion. A further cough, and then another and another, whereupon the plane began to shake and shudder as the cylinders, one by one, got the hang of it. Then, over a few seconds, the irregular reluctant coughing gave way to a deep throaty powerful roar. The propeller tips became a fuzzy circular arc in the reflected luminescence of the engine's glowing exhaust gases.

Jan started the right-hand engine. It gave no trouble and quickly settled itself down to a steady, even roar. A few minutes were taken up in letting the two engines warm up to operating temperature. Jan checked his vibrating gauges and moved his hands over vital controls in final preparation for the takeoff.

We had already tested the intercom sets built into our helmets and, at this point, having judged Jan to have completed his checks, I reminded him that Kedah Peak was dead ahead and only five miles distant. I had no desire to let him dash the Hudson to pieces against the jungle-clad eastern slopes of this dreaded obstruction.

He half-turned his head toward me and, giving a kind of light-hearted but sober laugh, said, "Relax, Peter. I spent half an hour last night studying the Sungei Patani landing chart and, in any case, I took a good look at the mountain yesterday afternoon when I flew in. I think I'll be able to miss it all right."

His words satisfied me, although his last remark left me with my brow deeply furrowed. Had I been able to see his face clearly I might have been able to decide whether or not he had been joking. As it was, all I could do was hope.

I strained my eyes to read the fuel gauges and saw that both were indicating full. The wipers had been used to clear the windshield of mist droplets. We were ready to go.

Jan released the parking brake and opened the throttles slightly. The Hudson lurched forward into darkness. Gradually the nose turned to face the far green light, then Jan scanned the instruments again. "Okay, Peter. Ready?" he asked, and with that he switched off the cockpit lights.

"Ready," I answered, already tightly gripping the warm metal side tubes of my seat.

He held the plane on the brakes and moved the throttle levers fully forward and then through the takeoff boost gates. At this the cockpit ceased to be acceptably quiet and comfortable but, instead, became a shaking, vibrating darkness with just the low-level lighting of the instrument panel to remind us what we were about. The engine noise, even though the earphones were keeping much of it from reaching our ears, was impressive. You could tell there was no way the Hudson was going to hang around for long with that tremendously powerful racket going on—providing the plane stayed in one piece. Personally I found thought and concentration difficult; therefore, I simply continued to grip my seat, watching that green light with one eye while trying to read the airspeed indicator with the other. I knew 115 knots to be the magic figure, but right now it was reading zero. At the magic figure, with a bit of flap down, the Hudson would, I hoped, be ready to rise up into the night sky and begin its crucial sharp turn to avoid Kedah Peak.

The powerful landing light came on, transforming the ground mist ahead into a luminous light-grey roadway. Jan released the brakes. The Hudson leapt forward, pushing me hard back in my seat. I gave up watching the instruments; at this point something else was more important. What held my attention was that distant green light. The Hudson's tail lifted and then we were urged along the luminous road that stretched out ahead, with the two massive engines roaring away at maximum power and seemingly malevolently dedicated to running the plane into Kedah Peak and oblivion.

Then a funny thing happened. Jan momentarily removed his hand from the two throttle levers and switched off the landing light. Now there was just the green light and it was coming at us fast. I leaned over toward Jan. The airspeed indicator was on the far left side of the instrument panel, and I could not read it unless I very nearly pushed him out of his seat. The needle was vibrating and so were the figures on the dial of the instrument. I gave up and immediately resumed my terrified interest in the green light now hurtling at us. It was, I vividly recall, no more than about two hundred feet away when Jan gently heaved the control wheel back quite a way, whereupon the Hudson left the ground without fuss. My relief at this was amazing. Suddenly I experienced a rush of renewed confidence.

"Don't forget the mountain," I reminded Jan, something that seemed to be reasonable for me to contribute at this juncture.

He gave a grunt but did not reply in words. He was at the moment fully occupied with the instruments. At last I was able to relax as I felt the aircraft bank to the left, its engines still pouring out great lumps of power. As we turned away from the mountain's hidden presence, I had the sensation of being lifted, not in a smooth and gradual way, but in distinct leaps as though the plane was on a switchback ride in which the dips had been leveled out.

A few minutes later the aircraft ceased its turn and its rate of climb increased to 1,500 feet per minute. The gyro compass indicated 080°—roughly east-northeast. Jan eased the power off a little, thus reducing the noise level in the cockpit and giving the engines an easier time of it.

"Well, Peter, we missed your mountain," Jan quipped. It was the first time he had spoken since commencing the takeoff.

He turned his head toward me, though in the darkness it was impossible for me to read his eyes. "I'm going up to seven thousand feet, then we'll continue on autopilot," he said.

"Is everything looking good?" I asked. My hands had stopped gripping the sides of my seat and were now in my lap—still trembling.

"Sure," he replied. "In five minutes or so we can have a smoke. From then on things may get a bit boring, I'm afraid." He then fell quiet until at seven thousand feet he leveled the plane off, reduced power even more, then engaged the autopilot. I studied the instruments—directional gyro 080°, altitude seven thousand feet, engine speed 2350 rpm, engine boost 31 ins.Hg.

"You won't need your helmet now," Jan advised as he took his off. I removed mine and was surprised to find that the engine noise now amounted to only a muted bearable roar.

"What about radio calls?" I half-shouted.

"What about them?"

"You won't be able to hear incoming calls without your helmet."

"There won't be any, Peter—I'm not expecting any, and in any case I'm not particularly interested."

For a pilot, Jan's words amounted to a cavalier disregard, contempt even, of accepted procedure. This I found worrying, for there were any number of reasons why various ground stations might wish to contact him. In effect, he was shunning the opportunity of picking up any instruction or advice that some authority might see fit to give him.

I thought about this for some time, but, as with a lot of things about this flight, I got nowhere.

"Let's have a bit more light," said Jan, turning up the cockpit lighting. His action improved matters inside the cockpit but just about ruined our visibility of the great outdoors. Instead of seeing vague shapes of clouds and the odd bright star, all I was now getting were badly distorted reflections of the two of us in the windshield and side screens.

"Can't see much now," I ventured.

"You're not missing anything."

"What about other aircraft?"

"Well, if they're using navigation lights we'll see them," he said.

"But what if they're not using lights?"

"In that case we won't be able to see them," he replied laconically.

I had another thought. Sundry thoughts had been coming to me at a rate of knots for quite some time. "Are we using navigation lights?"

"No," he replied.

"Well, isn't that a bit unwise?"

"Yes, it is a little, I suppose. But on this trip I don't use them."

"On this trip," he had said. Did that mean he did this kind of thing on a regular basis? I asked myself.

Once again I got nowhere. I stopped trying to worry about all these unanswered questions. Instead I sat quietly, juggling my misgivings. After a time something dawned on me. This volunteering thing—surely a reasonably sane person could volunteer only when that person had a fairly good idea what he was about to volunteer for. I turned this philosophical concept over in my mind, while scratching the extreme tip of my left little finger, which had started itching like crazy, and came to the conclusion that only an imbecile would volunteer for something that he knew nothing or very little about. And what did that make me?

He produced one of his cigars from a tube in his top pocket. Then he lit the thing with his fancy lighter and puffed at it until he got it going to his satisfaction. The cockpit filled rapidly with cigar smoke. "You can smoke if you wish," he said. He gave me a light for one of the Guinea Gold cigarettes he had gifted to me the previous night, and then I made myself comfortable.

"Go back and sit in the cabin if you like," Jan said. "There's more room in there."

Somehow I got the feeling that I might be happier exactly where I was, despite the space restriction. "Actually, I'd rather stay here, Jan," I replied. "But I think I should have a look at those Hudson maintenance manuals you mentioned."

"They're in the cabin," Jan advised. "You'll find them in one of the toolboxes. Get them and bring them back here when you're ready."

A little later I unbuckled myself, went back and found a couple of manuals, then returned to the cockpit. By the time I got back Jan had adjusted the ventilation and had substantially cleared the air of tobacco fumes.

I began poring through one of the manuals. It was printed in English. I found it hard going in that it was the wrong time of the night to take in facts that at any other time I would have found riveting. The engines were still in good voice, regular and smooth. The aircraft was flying level at seven thousand feet. But I noticed that our airspeed had fallen to 140 knots, around 160 MPH. I had finished my cigarette. Jan still had his cigar going. He spoke. "This is the only sane place to be," he said. I realized that he had been speaking from the heart, but, of course, under the circumstances I could not entirely agree with him.

"Huh," I grunted, not wishing to upset him.

"What did you make of that squadron leader?" he then asked.

"You mean Squadron Leader Palliser?"

"Was that his name?"

"You mean the officer who recommended me to you?" I asked. "The one who met us at the airfield?"

"Yes. What did you say his name is?"

"Palliser, or perhaps Balliser. At least that's what I was given to understand."

Jan went quiet for fully half a minute, then, "Funny," he said.

"What is?"

"His name. I don't recall hearing either of the names you've just mentioned when he introduced himself to me. It was something quite different—an unusual name—I can't remember it. I'm sure you've been misinformed, Peter—maybe it'll come back to me."

So there was another problem for me to worry over. Now I was even unsure of the name of the officer who had launched me into my present situation—a situation that was becoming more fraught by the minute. None of it made any sense. The more I mulled over all the ambiguities and uncertainties the less comfortable I felt. Meanwhile the Hudson was droning on into darkness, a mile and a half above the mountainous sleeping jungles of northern Malaya. I was becoming deeply anxious—and nettled. I wasn't just irritated—I was angry. It was time for a lot of things to be straightened out. It was a time for the two of us to do some talking.

6 To French Indo-China

Thursday, 4 December

"The squadron leader told me that we would be flying to the north," I said conversationally to Jan. "But we're heading more easterly, aren't we?"

"Yes," he replied. "For another fifteen minutes or so anyway. Then we'll change heading to the northeast. I don't want to fly over Siam."

I thought about that. Very shortly we would be passing over the east coast of Malaya; then, if we continued on the course he had mentioned, we would eventually reach French Indo-China.

"Do you know precisely where we *are* going yet?" I inquired, determined to find out as much as I could.

"Sure, at the moment anyway, but I may get further orders in a few hours time."

He was still keeping a lot from me. How could he be flying so confidently without knowing exactly where he was supposed to be going? I felt sure he was holding out on me.

"But, I mean, if you don't get instructions to the contrary, where will you be heading for?" I continued, still taking care not to reveal my displeasure.

Then came another of those silences—ten seconds or so of thinking time for Jan. Then, "French Indo-China," he said.

I started as his words sank in. "French Indo-China!" I exclaimed. "How come?"

In a split second my brain had reminded me that French Indo-China was now *Vichy* French Indo-China, meaning that the strings of its present French administration were being pulled by the Vichy French government which, in turn, danced to the tune of Nazi Germany—the enemy, engaged in mortal war against Great Britain, the regime that had overrun Holland, the Dutch Netherlands, back in 1940. It was fairly certain therefore that I, a serving member of His Majesty's Royal Air Force, would receive anything but a rapturous welcome on landing in Indo-China. And then there was the Japanese question to think about, it being fairly common knowledge that French Indo-China's government had been threatened and coerced by Germany and Japan into allowing free, unhindered access into Indo-China territory to Japan's troops and military aircraft. To all intents and purposes Indo-China was, at this very moment, a huge Japanese military base. Many airfields were now occupied by Japanese army and naval air forces. The whole country was bristling with Japanese troops, while ports and harbors had become homes for Japanese naval vessels, including large capital ships, submarines, and troop transporters. True, Japan was not a declared enemy of Great Britain, but, the political situation being what it currently was, I imagined the Japanese would in all probability not be as charitable and understanding toward me as I would have liked.

I thought about all this very carefully. It took me a long time—about five seconds flat.

"We can't go there," I continued even before Jan had answered my question.

He looked at me, laughing. *That* made me even more angry. "Yes, we can," he almost chortled.

"But the damn place is full of Nazi sympathizers and Japs. Have you got official permission to land there? Is that it?"

He stubbed out his cigar butt in the tin lid we had been using as an ashtray. "No," he replied. "I haven't got permission to land, but I've been doing this trip every six weeks over the past two years. I've never had any trouble." He leaned back in his seat again with a thoughtful smile on his dark features.

"But, Jan, the point is that I'm in an unsatisfactory position—I'm a serving member of the British Royal Air Force, but I've been relieved of my identification papers. I'd have difficulty proving to the Indo-China author-ities that I'm an RAF aircraftsman. They just might perceive me as an under-cover intelligence agent or something. In any case I'd be unable to explain what I was doing in Indo-China; I would find it impossible to invent any excuse for my presence. At best they'd be bound to give me a rough time; the *worst* is something I'm not prepared to risk."

I was working myself up to the point where my anger and anxiety were tak-ing control. No longer was I picking my words in an effort not to annoy him, or give him the impression that I was lacking in courage. No longer did I care if I upset him, or if he arrived at the conclusion that I was afraid. The plain fact was that I *was* afraid, and the sooner he realized this, the better it would be for both of us. It was not too late to turn back. I would have a good explana-tion for having persuaded Jan to do so, and as far as he was concerned—well, that was *his* problem. And that weird squadron leader would have a lot of explaining to do. Perhaps for some reason it was okay for Jan to land in Indo-China; after all, he was not British—at least this was pretty certain to be the case. It was high time I found out the answer to that particular question.

"What's your nationality?" I asked outright.

He did not hesitate, "Dutch," he replied. "I thought the squadron leader had told you."

"No, he did not."

He adjusted his seat forward, then dimmed the cockpit lights right down.

"So, you see, I'm really in the same position as you, Peter. The Dutch are friendly toward the British. We are your allies. The Germans hate us and so do the Japanese. The French in Indo-China are a bit different—most of them get on with we Dutch people quite well. However, I wouldn't wish to be picked up in Indo-China." He appeared about to say more. I did not let him.

"Then why are you going there?" I exclaimed. I must have sounded hys-terically furious because I made no attempt to disguise my emotions.

"It's a complicated story, Peter. But take it from me that there's a good rea-son for me to be visiting Indo-China."

"Maybe for you, but what about me?" I interrupted again. "I have no rea-son to go there. Indo-China means nothing to me."

"The squadron leader asked you if you'd like to volunteer to fly with me, I think. And you agreed to do so," Jan said quietly. I was only just able to hear his words.

"No!" I barked out. "He said nothing about Indo-China."

"Maybe, but you volunteered just the same. You volunteered for an operation in the interests of the RAF."

"No! It wasn't like that at all. The squadron leader expressly told me that this was *not* an RAF flight. He, in fact, gave me the clear impression that I should regard the time I spent away from camp as a 'spot of leave.' He said nothing about the whole thing being in the interests of the RAF."

"Well, perhaps he assumed that you would understand that—like he didn't wish to tell you everything," Jan said. "The fact is that our flight to Indo-China *is* in the interests of the RAF—or, maybe, the British—perhaps not the RAF especially."

My anger had subsided, just a little, but my anxiety still gnawed away at me as though some terrible, unthinkable but undeserving sentence was hanging over my head. In the past few minutes much of my hitherto-compliant attitude and naivete had evaporated, never to return. Since climbing away from the airfield at Sungei Patani I had grown up—I had put years on—I had become cynical and distrusting. I had undergone the ultimate lesson in how not to look after myself. The penny had dropped at last, yet I was still charging through a jet-black tropical night sky toward a reception, the quality of which I hardly dared to contemplate.

"Well, I think you'd better tell me all there is to know," I said, and my voice, even to me, sounded bitter and resigned. "Because if you don't do that I shall feel quite justified in queering things up so much that you'll have to turn back. Any consequent trouble I might get into at Sungei Patani would be nothing compared with what I might have to face in Indo-China."

I gave Jan a couple of minutes to chew on what I had just said. It gave me enough time to work out how I could force him to return to Sungei Patani. Easy—I could fiddle around with a few levers. I could mess about with the gyropilot control, the propeller controls, rudder and aileron and elevator trim tabs, all things that would make it well nigh impossible for him to fly the plane yet not place us in mortal danger. He would be obliged to rectify matters constantly. No pilot would be able to cope with such a workload for long. Of course he could always put a stop to my antics by laying something heavy on my head, thereby rendering me incapable of doing anything. But he wouldn't do that simply because he might need my assistance at some stage. As long as I kept monkeying around with a few selected controls he would have no option but to turn back. And I was not so dim as not to know, at any time, in which direction we were heading.

But it did not come to that, for Jan, having weighed my words and his options, decided to divulge a useful amount of very interesting information. I had no means of telling if what he revealed to me was genuine, accurate, or complete, but when he finished I had heard enough to convince me of the necessity of continuing the flight to Indo-China. What he told me hardly relieved my anxiety, but it did let me in on the reason for the operation. I could have done quite well without it, but now that things had progressed this far, with utmost reluctance I felt it incumbent on me to enter into the spirit of the undertaking.

Basically, what Jan told me was as follows. He acted as a courier for an organization involved in the importation of goods from Indo-China into Sumatra. For certain good reasons it was impossible to acquire and transport such goods by other than prohibited means, including clandestine air operations. This was doing no harm to anyone, according to Jan's word anyway, and had been going on, as far as he knew, for more than two years. Jan played no part in the commercial side of the dealing, contributing only his services as the pilot of the Hudson, the property of the organization for which he flew. He claimed to be ignorant as to the nature of the goods he picked up in Indo-China and to the amount of cash or other consideration he took there in exchange. Somehow his explanation rang true. It could account for the Hudson's lack of registration or other identification markings and for the night flight; also, I thought, it would account for Jan's style—his swish manner of dress, his jewelry, quality watch and cigarette lighter, his cigars, and, in fact, his whole calm and quietly self-assured manner. He projected the image of one who is capable, intelligent, and on to a good thing—a good thing that was paying off rather well.

Though his story intrigued me, it did not in itself alleviate my anxiety. I could not see how or why his contraband involvement (for that is what it undoubtedly was) should make me see the operation in a different light. I was getting nothing out of it—except, more than likely, a lot of serious anguish and grief.

However, before I could put this point to him he squared himself up in his seat, disengaged the autopilot, and banked the Hudson to the left. I watched the gyro compass as we changed heading, and I watched the magnetic compass swing. Then Jan leveled out on 050°, trimmed the plane carefully, and engaged the gyro compass again.

"Exactly where are we now?" I asked sharply.

"Just crossing the northeast coast," he replied. "We're probably twenty miles or so north of Kota Bharu, just inside the Siamese border. But let me give you the rest of my explanation. This is the part that makes it necessary for us to continue."

"Go on," I said hollowly, but with cold determination. I was waiting for him to spout a load of irrelevant crap, and *that* would be my signal to put out my right hand and disengage the autopilot, the gyro device that was automatically maintaining the aircraft's flying altitude and heading. At the same time, using my left hand, I would crank the aileron trim lever so that the Hudson would bank heavily to the right. If all that left Jan unperturbed, I would then abuse the elevator and rudder trim levers, thus causing the aircraft to stuff its nose down and begin to fly like a crab—unless Jan used his strength and flying skill to fight the control wheel. He certainly would not be able to cope with that for very long. And then, when he had straightened the aircraft out, I would do it all over again, and so on. He would simply have to give in and turn back.

He resumed his explanation. "We were approached by the Dutch authorities in Sumatra a few days ago and were informed that our business with Indo-China had been uncovered but that severe legal action would not be taken against us providing we carried out a certain service for the authorities. Apparently my flight over Malaya a month ago had been detected by the British RAF, and the Dutch authorities had been questioned because it was strongly suspected that the aircraft detected had carried on to Sumatra, though no Dutch flight over Malaya had been properly notified. Actually, the British fear had been that it was a Japanese plane that had flown over northern Malaya—something that does happen from time to time. Anyway, inquiries went ahead and eventually the Dutch authorities finished up at our door up near Medan. You can't keep an operation like ours totally watertight—we've been lucky when you think of all the possible leakage points. But, if it hadn't been for your RAF inquiry, we would probably still be in business. The service we were asked to carry out concerns the British. It seems there is a British chap in Indo-China who, for some reason, wishes to get out. Presumably he's been keeping his identity quiet; otherwise he would have been either deported or detained. I don't know what he was doing there, and I'm not very interested. The Dutch, in liaison with the British, have given approval to this last flight, providing I pick this British chap up in Indo-China and take him back to Malaya. He must be important in some way, otherwise why would they bother? I suppose the RAF wouldn't have attempted the operation—if one of *their* aircraft had been discovered in Indo-China, it would no doubt have been regarded as having been on a hostile mission of some kind, and may have provided an excuse for Japan to actually commence full-scale hostilities against Singapore and Malaya. Your lot wouldn't have risked that."

His words had put a different complexion on things. The way he had told it gave purpose to the mission. But I was still having difficulty trying to understand why *I* had become involved, and I was now mentally engaged in balancing my anxiety against my sense of duty. It took me just a few seconds to decide on the action I should now take. No effort of will was required, neither was any ice-cool sense of heroics. It was fear that made up my mind for me—fear of having to cope, forevermore, with a feeling of shame if I were to be the cause of the flight being aborted, rather like the shame one feels on refusing to jump from the top of a high wall when all of one's pals have already jumped, even if they have each wrecked an ankle. Some kinds of shame are harder to live with comfortably and become an ongoing, self-inflicted mental punishment that one is powerless to do anything about.

So I brushed aside my thoughts about interfering with the Hudson's controls. Instead I reconciled myself to being part of the bizarre operation. Still, my heart was not wholly in it. I felt I had been unnecessarily hoodwinked, and I was fairly sure that, had the full facts been put to me by the squadron leader, I would certainly have declined the opportunity. I had been trained for some things, but certainly not for this sort of lark.

"I see," I said. "Why the hell didn't that squadron leader explain the position to me before asking me to volunteer?" I was really just thinking aloud.

"Obviously he didn't want you to know the facts," Jan replied.

"Exactly! Because he'd know that I would turn him down."

"And then you might have gone around telling people about how you had been approached and he wouldn't have wanted *that* either."

"Well, I think it's a poor show. He was an odd-looking type anyway—he could have told me more," I grumbled.

"Anyway, are you happy now, Peter?" he asked, obviously relieved in that I had calmed down.

"No, I'm not a bit happy, Jan. I've been conned, and there was no need for it. But I'll go along with you and make an official complaint when I get back—if, in fact, I ever do get back."

He laughed. "You worry too much," he said. "In twenty-four hours time you'll be on your way back to Sungei Patani."

"I'll look forward to it," I replied.

The Hudson roared onward. Through the overhead perspex canopy everything was pitch black; no longer were there any cloudless patches of sky. Ahead and to either side it was the same. Every now and again I had the vague impression of clouds rushing at us and hurtling past the screens—in themselves deathly silent and a part of the vast darkness. The engine noise, satisfying and almost comforting, was not at such a level as to be annoying, though I found that it tended to spoil my concentration. I replaced my helmet but left it loose. The earphones blanketed the noise a little, yet without pressing on my ears.

I pondered all that Jan had said and arrived at the conclusion that he just *may* have made it all up—a conclusion that presented me with more problems than it solved. But it could not change anything. Things had now gone a bit too far for me to start getting stroppy again.

"About this person we're supposed to be bringing out of Indo-China," I remarked. "Where will he be? I mean, how will you contact him?"

"That's something I don't know. All I was told was that he'll be getting in touch with me. I don't know who he is or even what he looks like, but apparently he'll be able to convince me that he's the chap concerned."

"Sounds a bit dodgy." I said. "Are you happy with that?"

"I'll have to be, Peter. Don't forget, I'm doing the British and Dutch authorities a favor on account of that I really have no choice."

"What about your second man—the observer? Was he really taken ill on the plane?"

"Yes. Otherwise I wouldn't have had to land at Sungei Patani to put him off and request help."

"What do you suppose will happen to him now?" I asked.

"When he's well he'll get a flight back to Medan in Sumatra."

"Is that where you're from?" I asked.

"Yes," he replied.

Despite the engine noise and its adverse effect on my concentration, I got the feeling that something did not add up. How was it, for example, that the squadron leader happened to be on the camp, apparently for the very first time, just as Jan had found it necessary to fly the Hudson in—even though the latter, again presumably, had not been expecting to do so? *That* was another enigma for me to puzzle over while being sped, one and a half miles high, across the three-hundred-mile width of the Gulf of Siam.

"I notice you're not using your wireless at all," I said.

Jan turned his head. "Wireless?" he asked.

"Yes, your wireless, radio, or whatever you call it in your circles."

"Oh, that. No, I never use it when everything's going to plan. No need to use it."

"Of course," I murmured. He couldn't have heard me. If his explanations had any truth, the last thing he would do would be to divulge his presence and position. To do so would be to invite unwelcome inquiries—inquiries that could lead to certain trouble. Interception by other aircraft would be difficult at night, but, even so, keeping radio silence was, for him, the best bet. And yet there was still some doubt about where he was going—he would need to use the radio to find that out.

Then I thought about how the Hudson had put down at Sungei Patani in broad daylight. If it hadn't done so in order to drop off the observer, then surely it would have continued its flight to Indo-China in broad daylight. This probably meant that on his previous flights Jan had not, despite what he had already told me, even bothered to seek the protection of night's darkness. Perhaps he had never before done the trip in darkness. If so, how was he going to find his landing field? And how good was he at putting the Hudson down in night conditions? Still more questions to fret over. He had been amazingly fortunate to get away with it for such a long time. That is, if his explanation had been truthful.

"How are you going to find your way to your airfield in Indo-China?" I asked.

"Ah, radio," he answered straightaway.

"But you just said that you never use it."

"I don't mean that I have discussions with anyone, although, if necessary, I can be contacted," he went on. "I've got a radio compass. I can receive radio signals that will give me headings to steer."

"So you're proposing to land at a civilian airport—a place where they operate a radio beacon around the clock?"

"No. I have a special unit that allows me to let my destination airfield know whenever I want a heading. It's a bit like your usual radio-compass but with refinements, such as it transmits and receives in five-second bursts only. That's insufficient time for us to be detected and pinpointed by the authorities."

He was beginning to make sense, but there was one remaining difficulty—one of chilling proportions. The RAF in Singapore and Malaya had radar—not very sophisticated and somewhat unreliable, but nevertheless well capable of spotting a lone aircraft at forty miles, that is, if the unit was in use, and if the operator was fully alert and interested, and if the area concerned was free from lightning. It was reasonable to assume that the Japanese had radar of at least equivalent performance to that in use by the RAF. Therefore Japanese radar might spot the Hudson. If so, then we could well finish up flying into a hornets' nest.

"The Japs might have radar at strategic points on the Indo-China coast," I pointed out to Jan. "They'll have been informed of the Singapore 'state of emergency' declaration and they'll be on the alert for intruding aircraft. We'll probably be detected long before we reach the coast."

Jan made a little growling noise. I was, however, unable to judge whether this indicated irritation or contempt.

"I've heard that radar is unable to detect a plane flying below 1,500 feet," he said. "I can get right down when we're about fifty miles out—and put some speed on. We won't be detected very easily and, in any case, by the time they could get interceptor aircraft airborne we'll be down on the landing strip."

"As easy as that?" I asked with some doubt.

"Yes," he replied. And that was the end of that particular exchange.

We sat with our own thoughts for a further half an hour or so. Then Jan suggested sandwiches and coffee. I went back to the cabin for the ration box, and when we had finished our refreshment the time was 6:00 A.M. Airspeed 125 knots (140 MPH). Boost 31 Hg. Economic cruising conditions. Fuel consumption sixty Imperial gallons per hour, according to the operating manual.

"Where do you think we are now?" I asked.

Jan had a chart on his left side. He passed it over to me.

"See if you can guess," he replied. He turned up the cockpit lighting.

I possessed good vision, and I needed it to read the chart. I quickly located Penang Island and then Kota Bharu. Off to the right was the landmass of French Indo-China. We were flying, approximately, on a northeasterly heading and had now been airborne for about two and a half hours. I did a bit of mental arithmetic and arrived at the conclusion that the Hudson must have flown some 350 miles since takeoff. I pointed at a spot about a hundred miles from the coast of Indo-China.

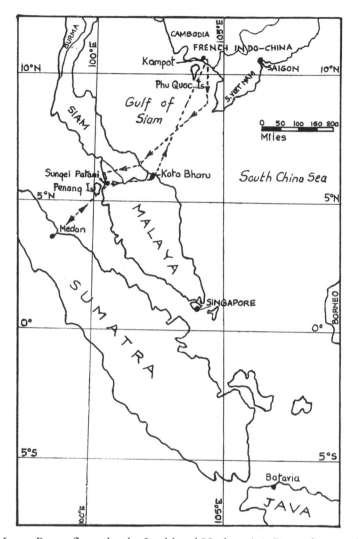

Map 2. Route flown by the Lockheed Hudson (4/5 December 1941).

Jan glanced down at my pointing finger. "You think we're there, do you?" he asked, his voice giving nothing away.

"Yes," I replied. "Roughly anyway. Not knowing the wind speed and direction I've made no allowance for that."

"Not bad," Jan said. "Quite good, in fact. I hadn't realized you were watching as closely as all that."

"But where do *you* imagine we are?" I asked.

"I'm not sure—but not a long way from where you think we may be. In thirty minutes or so I'll see if we can get any response from my friends over there. Remind me when it's about 6:30 A.M., please."

"I'll tell you when it's a quarter past the hour," I hastened to assure him, for I had no desire to find ourselves lost and within range of Japanese radar.

It had become noticeable that the Hudson's progress was not as smooth as it had been. A certain skittishness had begun to manifest itself. It had started as a kind of occasional unexpected lurch but had now progressed into a well-developed overall instability, rather like riding in a speed boat at sea. I checked my harness. It was tight enough to hold me secure, even if the turbulence worsened.

Jan motioned to me to fasten up my flying helmet. He did the same, then he switched off the cockpit lighting.

"We're running into a front, Peter," he said. "It's going to get a bit bumpy, I'm afraid."

Marvelous, I thought, and repositioned my hands on the frame of my seat again. Then it occurred to me that any would-be intercepting aircraft would find their task a lot more difficult in bad flying conditions. Thus cheered, I just rode the bumps, knowing the Hudson could take it.

For ten minutes we charged through light rain, then heavy rain, and then hail. The noise of the latter on the windshield, in some way, even sidetracked the canvas of my helmet and the protective cups of my headphones. It drowned the engine noise completely. Jan remained utterly unmoved by the noise and the leaping and bounding of the aircraft. At one point he relit his cigar, then sat soberly and reflectively in his seat, as though out on a rather pleasant train ride.

Then, suddenly, we were through it and out into still air once more. I could even see patches of clear sky and stars. I was glad to be able to enjoy the relative peace, and the now-steady ride restored some of my faith in nature. Then I remembered the radar threat and began fretting again.

"We'd better get things tidied up now," Jan said. "We don't want to be cluttered up with debris when we make our approach."

It was 6:15 A.M. I gave Jan the word, unbuckled myself, and took the ration box and its few remaining contents back to the cabin. Into one of my pockets I stuffed half a cheese sandwich, thinking that it might come in handy. I hurriedly ate the other half on my way back to the cockpit.

Jan reset his altimeter. "I'm putting it on low safe setting because I don't know what the sea-level pressure is out there," he explained. When he was finished, the instrument gave our height above sea level as being four thousand feet.

"This is where you can help," Jan said. He spoke authoritatively and urgently. He leaned to his left side, and when he was upright again he had in his hands a box the size of a large biscuit tin. He rested it in his lap while he turned up the cockpit lighting. Then he handed the box over to me.

"Don't drop the damn thing," he urged.

Attached to the box was a flexible conduit that draped across Jan's lap, then disappeared down on his left. He instructed me how to hold the equipment. On its face were a few simple switches and an instrument dial with a solitary needle, pivoted at its center. Jan flicked one of the small switches, whereupon the dial lit up. He operated another switch, and a point of amber light glowed on the face of the box.

"Now we're in business," Jan said.

He looked at his watch. "Dead on half-past," he growled. Then he adjusted the way I was holding the box so that its face was directed at him. He clicked another switch down and began counting aloud. "One, two, three, four, five." He released the switch and it flew back to its "off" position. No more than ten seconds elapsed before, as though by magic, the needle swung round to its left by some thirty degrees, hung there for five seconds, and then returned to its original position.

"Good!" exclaimed Jan. "They're awake anyway."

He looked at me, smiling, his dark eyes twinkling with good humor. The cockpit lighting made his fillings glint. He appeared to be a well-satisfied man.

"What now?" I asked.

"Well—I know the direction they're in, but I don't know how far yet anyway. It'll take five minutes or so."

He disengaged the autopilot, lowered the Hudson's nose, and opened the throttles. The plane's speed rapidly built up to 230 knots (260 MPH).

At two thousand feet Jan leveled out. "We're moving now, Peter," he said. "Using fuel like mad—that's the only problem."

Then it was time to use his box of tricks again. He operated the switches, the dial lit up, the amber light glowed, he counted to five and waited. The needle moved to the left again, but a little further this time.

"We've got about eighty miles to go," Jan announced. "We've drifted a hell of a lot."

He banked the speeding Hudson and took up a new heading of 010°. I began to get excited; if there were to be any problems, all the ingredients would now be being brought together in the darkness below.

"How much longer before we land?" I asked tensely.

"About thirty minutes, I reckon," he answered.

"What time does the sun rise over here?"

"Around 7:15 A.M.—but the sky will light up long before then with a bit of luck. You should see it any time now out of your side."

I looked out to my right. Total blackness—not even a small patch of cloudless sky to be seen.

"Nothing yet," I told him.

"Never mind. At least we're in the right area. We can hang around for an hour or more if necessary."

"And give the French or the Japs time to detect us, you mean," I said rather waspishly.

"There's no fear of that," he said. He was back on autopilot again—just sitting there, leaving everything to the aircraft.

During the ten minutes that followed I spent my time straining my eyes, looking for the very first signs of dawn.

Jan leaned over in my direction and studied the darkness that lay outside beyond my window. "The horizon must be obscured," he said. Then he looked at his watch in the dim light of the instrument panel. "7:10 A.M., Peter. Keep your eyes out for a bit of daylight."

"Are we clear of terrain obstructions?" I asked.

"Sure—there's nothing over 1,500 feet in this area—it's mostly quite flat down there—rice fields and swamps and that kind of thing."

"Are we over land now?"

"Probably—maybe just crossing the coast," Jan replied.

I looked down out of my window and immediately saw a group of tiny white lights.

"Lights down here, Jan!" I cried out with great relief.

"Good," he replied. "But keep a lookout for that horizon."

The Hudson continued to charge headlong into the unrelieved darkness, and then, suddenly, the night began to be swept aside. The change from overall blackness to darkest deep blue seemed to have happened in an instant. Over to the east there was even a faint horizontal smudge of lighter blue.

"I see it, Jan!" I cried. "Over here—look!"

Jan glanced through my window and grunted, then he motioned to me to present the radio-compass device to him again. He went to work on it as before. "Almost dead ahead now," he said. Then he disengaged the autopilot, banked a little to the left, and pulled back sharply on the control wheel.

The Hudson's airspeed fell back to 120 knots and Jan leveled off at four thousand feet. The engines were still running at near maximum power and the plane's speed quickly built up again. The light-blue narrow smudge on the horizon had now developed into a wide golden blue band with the definite line of the horizon clearly discernible.

"Five minutes to go, Peter," Jan advised, almost nonchalantly.

I noticed that he had suddenly become all eyes, first craning his neck to see forward and downward, then quickly turning to see what was on his left and then his right. I was busy crushing the frame of my seat again, wondering how the devil he was going to put down in the murk and darkness.

But it was becoming lighter by the second. I could now pick out dark patches below. A short line of lights came into view down on my right, then ahead a cluster of brighter lights emerged, disappearing momentarily from time to time as the Hudson passed through wisps of cloud.

Jan pulled the throttle levers back. The engine noise settled down to a rich, rhythmic burbling. The plane banked to the right and the approaching cluster of lights veered off the other way. The ground was becoming visible—or, at any rate, I could see a lot of ground mist. We were rushing through thinly scattered clouds, silent, ghostly, and almost luminescent vapors.

"Put the box down," Jan instructed. "We won't need it anymore." He had one hand on the wheel and the other firmly on the throttle levers. I did as he asked.

"Tighten up, Peter," he growled—as if I needed any telling, having been well and truly strapped in for the last half hour.

The aircraft was sinking fast. Jan prepared for the landing—wheels down, flaps down, fine pitch, and a few other essentials, while all the time searching the indistinct ground and mist ahead for the landing strip. I could be of no help, being clueless as to what kind of place he was looking for.

Jan had stopped talking. He was 100 percent, and more, immersed in what he was attempting to do, that is, find his landing strip, which as likely as not was obscured by mist, while coaxing the Hudson along at something perilously close to stalling speed. But he had done it before—if he were to be believed.

Then air disturbance hit us. Not violently but enough to prompt Jan to pour on a bit of power. He did so automatically, without thinking, then straightaway he took it off again. He dropped the nose and we hurtled down toward whatever it was below that appeared as a fuzzy dark-grey surface with patches of lighter grey.

The final moments of our now-hurried descent were swiftly over. Jan must have seen the airstrip lighting but kept quiet about it. At the very last moment I too saw it—just two rows of light that appeared to have little more output than motorcycle headlamps, their low beams slanting across and in the direction of our landing run. It was then that I at last became convinced that Jan had done this before.

The Hudson barely quivered as its wheels touched down. Then all engine noise ceased. I was immediately thrown forward into my harness as the brakes came on. Apart from a little bucking and minor swerving the landing went well. Half a minute later we were off the airstrip and taxiing toward a large workshed. The Hudson passed through gaping sliding doors into the dim interior, then Jan quickly shut down the engines. Outside, the two lines of runway lights were no longer to be seen. The eastern sky was ablaze with a dazzling suffusion of gold, orange, and red.

I just wanted to sit for a while, until my mind in addition to my body had returned to earth. But Jan was already out of his seat and making preparations to exit the aircraft. He did not seem at all elated, or even relieved that we had arrived in one piece. With me, however, it was different. I was marveling at the way he had managed to find the airstrip anyway. I was indescribably relieved that we had not been intercepted. But my main immediate source of pleasure was the simple fact that I was back on the ground.

I unbuckled myself, sat for a moment or two, taking deep breaths of air, then clambered back after Jan. He was opening the main hatch when I caught up with him. He glanced back at me and on his stubbly face was a good-natured grin.

"Okay, Peter?" he asked.

"Kind of," I replied.

My reply may well have suggested a degree of uncertainty—in which case, I have to say, it was not far off the mark.

7 Cambodia

Thursday, 4 December

It was a fairly large room, with a high, tiredly ornate ceiling with suspended propeller fans driving stifling air down over dining tables. The walls were papered but probably had been, at one time, bare plaster. A number of plaster moldings, sculptures of dancing girls, still remained on the walls, painted in gilt and frantic metallic colors and looking as though they would have been more at home on a fun-fair ride than gracing the walls of a back-of-beyond Cambodian restaurant. The floor was tiled—ceramic tiles with an overall pattern of green foliage on an otherwise off-white surface. There were twenty or so dining tables, arranged with ample space between them and laid with white linen tablecloths and surprisingly gleaming cutlery. The dining chairs were of dark hardwood upholstered with bottle-green velvet.

Suspended from the high ceiling were a number of chandeliers which, in their day, would certainly have been regarded as ornate and elegant. But those days had passed some thirty or forty years ago and now these unhappy-looking displays exhibited all the signs of modification, repair, and general decadence. Altogether the room's interior resembled that of a dining room in some sad, rundown Victorian hotel in the heart of rural Lincolnshire, or its French equivalent, though sundry Oriental decorations and appurtenances, along with spicy cooking smells, placed it firmly in Indo-China or thereabouts.

Four of us sat at one of the tables, only two of the other tables being occupied. In one corner a two-piece band played quaintly arranged songs from the shows. At the moment the two diminutive musicians were repetitiously grinding out the theme tune of the film *Gone with the Wind* on a violin and a flute of sorts. The result was oddly excruciating and distinctly pathetic.

With me sat Jan and two others, Paul and Henri. We were conversing in English for the most part and in low tones, just loud enough to be heard among ourselves over the musical caterwauling. The dinner, now over, had been good, although Jan had eaten hardly anything. I had enjoyed myself with, I recall, lamb curry and rice. The other two had eaten selectively and well, one of them, Henri, seemingly being reluctant to quit overloading his already ample paunch. Two bottles of French wine had been consumed, though both Jan and I had declined any kind of alcohol.

It was now 8:30 P.M. The two musicians must have decided it was time for a change and thereupon launched into "Roses Are Shining in Picardy"—this time on a saxophone but with a mouth organ as occasional backup.

Presently we left the dining room and proceeded along a short corridor, then up a curving staircase to a landing. There we were shown into a small lounge, comfortably and elegantly furnished in colonial style. We sat in wicker armchairs around a wicker table under a lazily turning propeller fan, with wood-paneled walls lending an atmosphere of hushed privacy and security. Subdued lighting gave the place a cozy feel. Against one wall was a heavy-looking wooden sideboard. It had a lot of intricate carving and was much blackened by age and use. But its most interesting feature was the wide selection of bottles exhibited on it. I eyed both it and the bottles, thinking how, yet again, my luck was out. I could have swigged the glowing contents of any of those bottles readily and with gratitude, but I was in the wrong place at the wrong time.

I sat scratching my fingertip, it having caused me a deal of anguish throughout the day. Now, as I looked at it, I could see a mosquito bite that had wasted little time in turning nasty. The end of my left little finger, right on the rounded part on the opposite side from the nail, was purple and swollen. Furthermore it throbbed and itched like the devil. It was by no means an average mosquito bite. The way it was going pointed to the need for an effective emollient or even hot fomentations. It was going fusty at a rate of knots. I would discuss the matter with Paul when the meeting was at an end. He was the kind of chap who would know best what to do, and would doubtless have the necessary stuff with which to do it.

A waiter appeared with coffee—a polite wisp of a youth in a spotless white uniform. He had, on his glistening brown Cambodian features, one of those frozen enigmatic smiles that can keep one guessing for long enough. He went about his business, setting out the cups and saucers and dispensing coffee noiselessly and unobtrusively, yet one felt compelled to hold one's tongue until he had finished and departed.

Jan lit a cigar. The other two smoked cigarettes. I just scratched my fingertip and began to sense that I was intruding.

It had been an unusual day, but one that had passed quickly. After taxiing the Hudson into the dark sanctuary of the workshed, we climbed out to be greeted by a Frenchman—a tall, slim fellow of, I would guess, around forty-five. Of marked intellectual appearance, he was plagued by an odd nervous tick in that, every half minute or so, he would lift his chin then jerk his mouth to one side quite sharply—twice, the first time as though for practice and the second time in earnest. The habit detracted rather from his otherwise normal, reassuring, and affable manner. It was something that could and should have been sorted out long ago, for I imagined it had been with him for quite some time. His countenance was somewhat gaunt, his dark eyes a little sunken, and he had, rather like Jan, almost black hair trimmed almost to the scalp. His name was Paul. He showed some surprise when informed that I was English and with the RAF. However he remained quiet about it, although his guarded sidelong look at Jan signified that he felt further explanation would not be out of place. The two conversed in English, by which I took it that neither was happy speaking the other's language. I was glad of that because my only other language was German, having learned it as a boy.

The three of us had walked to the Frenchman's residence—a kind of villa with a definite Oriental flavor. About two hundred yards from the shed in which we had secreted the Hudson, the villa was nestled among ornamental trees and shrubs on the side of a slight incline. After Jan and I showered, the three of us walked out onto a south-facing veranda where croissants and cof-

fee were brought to us by a Cambodian girl. She would have been eighteen
or nineteen, her dark features attractive and pleasing. Her figure was the
right shape and she walked with a kind of haughty grace. She wore a long
silk dress with a high neckline and short sleeves. It was a tight dress, like
the Malayan kebaya, which, as she walked, deliberately or by chance high-
lighted the long, full curve of her thighs. She had jet-black, strong, wiry hair
swept back into a bunch secured by a gold and ivory clasp that must have
set someone back a bit. At one stage I caught her examining me with eyes
that were even darker than her skin—black glittering oval orbs—as hard
as they came. I wondered who she was and where she came from. She was
never mentioned after that, and I never saw her again.

No business was conducted between Jan and the Frenchman over breakfast. Conversation was politely limited to trivialities, though touching now
and again on the Japanese situation. I learned that, after nightfall, the three
of us would drive over to a small not-too-distant town and that there we
would be joined by another Frenchman whom they had referred to as Henri.

Both Jan and I were feeling the lack of sleep and at around 9:30 A.M. we
were shown to rooms where we could sleep for a few hours. I slept for six
hours, then had another shower, and then took tea and cake on the veranda with Paul—this time waited on by a much younger girl, but one clearly destined to become as interesting as the breakfast girl. She could well
have been her sister. My mind was on the Hudson because I had agreed
with Jan that directly after tea I would go down to the shed and give the
aircraft the once-over.

Both Jan and Paul went down with me. Paul had arranged for me to have
the services of a couple of his Cambodian workmen. Then they left me to
it. I spent the best part of two hours inspecting the plane, the two locals helping me remove and replace panels as necessary. I topped up the two twenty-
gallon engine-oil tanks, using oil carried in five-gallon drums in the plane.
I was unable to check the running of the engines while the Hudson was
inside the shed; that would have to be done in the open air after dark. I finished my work just as the sun began to set. Looking back toward the short
airstrip, I was surprised to see that clumps of vegetation had been dragged
over it, which, along with a collection of plantation machinery strewn hith-
er and thither, had effectively blended it into the general landscape of mixed
scrub and cultivated plots. The Frenchman was evidently making sure his
occasional involvement with aviation could not be spotted from the air. But

he had workers to help him in whatever his full-time business was, and any one of them could spill the beans if ever he chose to do so. However, that was Paul's business and no doubt he had contrived to render his operation watertight. But his anxious demeanor and his twitch were perhaps both due to the fact that he had allowed Jan to use part of his land as a covert, illegal airstrip for the past two years. Perhaps it had all become too much for him.

The general surrounding landscape consisted of undulating terrain mostly given over to rice and green-crop cultivation. In the immediate vicinity very little appeared exotic or even tropical, yet the low hills seemed to be heavily forested, possibly with rubber trees or jungle. There were higher hills to the southwest. No other buildings were to be seen. The hot, humid air carried in it the smell of the East, of moisture and of warmth, of woodsmoke and fruit and vegetation. It had the smell of Cambodia, subtly different from that of Malaya. But to me it was a smell heavy with hidden threat for I was not supposed to be here. There were people here who, to say the least, were not my friends. All I had between myself and them was a Lockheed Hudson and a pilot who was not even English and who seemed unable to appreciate the particular gravity of our situation.

Alone, I commenced the short walk up to the Frenchman's villa. When I was about halfway there, the sound of aero-engines reached my ears. I stopped, looked upwards, and immediately saw a tight bunch of aircraft approaching from the north. I stepped back instinctively into a group of trees. The aircraft, at about one thousand feet, droned on in my direction. Two minutes later they were virtually overhead the residence, nine twin-engined jobs and unlike any I had ever seen.

I turned my attention away from the general outline of the aircraft and, instead, to their markings. I had never seen a Japanese airplane but knew vaguely that their identity was denoted by a red disc. Each one I looked at bore such an insignia. My blood ran cold. I had read in books of such and such an individual whose heart had been clutched by fear. Personally I had never experienced this, but on seeing those red emblems I understood precisely. My reaction was immediate—the clutched heart, the sudden coldness, the blood draining from my face, and the trembling of my hands and knees. The realization that all I had heard about the virtual takeover of Indo-China by Japan was manifestly true hit me like a savage thump on the side of the head. I stood, frozen to the spot.

I watched as the aircraft slowly receded south toward the coast. Then I heard more approaching. Again, another nine twin-engined aircraft of the same type came into view and droned lazily overhead, proceeding in the same direction as the others; those red discs were there as before. They, too, moved away toward the coast. But it was not finished, for yet another nine droned in my direction, passed overhead, and were then lost in the dazzling brightness of the evening sky.

I resumed my walk up to the villa, my heart now beating at a more or less normal rate but feeling crushed and as though it had just suffered a degree of permanent damage. On reaching the villa gates I heard the sound of more approaching aircraft. This time they were in groups of three; small single radial-engined fighter aircraft, all bearing the Japanese insignia disc. There were six groups of three—eighteen in total, all snarling across the sky at a ridiculously low level and at a speed I estimated at something like 250 MPH. These, though I could not know it at the time, were a version of the so-called Zero fighter—the fighter which, within a few days, was destined to prove much more than a match for the jinxed Sungei Patani Buffaloes.

Jan and Paul had stepped out into the garden, curious to find out what all the noise was about. The three of us discussed the matter after I washed and made myself presentable in a white duck jacket and trousers that Paul had loaned to me. Both he and Jan thought it not a good idea for me to turn up for the arranged dinner wearing anything other than the style of clothing worn by French people out here.

"They're the kind of airplanes I talked to you about earlier," Paul remarked to Jan. Evidently they had been discussing the growing presence of Japanese military planes while I had been checking the Hudson.

"Where do you think they operate from?" Jan asked.

"I can only guess—but every day there are more and more of them. Maybe they come from Saigon, or Phnom Penh. But I heard just last week that the Japanese have established an airbase on the island."

"Which island?" Jan asked.

"Phu Quoc, of course," the Frenchman replied irritably. "Why would they want a military airbase there if they were not preparing to attack Malaya and Siam?"

"God knows," Jan replied, and for the first time I detected in his voice and face an absence of that cool, confident self-assurance that up to now had so much impressed me.

I butted in. "Phu Quoc Island must be only about forty miles from here," I said, remembering having seen it on Jan's map. "About fifteen minutes flying time—even less for those fighters—and the Japs are bound to have radar there."

The Frenchman stood up abruptly and poured himself a large Pernod, which he then drowned with about three drops of water. He took a large gulp, which, judging by his expression, nearly blew his brains out. But it stopped his twitching for the next few minutes. "That was the largest number of Japanese planes we've ever seen," he grumbled. "It must mean something. Perhaps they're already on the move."

It was getting dark. At around 7:30 P.M. we set off in Paul's car for our rendezvous. The vehicle, I remember, was a monster of a thing. It smelled of damp leather and petrol and exhaust fumes and sounded a bit like a marine landing craft. It helped clear the air if the windows were cranked down. He drove it lovingly, at about twenty MPH. The massive headlights lit up the whole countryside whichever way they were pointed. Any approaching motorist would have had to pull off the road into the nearest paddy field to avoid being blinded by light and having his conveyance pushed to one side.

Those Japanese planes had left me jittery, although once again there was nothing I could do about it. The right thing would have been for Jan and me to leave the country directly after sundown, but instead here we were thubbering through the warm Cambodian night air rather like the Three Stooges, toward not quiet seclusion but habitation and people—and all just so that Jan could do a bit of dodgy business for the last time and also, it seemed, take delivery of a British chap who ought to have had enough sense to quit the country well before now.

We arrived at the restaurant some thirty minutes after leaving the villa, having first driven into the minuscule town of Kampot with its occasional bright lights and cafés, its mysterious little shops, its smells, and its people in all manner of excitement, misery, and endeavor. The restaurant itself was an aging, run-down stonework building, having what I imagined to be the stamp of French architecture. It resembled some of the English colonial buildings I had seen in Singapore and Kuala Lumpur. Whatever it had once been, it had now ceased to be quite that—no doubt it had long been taken over from some disenchanted French proprietor by a budding Cambodian entrepreneur, who for some reason had allowed it to sink more or less slowly until it had become what it now was—a weary-looking eating-cum-resthouse, languishing in an aura of Oriental decay and indifferent neglect.

I decided the time had come for me to leave the other three alone to get on with it, in addition to which I felt the desire to be alone for a while. Jan presented no problem to me, but the two Frenchmen were getting on my nerves. Paul had his twitch and his worried look and his general air of melancholy. Henri, the second Frenchman, was something else again. He was big—tall-big and heavy-big—maybe twenty stones or more and tough-looking with it. He was dressed in a smart light-grey silk suit and white silk shirt. His shoes were light-grey calf leather with white toe flashes. His voice was deep, rich, and oily. He had the habit of shaking his head from side to side when emphasizing certain points, and this set his jowls and full range of chins wobbling. His countenance was a healthy olive-brown shade, and his penetrating eyes were a matching brown. He was, due to his several remarkable characteristics, an easy individual to remember. His black hair was parted down the middle and slicked back and secured there with, I assumed, pomade. Yet another singular thing about him, but by no means the least, was his nose—a pretty big effort by any standards—long and fleshy and curved. The nose alone would have warned me off entering into any dealing of even the slightest significance with him. He looked far too worldly, intelligent, and artful for my taste. In his presence I felt about as useful and important as a trainee luggage porter on a disused railway station on a wet Sunday afternoon somewhere between Newark and Cleethorpes. He had that kind of effect on me. He walked with the brisk and erect gait of any guards officer, and he carried around with him the clinging aroma of eau de cologne or similar fragrance. The man was fascinating, but he looked pretty deadly.

I excused myself. Jan came out onto the landing and quietly told me he would find me when the meeting was over. He suggested I go back into the dining room, have more coffee, and listen to the music, but not to speak to anyone or drink any alcohol. He would be about an hour.

"What about the British fellow you're supposed to be picking up?" I asked.

"I was told that he'll be here at 10:30 P.M.," Jan replied, patting me lightly on the shoulder and turning away to rejoin the other two, thus making it plain that he had no wish to discuss the matter further.

Downstairs I found the washroom where I quickly stuck my stricken finger under a cold water tap. The wash basins were from another age—huge chipped and crazed things with unpolished brass taps. There were half a dozen or so of them. I remained alone for a minute or thereabouts; then the door opened and an Oriental person entered. He was too light-skinned to be Cambodian and did not strike me as being Chinese, being of short, solid stature with a wide face, an immensely strong lower jaw, and alert oval-shaped eyes under thick black, higher-than-usual eyebrows. The newcomer strode purposefully into one of the WC cubicles. I continued to let cold water trickle over my finger.

When he came out of his cubicle, the gentleman proceeded to wash his hands, an act in which he was most thorough. At one stage he darted a glance in my direction. Then he stepped back from his basin and shook his hands in an attempt to dry them. I thought the least I could do would be to acknowledge him. Consequently I turned and gave him a quick nod of the head. The result was amazing. He immediately straightened himself up, feet together, then bowed to me—a low bow that brought his torso parallel with the floor, a feat that must have brought considerable discomfort to his lumbar region. When he resumed his vertical posture I grinned at him, on the assumption that he had been fooling around, and he straightaway went into his bowing act again.

At length, having worked the near-acrobatic courtesies out of his system, the chap pointed at my finger and over his face there fell an expression of questioning and concern. I removed the offending finger from the streaming water and showed it to him; then, with my other hand, I described an arc in the air while making a sound like the whine of a mosquito. I then made little stabbing motions at my finger to indicate that it had been bitten, or, more accurately I suppose, injected. He examined it closely—about six inches closely in fact—then he smiled and exclaimed, "Aahh!"

The fellow produced an assortment of other noises which, rightly as it happened, I took to be expressions of commiseration. He seemed to be an intelligent individual and was blessed with not-unpleasant features, so that when he took my arm and politely led me to the door I felt no strong reason to object. Plainly he had some kind of helpful plan in mind.

We went out on to a wide veranda at the rear of the building. My newly found acquaintance found a convenient table and indicated to me to be seated, then gestured to me to remain there until he returned. He disappeared into the building and while he was gone I studied my surroundings. The veranda was dimly lit, with colored lanterns suspended from a low ceiling. It looked out over what appeared to be gardens, the dark shapes of shrubs and trees silhouetted by a bright moon. Beyond the gardens there was only darkness. In the warm, moist night air was the faint but unmistakable smell of the sea. The heady scent of sweet-smelling flowers gave to the atmosphere a suitable aura of tropical mystery, something I may have appreciated more had I not been plagued by an itching and burning finger along with a degree of nervous tension probably severe enough to be turning my hair white even as I sat there.

The chap returned very shortly, carrying a bottle and two glasses. These he put on the table and sat down opposite me. He had a grin on his face, not a malicious grin but one that denoted considerable satisfaction and pleasure. He appeared to be in his mid- or late thirties. His teeth were ridiculously even and white, and something about his complexion definitely confirmed him as some race other than Chinese. His cheeks, under prominent cheekbones, positively glowed and were tinged with a healthy pinkness. He filled the two glasses from the up-market bottle. I had no idea as to the quality of what the bottle contained, but the label stated it to be cognac. I could not drink this stuff so when my newly found friend put one of the filled glasses in my hand I inwardly groaned, then made a pretense of sipping some of the enticing amber liquid. He lifted his glass at the same time, but, instead of taking a cautious sip, he downed its entire contents in one massive gulp. Then he banged the glass on the table and treated me to yet another of his disarming grins. I liked the sip I had taken and, thinking to humor him, I took another. It burned my lips and throat but removed the sharp edge of my tenseness. I made a mental note not to imbibe more of the stuff but instead concentrate on encouraging him to produce his already hinted solution to my finger problem.

I pointed to my finger and winced. He got the message and dived into a canvas pouch he was carrying on the waist belt of his blue-cotton drill trousers. Taking a tube from the pouch, he indicated that he would apply some of its contents to my finger. I nodded, even though I did not know what it contained. It took him just a few minutes to smear a liberal coating over the end of my finger, cover it with a small piece of gauze, and then seal it with sticking plaster. Then he tidied up and went to wash his hands. I took the opportunity to look out over the edge of the veranda rail and, at the same time, empty the rest of my cognac into the bushes.

I was, of course, now planning how I could make my escape. He had done his good Samaritan thing and had given me a drink, but the time had come for me to give him the slip. I beckoned a waiter over and ordered coffee for two. Jan had instructed me to charge anything I ordered to Henri's account, thereby avoiding trouble due to my not having any local cash. The full truth was, in fact, that I had no cash of any description on me. The Cambodian waiter understood my message without difficulty—it not being too difficult to order two coffees from someone who can understand the mathematical meaning of two fingers held aloft. My plan was to slip the stranger a cup of coffee, and then at the very first opportunity do a bunk.

In a moment or two the waiter reappeared with the coffee. He also brought a small dish of what I assumed to be crystallized ginger. It was sweating and almost all the sugar had metamorphosed into syrup. My friend arrived back at the table at virtually the same time. Also in the same instant it suddenly struck me that the fellow might very well be Japanese. My heart put on a special hyperactive performance for a few seconds. My problems had suddenly increased a thousandfold.

He grinned cheerfully at me, refilled our glasses, then shouted, "Oi-oi," to the world at large before again slurping his drink down in one go. He pointed at my glass. His meaning was clear. I evaded the issue by dispensing coffee into the two cups and indicating that he should take one. Instead, he peered closely at the ginger and then popped a piece in his mouth and began chomping on it. He let out a cry which, I remember, sounded much like the noise he may well have made had a bull mastiff suddenly taken a slice out of his backside. The other individuals on the veranda cast alarmed glances in our direction. Leaning over, the fellow spat out his bit of ginger, or whatever it was, over the veranda rail, then took more cognac to get rid of the aftertaste. I sipped my coffee pensively and nodded to him to drink his.

I glanced at my watch. The time was 9:15 P.M. Music from the dining room drifted through to the veranda. Now it was "Sweet Sue" in a hectic quickstep tempo on violin and drums. The silver, almost-full moon kept disappearing behind clouds.

My hair was very fair, as was also my complexion. There was nothing about me that could have been seen as Gallic. Yet this thirsty gent must have jumped to the not-unreasonable conclusion that I was French. If so, it was evident that he did not speak French because from the very start he had communicated with me in sign language, gestures, and grunts. He no doubt knew that English people particularly were, perforce, something of a rarity in Indo-China, and he could hardly have expected to come face to face with an Englishman at a third-rate restaurant-cum-hotel in a fairly desolate part of Cambodia. That he almost certainly did not realize I was English did not help a lot. Even the slightest suspicion on his part could well result in words being said to, from my point of view, the wrong people. I was seized by an overwhelming desire to remove myself from his company. But there was the coffee that I had not yet finished—and the cognac, too, looked lonely in its stylish, beckoning bottle. I put on a brave face and, on impulse, topped off my coffee cup with cognac and took a generous gulp of the fortified beverage. It worked, so naturally I took another. Then I finished it off and was then ready to give my full attention to my good companion, who had begun to make certain gestures that suggested to me he was most desirous of communicating further.

The gestures and signs that he was making told me he wished to know what kind of work I did. It is easy to understand such sign language when you are receptively alert thanks to a sudden shot of brandy, and when the individual who is trying to get something across to you is determined and enthusiastic. It took me, I suppose, no more than half a minute to indicate to him that I was, broadly, in the engineering game. He held out his hands for me to inspect. They were equally as hard as mine, the fingernails trimmed right down and broken in places. He was clearly a manual worker of some kind. His further gesticulations made it apparent that he was curious to know what brand of engineering I was in, but I thought it better to withhold from him the fact that I was involved in aero engineering. To have told him that would have been to whet his curiosity even further, so I indicated that I was concerned with engines generally, along with pumps and such like equipment.

He had given the cognac a fair thrashing. It had not seemed to have affected him very much thus far, and he must have liked the taste of it. He dispensed himself another, drank his coffee in one go, then chased it down with the cognac. His face now glistened with perspiration, and his eyebrows had somehow moved up his forehead about half an inch. He had already consumed at least a third of the bottle of the cognac, and it was beginning to make inroads on his central nervous system. Yet he was still anxious to know more and, indeed, to divulge more.

With a good deal of gesturing and other appropriate body language he succeeded in imparting to me that he was a civilian engineer and employed by a big company engaged in metal fabrication for the aircraft industry. Then he again rummaged in his canvas pouch and pulled out a little book which, when opened, turned out to be a diary of sorts. He flicked the pages over, eventually finding the page he was after. It featured a map of the world that extended onto the adjacent page. He peered at it closely, then pointed to an area on the map. He looked up at me, his eyebrows still high up on his forehead. Clearly he wished to convey to me the fact that this was his homeland. Although the veranda was not overly lighted, there was enough light to enable me to see the spot at which he was pointing. It was Japan. Actually his fingers rested on the southern island of Japan.

"Ah," I said. "Japan."

He nodded his head, his face beaming with pleasure. Then he pulled a pencil from that useful pouch of his and positioned its point precisely on the southern island of Japan. There could now be no mistaking that he was Japanese. I felt numb with a kind of bleak fear.

He tapped insistently with his pencil at the map as though to make quite sure I understood his meaning. I nodded vigorously to confirm my comprehension and wished he would now calm down so that I could make my escape. But no such thing happened. Instead he turned to an empty page in the diary and began sketching something on it. Then he tore the page out and positioned it in front of me. He had, quite carefully and neatly, sketched out the islands of Japan. He pointed to himself, then to a spot on the southern island. It was there, presumably, where he either worked or lived, or both. He then did another thing with his pencil. He drew a chain of small islands extending even farther north of the main northern island of Japan. He then laughed—a kind of triumphal laugh that had in it something more like intense satisfaction rather than just happiness. Once again he pointed with the pencil at a point on one of the smallest islands he had painstakingly drawn.

He raised his head and gazed at me long and hard, his brow furrowed, perspiration trickling down his cheeks. He poured out more cognac for himself, picked up the drink, looked at it, and then put it down again.

At this point a bright-green lizard about four inches long appeared over the edge of the table, evidently having climbed one of the legs in search of sustenance. It shot across in the direction of my companion, stopped, raised its head high in the air, and froze. The engineer glanced at it and swept it from the table with a swift, impatient movement of his hand. The unfortunate reptile could hardly have had time to work out what was about to happen. It shot through the air, over the balcony, and into the bushes where, maybe, it rested for a time, wondering where it had gone wrong.

My Japanese acquaintance gazed at me again, as though collecting his thoughts before venturing into another session of his brand of sign language.

He spoke just one word, which sounded like "Hittocappu."

"Oh," I replied.

He banged the point of his pencil down again on the spot.

"Hittocappu," he repeated, but not so quietly this time.

"Ah-ah," I returned.

He pointed at himself, then at the spot on his drawing.

"Hittocappu," he said again, this time quite vehemently.

"Hm." I could hardly say more without blurting out some giveaway words of English.

Then he went to work on his diary and began explaining the relationship between himself and this Hittocappu place which, along with other tiny islands, was stuck out in the sea many miles north of Japan's main islands.

I sat, quiet and motionless, as he related his story by means of a remarkable miscellany of assertive grunts, hisses, and hand and eyebrow movements. He sketched in his diary such matter as he would have failed to convey to me by dint of body language alone and also used the diary to convey dates.

He had recently been engaged at the factory where he worked on the manufacture of bomb racks for aircraft of the Japanese navy. He had, along with a few others, actually been put aboard an aircraft carrier for the purpose of modifying the bomb racks on several of the aircraft carried on board. The job had been to lengthen the standard racks to accommodate new armor-piercing bombs. The work had been carried out while the carrier was sailing from Japan to "Hittocappu," a matter of several hundred miles, as far as I could estimate from his little map. They continued working on the bomb racks and, when the work was finished on 24 November, his workmates had been taken ashore by tanker. He and one other, who apparently was next door in the dining room at this very moment, had been transferred to a destroyer and brought at speed to southern French Indo-China and then by plane to Phu Quoc, where similar bomb racks were to be modified in the same way. He and his colleague had, I gathered, arrived yesterday but had been granted overnight leave on the mainland and would in the morning be taken back to Phu Quoc to carry out their work.

At Hittocappu, he explained, it had been bitterly cold with fogs and snow-storms, but he had been able to discern the presence, in the secluded bay, of a great many naval ships, including aircraft carriers, battleships, cruisers, destroyers, and tankers. There had been talk of the carriers being loaded to capacity with planes, bombs, and torpedoes, while the presence of the tankers suggested that the whole naval armada was about to embark on an extreme-ly long voyage. In addition to the ships, several submarines had been spotted on the surface.

As his story unfolded, my acquaintance drew in his diary little sketches of one thing and another, including planes and ships, the latter being charac-terized and identified by outline and relative size. He may have lost his grip on the notion of discretion, but he most certainly had not let go his hold on his engineering expertise, his neat and well-proportioned pencil sketches plainly demonstrating his above-average technical background and ability.

My interest was heavily tempered by the growing fear of being stumbled upon by either French or Japanese officials. Yet all that this fellow was di-vulging to me seemed to constitute such unique information that I felt com-pelled to follow his various meanings and explanations as best I could. To speed matters along, I topped off his coffee cup and gently pushed his glass of cognac toward him. He swallowed both drinks in quick time, then hurled the glass into the night—probably his way of denying himself any more of the potent amber poison.

Putting his now-blunt pencil down, he stared at me through those glit-tering slits of eyes. He was more than a little bewildered due to alcoholic intoxication, but I sensed that any second he would get his thoughts straight-ened out and then I would get to know more. I had no reason to dislike him; after all, I kept telling myself, he had taken pity on me. But he constituted a positive element of danger to me, and because of that I was anxious to cut adrift from him.

He grunted, "Huh," and began indicating with his worn pencil how many naval ships he had seen at Hittocappu, stabbing with his pencil on one of the pages, once for each ship. When he finally put the pencil down, I counted forty stab marks on the page. I held up my hands, fingers out-stretched to indicate ten. I repeated this four times and he beamed gleefully in the recognition that I had understood his meaning. He proceeded to do a lot of nodding, but this must have made him feel dizzy, because he stopped abruptly and held his head between his hands.

I waited—very patiently under the circumstances. The band continued to play a tune unknown to me on saxophone and drums, the former blasting out in huge, rich, sonoric tones curiously interspersed with half-hearted squeaks.

He cleared his throat mightily, once again causing others on the veranda to dart startled glances in our direction. And then he delivered the real goods, except that at the time I had little idea this was so. He picked up the pencil and drew with it an arc on the map. The arc started at the spot he had called Hittocappu, swept across the wastes of the northern Pacific Ocean, then turned to the southeast and ended in the Hawaiian Islands. He pushed the map under my nose. In the poor light I had to peer hard to see where his pencil line terminated. I knew nothing much about Hawaii, and his demonstration meant little to me at the time.

He snapped out of another short period of meditation and tapped his head—not the kind of tap that one would use to indicate that the head is aching, but rather to convey the notion of thinking. There was something in his mind that he wished me to know. Once again he riffled through his pouch and, before long, put a small magnifying lens in my hand. He pointed with his pencil at the spot where the penciled arc finished in the middle of the Pacific Ocean. I squinted through the lens but, owing to the poor light and the fact that the glass was somewhat in need of a thorough cleaning, I failed to read any of the place names that lay under it. I looked up at him, frowned, shook my head negatively, and put the lens down in front of him.

He grimaced—a facial contortion that held back nothing of his frustration and impatience. His fist came down on the table with a thump that, again, caused no little alarm among those at the other tables.

"Hawaii!" he shouted, then, again, "Hawaii!"

I nodded in agreement, having no intention of upsetting him further.

"Hawaii!" he said again, though this time in a confidentially sly and much less noisy manner. Then he tapped his head in the way he had done a few moments before—as someone does when indicating that they are of the opinion and of a particular belief. He leaned over the table toward me, raised his black eyebrows, and smiled knowingly. Perspiration stood out in miniature globules on his furrowed brow. He breathed in, then held his breath for a few seconds. Then, thrusting his head even closer to mine, he said, "Purhabba." The word came out in a low whisper.

I nodded, though I had no idea what he was talking about. He opened his eyes as wide as their natural geometry permitted. They glinted as with

intense excitement and satisfaction. "Purhabba," he repeated. Then he pointed at his sketches depicting the ships he had seen at the place he had called
Hittocappu; and he moved his pencil along the wide sweeping arc, starting
at Hittocappu and finishing at the place he had first called Hawaii and then
Purhabba. He then sat back, evidently pleased that he had gotten his
thoughts and notions off his chest. But he was not yet entirely through.
Seizing the pencil again, he poised it over the Hawaiian end of the arc, then
proceeded to move it repeatedly up and down over the spot. Then he suddenly spread his arms wide and shouted, "Wugh!"

I got the idea. He was telling me it was his view that all those ships would
set out from Hittocappu, sail across the vast expanse of the northern Pacific
to Hawaii, and there attack the island he had indicated. The particular significance of Purhabba escaped me in that I had never heard of the place.
What I did know, however, was that Hawaii was a U.S. territory and therefore he was telling me that he suspected that this Japanese armada was making ready to attack it—and evidently sooner rather than later, because he was
now pointing out imminent dates in his diary.

Mosquitoes continued to dance around the lantern above our table. The
perfumed smoke of unseen joss sticks wreathed slowly and silently about us.
The band was playing "Melodie d'Amour," an incongruously evocative and
sorrowful tune.

The man beckoned for my attention. I leaned toward where he was now
pointing his pencil at his diary map again. Then, with more gestures and
sundry vocal explosions, he indicated to me that Japanese planes would bomb
Singapore and Malaya and that Japanese troops would attack Malaya—all at
the same time that Hawaii was, he seemed confident, being ravaged by the
fleet of ships he had seen at Hittocappu.

I smiled, frowned, and shook my head as in disbelief, though inwardly I
had felt the sickening clutch of fear.

He gazed into my eyes, his lips pressed tightly together. His eyebrows
dropped and his chin assumed a fierce set. His rather wide nostrils flared. I
could tell that I had displeased him. I filled my glass, pushed it over to him,
and made a sign for him to drink, meanwhile trying to keep a disarming
smile going. He looked at the glass, then back at me, and then picked it up
and tossed the cognac down his throat in a courageous but unwise gesture of
defiance and contempt. Directly the liquor impinged on his internals. His
face crumpled with acute distaste. He retched convulsively, flung himself out

of his chair, leaned out into the darkness over the veranda rail, and proceeded to make loud, guttural, protesting noises of the vomiting kind.

This was the opportunity for me to split. I gathered together his diary,
pencil, magnifying glass, and the loose pages on which he had made his little sketches. Then I ripped the double-page map from the diary, folded it
with the loose pages, wrote the words "Hittocappu" and "Purhabba" and the
date 24 November on one of them and stuffed these in my trouser pocket.

Having rid himself of the best part of half a bottle of cognac, a spot of coffee, and whatever he had consumed earlier in the restaurant, my erstwhile
friend swiveled himself around and allowed me to restore his diary and other
things in his pouch. Still bemused and groggy and smelling pretty awful, he
slumped down at the table once again. I could almost have felt sorry for him,
but time was rushing on. I waved him adieu and backed away. He struggled
to his feet and bowed and even managed to smile for an instant. Then, as if
on cue, his buddy appeared, complete with a couple of local girls. He looked
up at them and heaved; but this time his luck was out—he well-nigh redec-
orated and retextured the entire tabletop, whereupon I withdrew into the
shadows and quickly made for the stairs.

8 Return Flight to Malaya

I knocked on the door of the small private lounge where I had left the three. Jan called out for me to enter. They were tidying up their papers and putting them away in their various bags. Jan's heavy grip was still very much in evidence. The time was around 10:15 P.M. I wondered when the fellow we were supposed to be taking to Malaya would show up. Jan had said 10:30 P.M., but this place was many miles from a town of any size; perhaps, for some reason, he would be delayed.

The overblown Henri said his farewells and, dabbing his outrageous nose with a perfumed handkerchief, departed.

A Cambodian chap whom I took to be the manager of the place appeared in the doorway. He drew Jan out onto the landing, Jan still hanging onto his grip. A few moments later Jan stepped back into the room. He was frowning.

"Let's go," he said. "There's no more business to be done here."

"What about . . .?"

"Nothing doing," he replied. "He's not coming. He left a telephone message with the manager a few minutes ago." Paul mumbled something in French to himself as the three of us went down the stairs; I imagined he was relieved at not having to risk the charge of helping to smuggle an undesirable person out of the country being added to his unlawful though presumably as yet undetected goings-on. Such goings-on would be bound to come to light should the covert use of his land as an airstrip come under investigation.

The moon was still riding high as we drove back to the villa, and bright enough to light the way ahead for the throbbing car. I sat in the back, anxious to get airborne again. My little finger had resumed its tormenting itching and burning, and I felt sweaty and scruffy. Jan sat in the front with Paul, who drove. Throughout the journey Jan said very little, but he did remark on the fact that Henri had divulged that southern French Indo-China was now riddled with Japanese military planes. The nearby island of Phu Quoc had many fighters and a large number of twin-engined bombers stationed on it. He had told Jan and Paul that the general situation had become very tense over the past few days and it was said that something big was about to break.

I wondered if I should mention my encounter with the Japanese engineer. I imagined that both Jan and Paul would be horrified and angered by the disclosure, so I ended my quandary by keeping my mouth shut. This left me in a funny position, for unless he continued to broadcast what he knew to all and sundry, I was likely to be the only uninvolved person who knew about Japan's remote naval task force way up in the north Pacific. He had said he and his colleagues had finished their work on 24 November. It was more than probable, therefore, that the Japanese ships were already well on their way to wherever they were going, and, on the basis of what my Samaritan had suggested, this might well be Hawaii. None of it made much sense to me, and yet the matter kept on niggling. But there was nothing I could do about it even if his belief was accurate, and it was an absolute certainty that the Japanese task force would be kept under constant observation by the United States by one means or another throughout its exceedingly lengthy passage to Hawaii, something that I had already roughly estimated at anywhere between three thousand and four thousand miles.

Back at the villa Jan moved into top gear. "We'll take off at 4:00 A.M., Peter," he said.

"Why don't we push off now?" I asked.

"Because if we did that we would reach Sungei Patani by four in the morning—inconvenient."

"They'd put a flare path down for us," I argued.

"And the visibility might be terrible. No, I want to land at first light, around 7:30 A.M."

I shut up again. Jan said we should check the Hudson and then have a few hours sleep before taking off. He and I walked down to where the plane was hidden. Two Cambodian workmen were asleep in the shed, clearly having been earlier instructed by Paul to hang around for us to turn up. They had a tractor on hand, and together we moved the Hudson out from its hiding place. We ran both engines for a few minutes and found everything okay.

"What about fuel?" I asked. "I reckon you'll need the best part of five hundred gallons to get you back to Sumatra."

"I've checked. With what's in the long-range tanks I've got enough."

"Why not fill up while you've got the chance?" I countered. "If you have to fly much faster than economic cruising speed, you'll burn fuel up a hell of a lot quicker. I think you should take on at least two hundred gallons to be on the safe side."

"It'll take time," said Jan a bit reluctantly, "around thirty minutes."

I told him he could go and that I would stay behind to see to the refueling. The two workmen brought a motorized fuel tank such as one would expect to find on a large farm or plantation where plenty of machinery and plant is used. I wondered if the fuel was the right stuff, that is, one hundred-octane aviation spirit. I found a mug in the shed and cleaned it out. Then I asked for it to be filled from the mobile tank. On examining it I found the color and the smell to be right—at least it wasn't diesel fuel or second-rate motor petrol.

It took over half an hour to take on around two hundred gallons; then I trudged back to the villa.

Jan had arranged with Paul for everything to be ready to facilitate our departure at four in the morning. It was now 12:15 A.M. At the villa I found Paul slumped in a wicker armchair. I think he was asleep because he was not twitching. A tall glass of Pernod was on a low table beside him. A couple of cigarette butts lay in an ashtray, one of them still smoldering. He looked gaunt and defeated—even in sleep. There was no one else about except a bright-eyed houseboy who indicated that Jan had gone to his room to sleep.

He asked me in French, and with his hands, if I wished for anything to eat or drink. I asked for tea and cake. I had no interest in sleep. To me this was very much the wrong time to be sleeping—wasting time in the enemy's camp when, under cover of night's darkness, we could be winging it back to safety.

I went to my room. The boy brought what I had requested and left me to it. I wondered what the devil I was going to do until 3:30 A.M., when it would be time to get moving. I drank two cups of weak lime-juiced tea, ate about half a pound of sugary cake, then undressed and lay on the bed.

I watched the slowly rotating blades of the ceiling fan, silent, soothing, and mesmerizing. I made a half-hearted attempt to count the mosquitoes and other insect intruders as they flitted and fidgeted about the room. I listened to the noise of the crickets, or whatever they were, making the most of the warm night air. I lightly massaged my distressed finger, the itching having subsided but little. I worried about things—a lot of things. I worried about what I had been told. I worried about the possibility of having raised suspicions at the restaurant. I worried about the possibility of someone having reported the presence of the Hudson to the authorities. I worried about all the things that could happen to delay or prevent our takeoff at 4:00 A.M. I worried about the possibility of Japanese planes assisted by their ground-based radar detecting and laying into us; and I worried about the four-hour flight ahead and whether or not the visibility would be in our favor when we reached Sungei Patani. On top of all this was the matter of Wan, whom I was going to let down. The bedroom light was still on. I could not sleep. I had far too much on my mind. The noise of the crickets grew louder, and the fan blades seemed to be flicking in and out of my vision with a motion suggestive of mockery.

I covered my eyes with my hand and awoke at 3:30 A.M. to the sound of voices and the chink of teacups. Someone was knocking on the bedroom door. Before I could speak the door opened and Jan stood there, in his flying overalls, with a smile on his face. He needed a shave. I washed and within thirty minutes he and I had hurriedly refreshed ourselves with coffee and croissants and were on our way down to the Hudson, accompanied by Paul, who looked as though he was carrying all the worries of the world on his shoulders.

In the air hung the faint clean smell of the sea and of vegetation. The crickets had evidently reached the end of their shift and were now quiet. There was absolute silence—nothing stirred.

Jan and I shook hands with Paul and climbed in the Hudson. As I closed the hatch, I caught my last shadowy glimpse of him standing back to one side, holding the lantern high and looking infinitely weary and grave-faced. I could not help wondering what the fates held in store for the fellow.

Both engines roared into life and once again the familiar and exciting smell of exhaust fumes wafted into the cockpit. In a matter of a few seconds Jan completed his lining-up turn onto the runway. He pushed forward on the two engine throttles, then immediately switched on the powerful landing light. The runway lit up instantly, low slanting lights shining across and along the strip throughout its length. The Hudson strained and bucked impatiently against the brakes. Jan eased the throttles fully forward, took another look at the engine instruments, and let the plane off the leash.

One by one the runway lights came and went, and I then felt the wheels lift off the ground. Jan held the Hudson in the shallowest of climbs and leveled off at five hundred feet.

In no time at all our airspeed reached almost 200 knots with the two Cyclones still pushing power out at maximum boost. Very slowly we turned on to a southerly heading, then, at reduced power, stayed on this course for the next thirty minutes, during which time the plane's airspeed steadied at 170 knots.

We were away from Indo-China and were now around one hundred miles out over the sea. We had avoided flying close to the island of Phu Quoc, where Japanese fighters may have been ready to get airborne at a moment's notice, and had stayed so low that no radar could ever have registered us on its scope. Jan's attention had been riveted on his instruments, and we had refrained from speaking since commencing the takeoff run. But he suddenly relaxed.

"Easy," said Jan through the intercom.

"What was?" I asked.

"All that lot."

"How do you mean?"

"Getting away from there," he replied.

It was evident that he was assuming we were now out of danger. I was not so confident.

"How can you be sure we weren't picked up on radar?"

Jan's eyes never wavering from the artificial horizon. "I can't be sure we weren't picked up, Peter, but they'll never find us now. Anyway, why should the Japs bother to chase us?"

He had a point, of course, but it was a very poor point and one hardly based on a full knowledge of the latest circumstances. As a matter of fact, it so happened that, forty-eight hours later, an RAF No. 205 Squadron Catalina flying boat from Seletar, Singapore, was spotted by Japanese fighters close to Phu Quoc Island, They attacked without warning, quickly sending the blazing flying boat and its crew of eight into the sea. There were no survivors.[1]

I answered Jan's question. "Because they might think we were on a spying mission. If the situation is as fraught as your French friends seem to think, the Japanese are unlikely to tolerate uninvited planes flying over their installations."

The more I thought about it, the more I convinced myself that the Japanese may well have detected the Hudson. Hence I commenced a long vigil—all the time anxiously peering out of the side screens for signs of other planes. Out there it was pitch dark, but I knew full well that an aircraft's flaming exhaust gases could often be seen from a good way off. While the Hudson was in a high-power setting, its exhaust gases would be as good as a beacon to the sharp eyes of Japanese fighter pilots.

"Might be best to reduce power, Jan," I suggested. "Our exhaust is a dead giveaway as things are—plus you're burning two hundred gallons of fuel an hour at this speed."

Jan growled. "Okay, I'll climb to 1,500 feet, then go on to economic cruising speed."

"Make it 1,000 feet, Jan—safer from the radar angle," I said.

He climbed and a minute later the Hudson's speed had slumped to 130 knots. By comparison with the earlier top-whack power setting it sounded as though the two engines had been shut down. Jan engaged the autopilot, pushed his seat back, and lit a cigar. I continued to search the surrounding darkness for the first petrifying glimpse of company. We had flown into a certain amount of cloud. There were no stars to be seen, and I drew comfort from the fact that, in such conditions, it would be next to impossible for other aircraft to spot us even if they were being assisted by radar.

The plane droned on through the night. Miles off to the far distant left colorful flashes of lightning lit up the sky in an impressive and fascinating, virtually nonstop performance. We had been flying for two hours when Jan increased our height to seven thousand feet which, for a while, brought us out on top of the clouds and into a starry sky.

Jan at last spotted my finger with its surgical dressing.

"What happened to your finger?"

"Oh," I replied, "only a mosquito bite. One of the waiters at that restaurant took pity on me and fixed me up with some balm and a dressing."

I still felt disinclined to divulge that I had spent the best part of an hour being entertained by a Japanese engineer who evidently spent his time making bomb racks for Japanese war planes. Besides, Jan was not British and in fact, if I were to believe what I had been told, he was some kind of big-time law-breaker anyway. Not that I minded a lot what he did—but he was not British and, in some way, that made a difference.

"Are you planning to fly over Kota Bharu?" I asked, wondering what action the RAF boys there would take when they spotted us on radar.

"No," he replied. "This time we'll be going over Siam—we'll miss Kota Bharu by about fifty miles."

"You said on the way out that you didn't want to fly over Siamese territory."

"Yes, I know, but as this is my last trip I'm not much concerned about the Siamese lot now. They'll take no action against us. It's just that if I'd made a habit of overflying them by way of a short cut on a monthly basis, they might well have been waiting for me at some time. This way it'll shorten our journey by thirty miles or so."

Jan's knack of finding his way around in pitch darkness astounded me. I'd heard of pilots who simply climbed into their machines and blasted off into the night, or into fog, or whatever, using nothing but their compass, yet had managed to arrive at their intended destination several hundred miles away without difficulty. Some, I had heard, didn't even bother to use their compass.

"What are you planning to do if we find the weather lousy when we reach Sungei Patani?" I asked.

"How do you mean?"

"Well—what if we can't find the airfield owing to heavy rain like it was the other day just before you arrived?"

Jan hesitated for a moment or two. Then, "Oh, that," he said. "I'll speak to them on the wireless. I've got their frequency written down." He patted a notebook in the thigh pocket of his flying suit. "Perhaps they can transmit something that I can pick up on our regular radio compass."

"We could always divert to some other airfield," I ventured. "There are quite a few RAF airfields within fifty miles radius of Sungei Patani." I just wanted to be sure that he knew of these alternatives because the idea of groping around overhead Sungei Patani and Kedah Peak in a raging thunderstorm did not appeal.

"I know them all, Peter—at least I know of them," he replied. "But there'll be no problem. Actually, if the worst happens, and we can't get down, I can always take you with me to Sumatra."

This last idea did not appeal either.

Jan at length announced that we were probably approaching the Siamese coast. We had at last run into heavy rain. We went up to eight thousand feet and rode out a lot of robust buffeting. The engines throbbed on despite being exposed to tearing, near-freezing rain and hail.

"Pity about this," he remarked.

"The rain?"

"Yes—and the cloud. We ought to be seeing a bit of light by now."

"But the dawn will rise behind us, surely," I said.

"Of course, but we would still notice a general reduction in the intensity of darkness. We've got about another hour and a quarter to go," Jan growled, his seat still pushed right back. "It's 6:45 A.M."

"Yes," I replied and lapsed back into a state that lay uneasily somewhere between exhilaration and acute apprehension.

Half an hour later the Hudson emerged from the clouds and, in an instant, the rain and the turbulence ceased and the sky quickly turned a shade or two lighter than dark blue.

"I'm hungry," Jan remarked. "And thirsty."

"Me, too."

"There's plenty of water in the dinghy stowage locker. I'm not desperate yet. I can wait till we get down. But what about you, Jan?"

"No, it's okay. Forget it—we'll be down in forty minutes or so."

Jan pushed his seat forward. We fastened our helmets and resumed speaking through the intercom.

Darkness was being overtaken by dawn's early light. It happened quickly, as it does in Malaya. Then, suddenly, I was able to make out the rolling jungle with its meandering rivers. A few minutes later we caught sight of the sea, about ten miles ahead, dull and grey in comparison with the darkest of greens and the wispy blues of the now-emerging terrain below.

Jan strained his eyes and took over manual control of the Hudson and turned it south, along the coastline. He eased back on the throttles whereupon the plane's nose sank a little and the ride became very quiet and relaxing. Over to the left dazzling shafts of sunlight thrust upwards into the sky and the whole eastern horizon turned into yet another miracle of gold and orange fire. Down below, my friends and workmates would already have had breakfast and would now be making their way down to the airfield to start work. I was glad to be about to rejoin them.

The Hudson was slowly but surely losing height and it was now almost broad daylight. To our right the sea was a vast spread of steel grey on which fragmented reflections of sunrise shimmered like millions of tiny silver sequins. We could see for miles to the south, and it was not long before Jan called out, "Penang!"

"What about Penang?" I asked.

"Straight ahead, Peter," he replied. "About twenty miles."

He had obviously become accustomed to recognizing things like a small island from twenty miles away.

"Yes, I see it," I replied at length. "At least, it might be Penang."

Jan laughed. "It is Penang. I know because we passed Langkawi a few minutes ago."

"Where's that?"

"A little island back there—convenient for recognizing where you are when you're a bit uncertain of your position off this particular part of the west coast."

"Well, we must be fairly close to Sungei Patani then!" I exclaimed excitedly, searching the terrain below.

"Of course," Jan replied. "In case you hadn't noticed, there's your Kedah Peak off to the left."

I turned and looked through Jan's side screen. Sure enough, there was Kedah Peak with the tiny town of Sungei Patani just a few miles to the south.

Jan banked the Hudson, sweeping ever lower over the southern slopes of Kedah Peak, then over the town straddling the north-south road and, finally, over the plantations to the east of the airfield. We were established on the final approach, a mile out, when it struck me that Jan had not made any radio call to the control tower.

"Aren't you telling them we're coming in?" I asked.

"No," he replied. "They'll know it's me. That squadron leader, whatever his name is, will be with them."

"But—I mean—just to be on the safe side. It is a fighter base, remember."

"There's nothing going on down there. Look! Nothing's moving."

He was correct, as it happened. I could see the Blenheims grouped together near those two brightly gleaming petrol tanks, and the line of Buffaloes along the west side of the airfield. Nothing had changed. Even so, I did not approve of the way Jan shunned the use of his radio. One day it was going to get him into trouble.

He selected full flap, slipped the propellers into fine pitch, added a bit of throttle, and lowered the undercarriage. While he was doing all this, he found time to say, "You worry too much, Peter," something with which I agreed when, as now, we were about to land on an RAF airfield without first seeking permission to do so. I kept quiet and just hoped he was right about the squadron leader being there to argue our case.

Once over the perimeter the Hudson rounded out sharply and straightaway touched down and stayed there. Jan turned the plane in a wide sweeping semicircle and taxied back to the eastern perimeter and switched off the engines.

An RAF van motored over to us. Out of it climbed the squadron leader, looking little different from how I had last seen him around thirty hours ago. This time he wore a hat, a pith-helmet devoid of any kind of RAF insignia. In poor shape, it looked as though he had rescued it from a wastebin in some kampung bazaar.

Jan had gone back into the cabin by the time I struggled out of my harness. I found him taking deep swigs of water from an emergency can he had wrestled from the dinghy locker. It must have been lukewarm and of doubtful vintage, but there was no doubting that he found it hugely satisfying.

I was so pleased to have arrived back safely on my home ground that all my earlier animosity toward Jan vanished. I almost felt grateful to him. "We made it okay," I said a little sheepishly.

He grunted, a kind of subdued laugh. "Yes, we made it, Peter. I expect you're glad to be back."

"Too true," I replied. "It's been interesting, but—well, yes—I'm bloody glad to be back. Thanks anyway. . . ." My voice trailed off; I was in danger of being too polite.

Through the open hatch I caught a glimpse of the squadron leader standing back, awaiting Jan's appearance. Jan reached for something in one of the deep pockets of his flying suit. He produced a largish manila envelope and handed it to me.

"For you, Peter—for all your help—and your company, of course. Put it in your pocket before you get out. No need to let the squadron leader know our business."

I had no idea what the envelope contained, but never before having been handed a largish manila envelope along with a clear expression of gratitude, I straightaway poked it into my trouser pocket.

"Thank you, Jan," was all I said. I had no wish to seem too happy about things lest he recommend me to the squadron leader for more trips of a similar nature. Now was the time to make myself clear in this regard. What's more, I was going to have a polite but suitably cutting word with the squadron leader.

We jumped out of the Hudson. The squadron leader stepped toward Jan, a curiously mystified expression on his face. Then he pulled Jan away from the plane and the two of them remained in quiet conversation for some minutes. I stood by myself examining my left shin, which I had scraped on a piece of metal as I had moved forward to climb through the plane's hatch. It was a nasty scrape—about an inch and a half long and right along the sharp edge of the shin bone. There was quite a bit of blood and the pain was considerable. I pulled my stocking over it in an attempt to keep the wound clean.

The squadron leader came over to me. He acknowledged my salute with a half-hearted and dismissive wave of his hand. He also stared through me. I had almost forgotten his unique way of staring through me. "Hello, Shepherd," he said, affably enough. "Good trip?"

"Yes, thank you, sir," I replied in automatic response. Then I remembered that I had a few things to say to him. "But there are a few matters I should like to make a statement about, sir."

"A statement?" He gave me a puzzled look.

"Well, yes, sir—if that's convenient." I was being too polite again and did not quite know how to express myself.

At this point Jan strode over to me and held out his hand for the departing handshake.

"Thanks again, Peter. All the best of luck for the future. Perhaps we may meet again some day."

We shook hands. He smiled and showed his gold fillings. Then he turned to the squadron leader and said, "Look after him. You've got a good one there."

The officer stared at Jan, his face expressionless and with pale eyes that appeared to gaze into infinity. Jan gave a little wave and climbed back into the Hudson. I stepped toward the open hatch.

"Jan, have you got enough fuel?" I asked.

He peered at me, his eyes glinting in humorous slits accentuating his high cheekbones. "You and your fuel, Peter," he replied. "I've got enough to get me to Medan and back again, if necessary."

Jan closed the hatch. The squadron leader and I walked over to the van whose driver was standing alongside it. Presently the two hardworked Cyclones started up and Jan wasted no time in swiveling the plane around to face the Buffaloes and the mountain. He waved to us and roared off, leaving a blast of shimmering, barely visible hot exhaust gases behind him. I guessed he had not bothered to obtain permission from the control tower before taking off.

That was the last I ever saw of Jan. He departed as unceremoniously and nonchalantly as he had arrived less than two full days ago.

"Well, what is it you wish to say, Shepherd?" the squadron leader asked, squinting against the low morning sun.

I threw a quick glance at the van's driver. My unspoken meaning did not escape the officer. He walked away from the van, his head half-inclined back at me, and gave me the nod to follow him.

He stopped and treated me to another of his odd looks. "Okay, Shepherd—you can speak now," he said.

Where to begin? Which was the more important? My grumble about the way I had been conned into flying into territory that was to all intents and purposes alien? Or should the facts that had been divulged to me by the Japanese engineer take precedence? Which of the two should I raise first? I decided to start with the latter news.

"Sir," I began, "you are no doubt aware that we flew to Indo-China and that we landed in Cambodia." I thought it reasonable to assume this much.

"Yes, Shepherd, I know that," he replied guardedly. It was at this point that I noticed he was wearing squadron-leader stripes on one epaulette only. I thought this very odd, but now, in midstream, I put the observation to the back of my mind.

"Well, sir, I inadvertently got into conversation with a gentleman who turned out to be Japanese."

"You did what?" he breathed icily, his eyes focused on a point miles beyond me.

"I got into conversation . . . ," I started again.

"Yes, yes, I heard you say that. But how the devil did that happen? Didn't the pilot tell you not to speak to anyone?"

"Well, sir, what happened was this. . . ." I began my story, starting from the time that Jan, Paul, Henri, and I had entered the hotel outside Kampot. I told the officer precisely what had transpired, including details of the "discussion" I'd had with the Japanese engineer. It took me about ten minutes but, feeling relieved, and I suppose a bit pleased with myself at being able to impart information that I perceived as potentially valuable, I felt only minimum discomfort and inconvenience at having to stand to attention in the dazzling sunshine in order to deliver my message.

I had shown the squadron leader my finger with its now very grubby dressing. It was still angry but had now been eclipsed in the discomfort stakes by my shin injury.

"But how did you manage to converse with this Japanese chap? You don't speak Japanese, and he, you say, couldn't speak English. Neither of you spoke French—so how on earth did you manage to discuss anything?"

I was able to convince the officer that there had been no great difficulty in the Japanese and I making ourselves understood to one another. "Don't forget," I said, "that he was using a map and a diary, also a pencil and paper."

I produced from one of my pockets all the diary pages I had picked up from the table at which we had been sitting. "There, sir," I said. "Perhaps you'd like to look at these."

He took the pages from me and studied them. There was the two-page map of the world with the penciled arc linking northern Japan with the Hawaiian Islands, and there were the pages on which he had made adept thumbnail sketches of the several different classes of naval ships he had seen while at this Hittocappu place. There was even a rudimentary sketch of a bomb rack he had penciled out to help him explain the nature of the modification work he had carried out on the way to Hittocappu, and for which same purpose he had subsequently been shipped and flown down to Phu Quoc Island. And also there was the page on which I had printed in capital letters the words HITTOCAPPU, HAWAII, and PURHABBA.

He refolded the pages and began to hand them back to me, but then had second thoughts. "I'll keep these if I may, Shepherd," he said, and put them in his shirt pocket.

I went on to explain that the engineer, although significantly the worse for drink, indicated that in his opinion the massing Japanese fleet was preparing to attack the place he had repeatedly referred to as Purhabba. I added that he had, with obvious conviction and satisfaction, impressed on me that Singapore and Malaya were also about to be attacked by air, land, and sea. I said that he had positively gloated at the revelation and, in fact, had turned quite belligerent when I had unwisely attempted to disenchant him in the matter.

"About these naval ships—did he say how many he had seen?"

"Yes, sir. He told me, or rather showed me by means of pencil marks, that there were forty of them in the bay in which his aircraft carriers has been anchored. There were aircraft carriers, battleships, cruisers. . . ." The squadron leader cut me off irritably.

"Yes, yes, Shepherd. You said all that earlier. Did he say how long he'd been on the carrier?"

"He didn't say in as many words, sir."

"Well, did you get any idea at all how long he might have been aboard doing this bomb-rack modification work?"

"Yes, sir. I imagine he must have been aboard the carrier for around two weeks."

"Why do you imagine that?"

"Because of the diary, sir. He used the pages to indicate the passage of time—that is, from the time he was put aboard to the time he was transferred to a destroyer when his work was finished."

Then I remembered what he had said about civilian engineers having been aboard the carriers for the purpose of modifying air-launched torpedoes—something to do with making them run more shallow than usual on entering the sea, instead of plunging deeply before rising and then stabilizing at an effective running depth. He had indicated, by his unique brand of gestures and alcoholic grunts, that this meant the torpedoes were probably to be used not at sea but at some point where the target ships were already in quite shallow water—such as, for example, in a naval base or docks. I carried on with my dissertation, all delivered while standing uncomfortably to attention.

I stopped as another thing entered my mind. "He explained that the bombs to be used in his modified bomb racks had been made from naval shell casings—hence their unusual dimensions and consequently the need to modify the bomb racks. He said they had been specially made so as to pierce the armor-plated decks of large naval ships."

The officer did not seem too interested in my technical ramblings for he screwed his eyes up a little, as in pained boredom. I continued, "The two Frenchmen spoke of a huge buildup of Japanese military aircraft in Indo-China, sir. I actually saw for myself a loose formation of eighteen fighters, and also twenty-seven twin-engined machines which can only have been bombers. The Frenchmen told Jan and me that numerous aerodromes in southern Indo-China now have squadrons of twin-engined bombers stationed on them. It's been building up rapidly over the past month."

The squadron leader appeared to be at a loss as to what to say. Then he spoke. "Good chap, Shepherd. Thanks. Oh, by the way, you don't need to say anything to anyone about any of this. If anyone says anything to you, or asks you any questions, simply tell them you are under orders to say absolutely nothing. You do understand that, don't you?"

"Yes, sir." I replied meekly, though suddenly beginning to enjoy the faint but distinct whiff of some kind of conspiracy and of having become entangled in it.

"Okay then, Shepherd. Perhaps you'd better carry on now."

"Yes, sir," I saluted him. He gave me one of his waves, then walked back to the van and jumped in. It drove off, leaving me standing there with my canvas haversack slung from my shoulder and my shin hurting like mad. My Indo-China trip was over; Jan was now presumably well out over the sea and heading for northern Sumatra; over in Cambodia my Japanese Samaritan would be, about now, setting out to modify a few more bomb racks for bombs designed to punch deep into the bowels of even the toughest of ships before exploding.

My shin needed dressing. I walked to the medical room. I felt tired, dirty, and hungry, but the wound needed urgent treatment. The corporal sickbay attendant, having decided stitches were not required, cleaned the wound and applied a dressing. I inquired as to the progress of the chap who had been taken off the Hudson on account of his stomach problems. He told me he had no knowledge of the individual. He checked the entries in the daily report book and found nothing in it to confirm that the man had ever visited the sickbay.

"Perhaps he was taken straight to a civilian clinic," I suggested.

"No. If he had been it would have been recorded in the daily report book," he replied. "Anyway, why the interest?"

He had caught me in a tricky spot. Rather than make up a hurried story that might be seen as lacking credibility, I decided to come clean but in a manner that would give nothing away.

"Oh," I said, "someone was saying that a civilian plane landed here a couple of days ago. Apparently there was a chap on board who was incapacitated due to stomach cramps or something. I was told that he had been taken off the plane and brought to the sickbay."

"There's nothing recorded anyway—probably one of those stories that get around."

"I suppose so." I replied, giving the impression it mattered little to me, although inwardly I was puzzled.

It was now 9:00 A.M. I had missed breakfast and was in anything but sparkling condition.

I decided to go to the airfield and report my presence. If any awkward questions were asked, I would just mention the squadron leader, then say no more. On the way to the airfield I remembered the envelope Jan had given me. I tore it open. It contained a wad of Malayan five-dollar notes which I estimated to be worth as much as I was normally paid in three months. I was amazed and overjoyed. At last, for a time anyway, I had the means with which to purchase the necessities of life—like beer, cigarettes, and bananas. It was an utterly splendid feeling and one that buoyed me up a miraculously.

At the airfield my belated limping appearance raised a few eyebrows among my colleagues. My corporal greeted me with a curious mixture of suspicion and respect. He said nothing but simply reacted as though it had been the natural thing for me to go missing for twenty-four hours. I said nothing to him except that I wished to go and get changed. He put no objection in my way. George had, of course, missed me and told me that he had thought I had perhaps pushed off to Penang to see the Malay girl. He had, however, said nothing to anyone about this, just in case it was precisely what I had done and had managed to get back into camp without being found out. I was able to put him right on that score but offered him no other explanation. He was a bit peeved by this, thinking no doubt that, as we were buddies, I would be gracious enough to tell him what I had been up to. When I said, for the third time, "I can't tell you anything, George," I got the impression that it suddenly dawned on him that I had been officially involved in some hush-hush scheme or other on camp. At any rate he pressed me no further in the matter. I felt all the more sensitive about it all on account of the wad of five-dollar notes bulging my pocket.

I was halfway up the incline when an airman on a bicycle weaved through the rubber trees toward me. He stopped and asked me if I had any idea where he might find Aircraftsman Shepherd—575176, Fitter Engines. I replied that he had found him and prepared myself for an invitation to the orderly room to explain my twenty-four-hour-plus absence. It was no such thing. I was to report to a Squadron Leader Mattinson at the control tower immediately.

"Mattinson?" I asked.

"Yes. At least I think that's what the orderly room sergeant called him."

"Could it have been Pattison—or perhaps Battison?" I inquired.

"Maybe, I'm not sure. Anyway, you've got to report to him right now—at the control tower."

I changed direction by ninety degrees and tramped off down to the airfield and the control tower. The squadron leader was standing inside the open doorway out of the sun in conversation with a flying officer whom I took to be the duty pilot.

"Ah, Shepherd!" he said sharply, directly he saw me. "Just step over here please."

The flying officer, sensing he was no longer welcome, took to the stairs leading up to the lookout tower. The squadron leader addressed me urgently.

"Look, Shepherd. All that stuff you told me this morning. Well, I've been talking to someone about it and I'm afraid that you and I have been called down to Kuala Lumpur to make a full statement. I've cleared it with the people here. How quickly can you be ready?"

My heart sank. A trip now to Kuala Lumpur—and me hungry, tired, and dirty. Six or seven hours on a sweltering train would be sheer hell. He would travel first class while I sat in a cramped compartment without food or drink.

"I haven't eaten yet, sir—haven't even had time to have a wash." I stood there waiting for him to come up with an understanding reply.

"Never mind that, Shepherd. Perhaps you'll be able to find something to eat at Kuala Lumpur. You can have a drink of tea or something here before we leave. And I should use the toilet, too, if I were you. There's a Blenheim ready for us now, so hurry along."

A Blenheim! So we were going to fly to Kuala Lumpur! That put a different complexion on things.

He saw that I was limping a little. "What's wrong with your leg?" he asked.

"Bumped it climbing out of the Hudson, sir. I've just had it dressed at the medical room—that's why I missed breakfast."

"Oh, I see. Well, get cracking, old chap. We've a bit of sorting out to do and not a lot of time to do it in."

A few minutes later, as we approached the Blenheim, I received a few looks of surprise from the waiting ground crew, they being the three chaps whose job it was to help start the Mercury engines. They possibly thought that I had been arrested and was being whisked away for questioning. I nodded to a couple of them but said nothing.

In the plane it was baking hot. Although a third member of the crew, the wireless operator/air gunner, was unusually absent, space was restricted to a near-impossible degree. The squadron leader, however, quickly found himself somewhere to sit, a place in which he would suffer only minimal discomfort apart from the heat, the drafts, and the nonstop engine noise. I was not so lucky, finding myself jammed in a kind of metal latticework labyrinth in which I found it impossible to sit, stand, or crouch without experiencing sundry pains in addition to cramps in the neck and legs. My parachute harness chafed me here and there, but the parachute pack itself, under my backside, at least protected my rear from the keen edges of the many metallic structural components in which I was jammed. The Blenheim touched down at Kuala Lumpur in the late morning, having flown a little over two hundred miles from Sungei Patani.

9 Interrogation at Kuala Lumpur

Friday, 5 December

At Kuala Lumpur the morning was sweltering and sticky. There was not the slightest movement of air and the surface of the small grass airfield shimmered with heat. A lazy silence hung over the whole scene. A couple of private light planes were parked to one side. Our Blenheim taxied to a halt alongside a de Havilland Rapide biplane. I knew that the airfield was home to the local flying club but heard that the RAF had been considering converting it to service use. There were a few very small hangars. A number of wooden huts stood adjacent to the airfield, along one side of which was a line of coconut palms.

An RAF sergeant strode up to us when we jumped out of the Blenheim. The squadron leader waved his hand in acknowledgment of the sergeant's salute, then stood waiting for me as I endeavored to stretch my neck and leg cramps away. The three of us walked over to one of the huts, led by the general duties sergeant. The sergeant offered to carry the squadron leader's canvas bag for him, but he declined. I was hampered by my haversack and my aching shin.

We reached the door of the hut. The sergeant knocked loudly on it, opened it wide, and stepped back to allow us to enter.

"Are they in here?" the officer asked the sergeant.

"I believe so, sir," came the reply.

The squadron leader walked into the hut. I followed, a few paces behind. A figure within approached him—a short figure dressed in a white duck suit.

"Ah, hello there," the short figure said with about as much enthusiasm as a hungover debtor welcoming in the bailiff.

"Good morning, sir," replied the squadron leader.

They shook hands. I stood back deferentially. They both looked at me as though undecided as to what they should do with me.

After a second or two the squadron leader smiled at me. "Oh, Shepherd," he said, "just a minute or two, would you please. Outside if you don't mind—there's a good chap."

Like a good chap I stepped outside into the raging sunshine. The door closed behind me and I was left standing alone. I wandered around a corner of the hut into some shade and sat on the grass in a position where I could more or less keep an eye on the door.

Ten minutes elapsed. The squadron leader stuck his head out of the door. I bounded to my feet and joined him.

"Come on in now, Shepherd," he said.

"Yes, sir. Thank you, sir," I replied, glad that things were at last moving.

Along a short corridor we came to an open door. The squadron leader walked through and into an office. I followed. Two civilian men were sitting at opposite ends of a desk in a small, baking-hot office. The side window was wide open, but little or no fresh air seemed to be getting in. The two men wore white duck suits, and each wore a wristlet watch on a white canvas band. The one who had extended the cool welcome was about thirty-five and five-four in height. His face, probably naturally pale, was flushed with the heat of the office. He had silky-looking gingery hair and gave the impression of being somewhat discomposed. His eyes merely flickered at me as I entered the office. It was not long before I began to suspect that he would be relieved when the meeting came to a close.

The second man was bigger and older and looked closer to fifty than forty. His face was perspiring, but he did not exhibit any of the fluster or discomfiture that seemed to be troubling his younger colleague. He had a full head of greying black hair. His was the face of one who is of a serious but cheerful disposition and who, due to having darkish skin, is not all the time seeking to hide from the sun. He looked well fed and fit. There was no doubt which of the two was the boss.

The squadron leader quickly found himself a chair underneath the open window. He sat down without saying a word, leaving the office door wide open. As I had been the last to enter the office, I thought it appropriate to close it and I did so.

"Ah, thank you, Shepherd," the larger of the two said. He spoke in a voice that was strong and clear and nicely modulated—a voice that one could listen to for some time without becoming in any way irked or bored.

He nodded to the only remaining unoccupied chair. "Pull that chair over to the desk and sit down."

I did as he asked. Now there were three of us at the desk, with the squadron leader to one side against the window. He, the senior of the two, had a few notes in front of him, but he sat back in his chair, his jacket unbuttoned, and regarded me with a disarming smile on his perspiring face.

"Shepherd," he began. "We thought we'd like to talk with you about the matters you mentioned to. . . ." Here he stopped and nodded very slightly in the direction of the squadron leader, "That is, the matter you mentioned this morning on your return to Sungei Patani. We understand that you were in French Indo-China yesterday. Is that so?"

I glanced sideways at the squadron leader. His face was an expressionless mask. His eyes were staring at nothing, not even catching mine. It was then I realized I was on my own. There was no point in my denying I had been in French Indo-China—I had already told the squadron leader and evidently he had told the two who were now sitting at the desk.

"Yes, sir. That's correct," I replied.

The big man leaned forward. "Well, we would like you to tell us what happened there. Apparently you got into conversation with a Japanese person."

"Yes, sir." It immediately struck me that he had not inquired as to how I had managed to be in Indo-China in the first place. The answer could only be that he already knew.

"Right then, Shepherd—tell us briefly how you got into conversation with this chap." He leaned back in his chair again. I gathered myself together and began to relate my story, starting from the time Jan, Paul, and I had arrived at that restaurant on the outskirts of Kampot.

The three of them remained silent as my story progressed. I of course exhibited my little finger, its dressing still in place, as a kind of testimony to the accuracy of the first part of the account, and continued speaking without interruption for two or three minutes. My mouth was very dry, and it became difficult to continue with a good, confident flow of words. Not wishing to detract from what I had to say by cutting my statement short owing to dryness of mouth, I asked if I might have a drink of water.

"Of course you can," the larger man exclaimed affably. "In fact, perhaps we should all have a drink." He turned to his flushed colleague and instructed him to see what he could do. The junior, as I had perceived him to be, got off his chair and left the office.

In the meantime I carried on as well as I could, telling the big chap how the Japanese and I had contrived to make ourselves understood to one another. Then I progressed on to how we had exchanged facts concerning our occupations, and then how he had opened up with regard to his involvement with bomb racks and the aircraft carrier and, in fact, if he were to be believed, the best part of the Japanese navy.

The agitated pink-faced character returned, followed by a Chinese boy carrying a tray on which were glasses and two large bottles of what turned out to be chilled lime-juice water. The boy set the tray down on the desk and then made himself scarce.

The lime-juice drink was like nectar. I resumed my story, this time telling how the Japanese had made sketches of naval ships on pages of his diary and had indicated on a map the route the armada of ships would, in his judgment, follow in order to achieve, also in his judgment, the purpose that it had been covertly assembled and made ready to carry out. Then I went on to describe how he had made gestures that had left me in no doubt whatsoever of his unshakeable belief that the Japanese task force was planning to attack Hawaii and, more particularly, a place there which he had referred to as "Purhabba"; also how, in his view, and at the same time, Japanese military forces would attack Singapore and Malaya. I explained how, when I had imprudently made signs indicating that I thought he was giving me a load of eyewash, he had become somewhat disagreeable.

I had just about come to the end of my story, having not yet mentioned anything about the Japanese military aircraft I had seen or what the two Frenchmen had told Jan and me about the recent heavy and sinister buildup of Japanese warplanes in Indo-China.

The large sunburned chap suddenly broke in on me. "I understand this Japanese person was drinking heavily. Is that right?"

"Yes, sir. He was."

"Was he drunk?"

"In the end he was, sir," I replied.

"But *how* drunk? Do you think he was talking piffle?"

"If he was making it all up, sir, he was not *talking* piffle—he was gesturing it *and* sketching it. I'm convinced that everything he imparted to me, in signs, gestures, and sketches, was genuine fact."

"But you say he was drunk," my questioner said.

"Yes, sir, he was, but he struck me as the sort of individual who would be only too happy to divulge to others what he had been up to. He wasn't so drunk that his reasoning was significantly impaired. It was just that the cognac had very much loosened his tongue. As I say, he was merely full of himself, pleased, proud, and satisfied. His judgment had been affected, of course, and obviously this is how he came to divulge to me all the facts I've just told you about."

"So you feel he could have been talking sense, and that everything he told you was more or less accurate?"

"Most definitely, sir," I replied.

"How did you leave things with him?"

"I don't understand, sir."

"Well, what was his demeanor when you parted company with him? Was he still being awkward?"

"No, sir. He'd calmed down a good deal by then. He'd just finished being ill."

The two at the desk became noticeably more alert at my last remark.

"Ill? What do you mean?" the big man asked.

"He was sick, sir—spewed up."

"I see. Spilled his guts in more ways than one then," my questioner quipped.

I glanced at his colleague and saw him give a brief, mirthless grin. The squadron leader's face remained impassive. Then, the moment of strained humor over, the senior of the two said, "Is that about it then, Shepherd?"

I had a little more to say. "Well, yes and no, sir. There are just a few further matters that may be of interest to you."

"Such as what?" he asked.

I told him about the Japanese aircraft I had seen, and I told him what the two Frenchmen, Paul and Henri, had said about the massive buildup of Japanese planes in southern Indo-China.

He rose from his chair, picked up a roll of maps from the floor behind the desk, and laid them flat on the desk. Then he produced the diary pages I had passed to the squadron leader when I had landed at Sungei Patani earlier that morning.

"Let's go into a bit of detail, shall we?" he said quietly. "I mean about all those ships."

The discomforted chap was now mopping his face with a handkerchief; it was plain that he was still suffering on account of the heat. The big man looked at him, smiled, and asked, "Are you sure you're all right?" I noticed that he had not addressed his colleague by name.

"I'm all right," the younger chap assured him. "It's just that it's so bloody hot in here, isn't it?" He turned to the squadron leader as though seeking his agreement, but the latter, sitting there deadpan with his disreputable topi resting on his knees, simply raised his eyebrows a millimeter or two and remained silent.

"Open the door if you think it'll do any good then," the big one said. But stand by it—you know," he added meaningfully.

The harassed junior opened the door wide and stood half in and half out, making sure that no one was hanging around who might overhear what was being said inside the office.

"Tell us about these pages, Shepherd."

I told him precisely what had taken place and how at the last minute, when the Japanese had been leaning over the veranda rail being sick, I had swiftly collected up the pages and put them in my pocket.

"Nice work," he said. "But, now, let's take a look at this map." He had before him a large map covering a good deal of the Eastern Hemisphere. It included China, Japan, Indo-China, and the East Indies. Hawaii, I noticed, fell just within its eastern margin.

The other two had joined us at the desk. The map, about four feet by three feet, was clean and legible.

"Now, Shepherd," the big man began, "where was this aircraft carrier when your Jap joined it?"

I leaned over the map. "About here, as far as I could gather, sir." I pointed to the area my Japanese acquaintance had indicated.

He continued. "And he told you he had sailed on the carrier to the north of Japan—to this Hitto-what's-it place you mentioned."

"Yes, sir. Actually I gained the impression that he went aboard the carrier a few days before it sailed north, which was on the eighteenth of November. Before the carrier sailed, huge amounts of stores and equipment were taken on, including a great many torpedoes. Apparently the torpedoes were just about the last items to be taken aboard, and as soon as their loading had been completed the carrier weighed anchor and sped north to Hittocappu to join, as it turned out, the main body of naval ships already there. It seems that although some of the torpedoes had already been modified at the factory in southern Japan, many still required this modification and consequently civilian engineers traveled north on the carrier for the purpose of carrying out the work en route to Hittocappu."

All three were listening to me intently. I had these three people, each very much older than I, concentrating on my every word. What I was telling them was, I imagined, of considerable significance and gravity.

Then I made a point, one that I had been turning over in my mind for the last hour or so. It was a point that, the more I had chewed on it, the greater its significance had seemed to become.

"There's a point I've been thinking about, sir," I said.

"What's that, Shepherd?" the big man asked.

"It's just that this torpedo modification work must have been very important, I mean, to necessitate civilian engineers being taken on board the aircraft carrier."

The junior civilian spoke up at this. "It's not unusual for civilian engineers to be carried on naval vessels." That was all he said, but his words tended to diminish the urgency and weight of my own brief assertion.

"But what I mean is that some of the torpedoes had been modified at the factory, yet, for some reason, it had been found necessary to modify the rest at sea. The most likely explanation for this is that time had been running out. I suggest that the torpedoes had to be completed and ready for distribution to the five other carriers by the time our Jap's carrier reached Hittocappu. This, surely, points to the possibility that time was of the essence, that is to say, a firm date had probably already been set for the task force to move out.

Our Jap's carrier, in such case, *had* to reach Hittocappu sometime before that date in order to distribute the torpedoes. The Jap was taken off the carrier, according to his story, on the twenty-fourth of November, the torpedoes having by then been distributed."

The junior civilian was manifestly unconvinced. "But *that* tells us nothing," he snapped petulantly. Then he dried up again.

"But I think it probably does, sir," I said, turning to face the older man. "It could mean that the fleet of Japanese ships probably weighed anchor and proceeded to sea as early as the twenty-fourth of November. This allows an estimation to be made of the earliest possible date of its arrival at Hawaii. On this reckoning the fleet will now have been at sea for"—I did a quick mental calculation—"eleven days."

"How on earth did you work that one out, Shepherd?" he asked. Even *he* was beginning to look a trifle uneasy.

"Well, sir," I explained, "today is the fifth of December. The elapsed time, from midday on twenty-fourth of November to midday today, amounts to eleven days. Wherever this fleet was planning to go, it's certainly had plenty of time to get there."

The junior spoke up again. "But we're discussing the matter as though the story of this alleged Japanese gas bag was genuine," he griped.

"No, we are not," said the big one. "Shepherd here is doing the talking—we're simply listening and questioning."

"Well, then," added the junior, and that was the end of another of his deflating and petulant interjections.

"If this information can be relied on," the big man continued, "I mean, if it's generally true and accurate, it certainly means the Japs are up to something. However, that's for others to worry about. If they're. . . ." He ceased speaking. I was bright enough to realize that this was not because he had run out of words but because he had suddenly remembered *I* was present; it was not for me to know any more than I already knew.

"How many ships did he see at this Hittocappu place?" he asked.

"Forty, sir. On one of the pages there's a penciled stab mark for each ship he counted. He indicated to me that he had seen no less than six aircraft carriers, including the one he was on. There were also battleships and, I reasoned from his gestures and sketches, a whole load of cruisers and destroyers—the sketches are all there, sir."

"Some armada, if it's to be believed," he breathed. He went quiet for a few seconds, then drew our attention to the map spread out on the desk. "Where's this Hitto place, Shepherd?"

I pointed to the northern group of islands the Japanese had shown me on the little map in his diary. "Somewhere up here, sir," I said.

My eyesight must have been a great deal better than his; I could read the names of even the smallest islands. There was not one with a name anything like Hittocappu. The high temperature in the office was beginning to make me feel terrible. My mouth was as dry as dust again. I just wanted to walk out, have a drink of water, then sit with my head between my hands, preferably in a cool place. I asked to see the diary map, and I then tried to relate the spot he'd marked on it to the islands shown on the large map laid out before us. Then I saw something.

"Look here, sir! There, sir!" I cried out. I pointed to one of the islands.

He said, "Where?" Then he leaned low over the map, at the same time dragging a pair of spectacles from his top pocket.

"There, sir!" My finger lay adjacent to two tiny words that were printed sideways in relation to the position from which we were viewing them.

"Hell," he said loudly. He turned to the other two, that is, his red-faced junior and the coolly impassive, ill-dressed squadron leader. "It's here all right." He peered again at the words alongside my finger and read what was there. "Hittocappu Bay." He spoke the words softly, almost reverently, as though uttering some esoteric code word.

I noticed the spelling. On the big map the place was designated as Hitokappu Bay. My acquaintance had merely spoken the first of the two words and which I had phonetically interpreted as being approximate to "Hittocappu"—this being the spelling I had used when printing the word on one of the pages in his diary. It gave me some satisfaction to see that, under the bizarre circumstances, my spelling had been pretty well on target. I noticed, too, that Hitokappu Bay was located on the small island of Etorofu, a comparatively short distance northeast of Hokkaido, the latter being one of the larger of the Japanese islands.

The other two crammed around to see for themselves.

The big man continued, "And this Japanese fellow said he anticipated that the fleet would sail right across the northern Pacific, then sweep down and attack Hawaii. Is that right, Shepherd?"

"That's correct, sir."

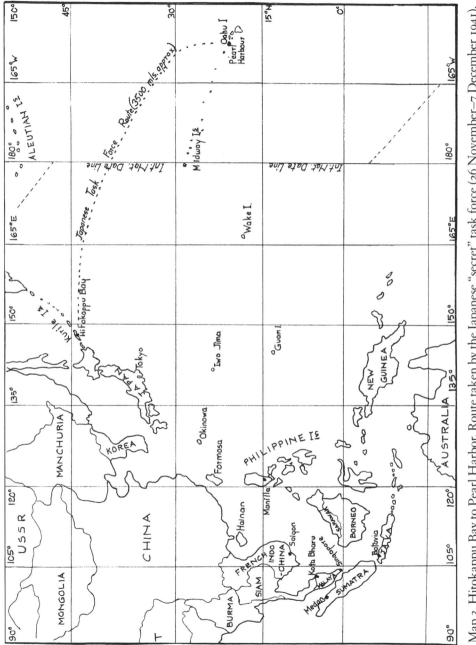

Map 3. Hitokappu Bay to Pearl Harbor. Route taken by the Japanese "secret" task force (26 November–7 December 1941).

"Right then," he carried on. "Here's Hawaii, look; now where's this place you mentioned, Pur . . . something, wasn't it?"

"Yes, sir—Purhabba, it sounded like."

"That's it, but there's no place with that name here," he said. "But, hang on a minute—on Oahu Island there's Honolulu and Pearl City and Pearl Harbor."

"Pearl Harbor, sir?" my question echoed his words.

"Yes," he said, "but there's no Purhabba or whatever you called it."

The hot and flushed junior butted in again. "But," he said, "from where I'm standing, your words 'Pearl Harbor' sounded rather like 'Purhabba.'"

"Yes, that's exactly what I was about to say," I added excitedly. "Perhaps the Jap was pronouncing the words 'Pearl Harbor' in *his* way—the way the Japanese pronounce it—or, rather, that may be the way it sounds to us when they say it."

"Could be," the big man said thoughtfully.

He lit a cigarette, drew in deeply, and then exhaled slowly. The smoke not only wreathed from his mouth but also curled from his nostrils. It looked for all the world as though some kind of spontaneous combustion had occurred inside his head.

"That'll be it, sir," I said. "For Purhabba *read* Pearl Harbor."

The three of them stood there listening to me, no doubt wondering how and why I was apparently so interested in what the Japanese might be up to. An eighteen-year-old half-trained aero-engine fitter could hardly be expected to worry his head about such matters, let alone develop his own theories as to what might or might not be going on in a really big-time military sense.

"Yes, I'm sure that's it. Pearl Harbor, the U.S. naval base," said the big man.

My brain was working overtime. I had never heard of Pearl Harbor, but I was doing a few calculations in my head and I carried on speaking as I did so. "Sir, Hawaii is U.S. territory. If the Japanese intention is to attack Pearl Harbor, their fleet will have to sail the best part of, say, four thousand miles. Allowing an average speed of fifteen miles an hour, that means a journey time of around eleven days. So that, if the fleet pulled out of Hitokappu Bay on 24 of November as already suggested, it means that today the ships could now be within striking distance of Pearl Harbor."

I broke off and used my fingers to check my calculations. "That's correct. They could be close anyway," I added.

All three of them stirred themselves at this soundly reasoned revelation. The red-faced one tossed his head and the squadron leader gave me a hollow stare.

"Well," said the big chap, "nothing's happened as yet. At least one's heard nothing."

"No, sir," I went on, undeterred. "But, providing the Jap fleet has not been detected by the Americans, it could be just hanging around for the right time to strike."

"But Japan hasn't declared war on the U.S.—not to my knowledge anyway," growled the chief. "What's more, I can't imagine her leaders being so imbecilic as to do so."

"Hitler didn't declare war before invading Poland," I replied, still going great guns. "Why should Japan do differently? If Pearl Harbor is a U.S. naval base, the last thing the Japs would do would be to, in effect, announce their intention to attack by first declaring war on America. I should think that a surprise attack would definitely be the Japanese intention."

The red-faced junior chap sat down as if having heard enough of my twaddle. The squadron leader continued to gaze at me as though finding it hard to decide whether or not I was talking nonsense. The big man looked worried. He took another great drag on his cigarette and did his spontaneous combustion bit again.

"Well, what does all this add up to, gentlemen?" he asked.

"Sir," I broke in again. "If a surprise attack on Pearl Harbor is Japan's intention, I suggest it will be delivered at first light, that is, at dawn—providing, of course, weather conditions are favorable. Also, I suggest the best time, as far as the Japanese are concerned, would be on a day when the harbor is at its quietest—like on a weekend. Sunday morning would perhaps be the most favorable time for the Jap fleet to strike; a lot of the American naval personnel would most likely be having a lie-in after having spent Saturday night out."

"Yes, all right, Shepherd. But we can't take it any further just now, I'm afraid," the boss man said. He sounded just a mite irritated.

"Just one more thing, sir," I said.

"What might that be?" This time he did not even look at me.

"If the Japanese *were* planning on a Sunday morning attack, then this coming Sunday may well be a possibility."

Then it occurred to me that the International Date Line lay between Malaya and Hawaii. This meant that in Hawaii the date would be different from that in Malaya. I struggled with the problem and finally dealt with it by announcing, "Well, actually, Hawaii is almost a full day behind us here in Malaya. What it means is that when it is Sunday morning in Hawaii it is Monday here, which means that when it is dawn on Sunday morning on the seventh in Hawaii, it will be a few hours *before* dawn on Monday here in Malaya. Monday morning in Malaya will be the eighth, but in Hawaii it will be Sunday the seventh."

The big man stared at me hard, but although there was a hint of comprehension in his eyes, I could plainly see that he had not entirely grasped my argument. "Is that so?" he said politely.

"Yes, sir," I replied. "So, if they aim to attack Pearl Harbor, Singapore, and Malaya at one and the same time, it means we can expect trouble here in the early hours of Monday morning, that is, on the eighth, which is less than three days away."

"Just go over your reasoning again concerning the time and date difference between Hawaii and Malaya," said the senior man, directly addressing me.

I went over it again, slowly and as methodically as the atmospheric conditions in the office permitted.

"Okay, Shepherd. I think I understand what you're driving at. Thank you. According to your theory we have only three days left before the Japs start on us," the chief said.

"Well, it's really only what I deduced from what that Jap told me," I replied.

Misery guts, the flushed junior, did it again. "He didn't *tell* you, Shepherd. It's only what you inferred from his alcoholic raving, or, more probably, what you're claiming to have inferred."

I was infuriated by this last remark but, turning to his chief, I said, "As a matter of fact, sir, we have rather less than three days—about four hours less if we're talking about the possibility of Japanese dawn attacks."

He looked at me as though trying to understand my thoughts. Then, on impulse I added, "Of course, sir, it may all be of absolutely no interest to anyone." This was just my way of getting back at the cavilling twit, the junior of the two, who had been getting up my nose for the past half hour or more.

The meeting was as good as over. It was 12:45 P.M. The squadron leader who, oddly, had played a low key role throughout spoke to me. "Shepherd, I understand the Hudson pilot told you he'd be bringing a certain person back from Indo-China." The other two appeared not to be paying attention.

"That's correct, sir," I replied.

"Did he tell you why he didn't bring this person back?"

"Yes, sir, he told me that the person concerned had telephoned and had left a message saying that he wouldn't be joining Jan as had been arranged."

"When and where was this telephone message received?"

"At the restaurant near Kampot, sir . . . last night." It was then that I realized that the other two, although paying no obvious attention to what was being said, were hanging around within earshot. It was clear to me that they were in fact carefully taking it all in while at the same time trying to give the impression they were totally disinterested.

"That's all right then, Shepherd," the squadron leader said. "Thank you. By the way, I won't be flying back to Sungei Patani with you. You'll find the Blenheim crew somewhere, I'm sure. Try the flying club restaurant. Have a good trip and thanks again. Remember, Shepherd—not a word to anyone. That's an order."

I put on my sun-helmet and saluted. He tossed me one of his half-baked waves. I glanced at the two civilians before making for the office door. They were both staring hard at me as I left.

I walked out into the scorching midday sun, then immediately went back in again because I had forgotten my haversack. The squadron leader was taking things from his canvas bag. On the desk were a pair of white trousers and on these lay the epaulette stripes he had up to now been wearing on just one shoulder. In his hands was a white jacket similar to those being worn by the two civilians.

"I left my bag," I said abruptly, somewhat embarrassed at having to return.

"Ah," someone replied.

Back in the sunshine again I limped off toward a hut that looked as though it might be the clubhouse. I found the Blenheim's pilot and observer in a part of the clubhouse where refreshments were on sale. I bought some sandwiches and a mug of tea. The Chinese counter-boy's eyes lit up when he caught sight of my wad of five-dollar notes. The two aircrew sergeants were anxious to get off back to Sungei Patani and were keen to know what I had been doing, and why the squadron leader was not joining the flight. I simply told them what he had told me. They stopped asking questions.

"I've never seen that squadron leader at Sungei Patani before today," the pilot said at one point.

"Nor me," I said.

"Funny chap—a bit scruffy."

"Weird," I agreed.

We took off half an hour later. The Dragon Rapide had just beaten us to it. I had watched its three passengers climb aboard—the big man who had questioned me so closely, his ill-dispositioned junior, and the squadron leader, the last seemingly now having been transformed into a civilian complete with immaculate white trousers, jacket, and sun-helmet.

An hour or so into the return flight I struggled out of my latticework accommodation and struggled up to look out of the gun turret. We were over the coast. Some way ahead lay Penang Island and a little later I could see Georgetown and the coastline extending up to the beach at Springtide and beyond, and I spotted the ferry terminal. I thought of the Malay girl, Wan, who would still be at the Springtide Hotel and expecting me to be waiting for her under the palms outside the place at midday tomorrow. That view, from around five thousand feet, of the enchanting island of Penang was, as it turned out, the last I would see of the place for half a century.

The sandwiches and tea had helped to rally me round. Now what I needed was a shower and a few hours sleep, a sleep during which I might clear my mind of many things, such as flying through the night with hailstones clattering on the windscreen; two Frenchmen, one with a gaunt, worried face and a nervous twitch, the other smooth and fat and smelling of attar of roses or something similar; a kindly Japanese engineer who drank and talked too much and who saw nothing wrong in honking his insides up over someone's carefully nurtured hibiscus bushes; and an armada of Japanese ships sneaking out of a cold and cheerless, windswept bay with well over three thousand miles of fog-ridden ocean to traverse before, as seemed likely, delivering a blow in the name of the Japanese emperor.

The Blenheim touched down at 2:30 P.M. The searing disc of the sun bore down mercilessly on the airfield, but in the east the sky was once more filling with dark grey clouds. There was hardly a soul to be seen on the airfield.

10 Guarding the Airfield

Friday, 5 December

Immediately on landing at Sungei Patani on my return from Kuala Lumpur, and having simply walked away from the Blenheim without being greeted, accosted, interviewed, or grilled by anyone, I walked up through the rubber trees to my hut. I found the place almost deserted. Someone told me that most of the aircraftsmen were at work down on the airfield. I had, in effect, put in a full day's work and I needed sleep, but I would have to report my presence before I could even hope to take a few hours rest.

I showered, taking care not to saturate the dressing on my shin, and changed into working overalls. My little finger, it appeared, was now out of trouble, both the swelling and the inflammation having subsided to such a degree that I immediately ceased to worry any further about it. Either the Jap's unguent had been effective or nature itself had worked the oracle. As I changed, my mind rapidly went over all that had transpired at Kuala Lumpur.

The two civilians in white had interrogated me in the presence of the unusual squadron leader—unusual because, on many counts, he had appeared unlike one and

in the end had even divested himself of anything faintly resembling RAF officer clothing and instead had put on civilian whites. The proceedings had
taken about forty-five minutes, but at no time had I been informed as to
which official or unofficial unit they were from. Had I been older and wiser
I would, of course, have asked, but it will be remembered that I was just a
youngster, immature, and barely yet emerged from the natural state of
youthful callowness. The two had behaved toward me in a straightforward,
businesslike manner, and at no time had I gained the slightest impression
that they may have had any object in view other than to elicit from me all that
I had by mere chance learned while in Indo-China. The squadron leader's
presence had lent to the proceedings a certain official and authoritative legit-
imacy. I'd had no reason to feel insecure or uncertain in any way, nor had I
felt any reservations about divulging all the information I had acquired.
Indeed, it had been incumbent on me, my duty in fact, to do exactly that. The
elder of the two civilians had, it is true, faltered when attempting to put a
name to the squadron leader, and this had struck me at the time as being
rather odd. The most likely explanation for this could perhaps have been that
they had only recently met, maybe that very morning. If this were so, then
it would seem to suggest that they were not both attached to one and the
same organization.

There had been something else about the squadron leader, something
that might have led a cautious person to worry a little: simply, that his appearance had not been that of an RAF officer. Something about his bearing
and demeanor had not been quite right. Whoever he was, and whatever he
was, the fact remained that he had pretty quickly made contact with the two
civilians and had had enough clout behind him to enable him to have a
Blenheim placed at his disposal. As far as the two civilians in white were
concerned, they may well have flown up all the way from Singapore for all
I knew, but they had had to make do with the Dragon Rapide, a rather old-
fashioned passenger-carrying biplane, and a civilian one at that. If they had,
in fact, flown from Singapore, the trip would have taken at least a couple of
hours in each direction. Anyway, whoever the three were, they had evidently thought it worth listening to my story. But, now, the question was,
what would they do with it? If what the Japanese had given me to understand was, in fact, genuine and reasonably accurate, a lot of communicating
and preparing for major action would have to be carried out by the British—
and fast! On the basis of that which my informant had suggested, I had

worked out that barely two and a half days now remained before the surmised Japanese onslaught on Singapore, Malaya, and Pearl Harbor would be unleashed. This would be in the early hours of Monday, 8 December, in Singapore and Malaya, and shortly after dawn on Sunday, 7 December, in Pearl Harbor.

If I were to be questioned by anyone in authority I would, as instructed, refer him to the squadron leader. But right now I had to report for work. I tried to rid my mind of swirling thoughts about this and that. I was well nigh physically and mentally exhausted, and it did not help that I was unable to discuss my experiences and present condition with anyone. It was now 4:00 P.M. and the sky had blackened. The grumble of far-distant thunder reached my ears, depressing and, in an odd way, defeating. It meant that the storm would be just about overhead as we were finishing work for the day.

I walked down through the plantation to the airfield. This time my corporal, normally a decent and quiet type, greeted me with an obvious lack of pleasure. I was, of course, conscious that I had been withdrawn from his ground-crew strength and presumably without explanation. He must have been peeved by this, yet there was nothing I could venture to say to smooth things out. I do recall saying something like, "Sorry about that, Corporal. . . . You were told, I suppose." And I remember him lifting his arms in a gesture of reluctant acceptance, but saying nothing.

After an hour or so the tension engendered by my return to the fold abated. Not so, however, the thunderous storm that had now arrived in no uncertain terms. There were six of us in the pen working on one of the Blenheims that had had the major servicing of its two engines hurriedly brought forward. Torrential rain hammered down on the corrugated iron roof and, through numerous gaps and imperfections, flooded onto the floor. We labored on in the dimness of the pen, sweating, swearing, and grousing at having to work through what remained of the uncomfortable afternoon with yet another thunderstorm raging around us.

At about 5:30 P.M. an airman on a bicycle appeared at the open front of the pen looking for Aircraftsman Shepherd. I was listening and naturally thought that I was about to receive the call for further questioning. But it was nothing like that. Instead, I was informed that I was required to report for special guard duty at 6:00 P.M. that evening. My heart sank because I knew of no way I could get myself excused. It meant, virtually, having to remain awake until 6:00 A.M. the following morning and with the added possibility of having to work all the following day, Saturday the sixth.

I was allowed to knock off early from my work on the Blenheim so that I could have a hurried evening meal before reporting for this guard-duty thing. The way it worked out gave me four hours rest before starting the first of my two shifts out on the airfield. So, between the hours of 6:00 P.M. and 10:00 P.M., I found myself within the oven-like confines of the guard room, where I stretched out on a mattress and sweated.

At 10:00 P.M. I went out on to the airfield accompanied by an Indian private soldier who was, I guessed, in his mid-twenties. His command of the English language was virtually nonexistent, but he made up for this deficiency by intoning in a variety of nasal modes and in a surprising number of intricate rhythms, songs, and tunes from his home country. From time to time he would even stop in his tracks and do a bit of arm waving—acting out, as it were, the message contained in the song of the moment. When arm waving struck him as inappropriate, he resorted to dancing.

After a time enough was enough. "Chabbarow!" I cried out, invoking one of the few words of Hindi I had picked up since arriving in Malaya. It meant, "Shut up," and carried real meaning and fervency. His warbling ceased immediately and was not replaced by any other of his nose-flute type noises. I think I hurt his feelings.

A little later the bright blinding light of a striking match suddenly hit me in the eyes. It was my Indian colleague lighting up a cigarette! I snatched both match and cigarette from him and stamped on them. Then, in the darkness, I gained an indistinct impression of him crouching down beside me, whimpering. It was some time before I managed to sort him out, his rifle once again slung over his shoulder. I made sure the safety catch was on. I was carrying a Tommy gun on which I had received no more than fifteen minutes informal tuition.

Toward the end of our two-hour spell of duty the clouds broke up and the moon shone down on us, thus lighting up the whole scene. The Blenheims and Buffaloes stood silent. The great mass of Kedah Peak stood out sharply against the sky. The only sound, apart from the crickets and bullfrogs, was the rhythmic throbbing of the camp's electricity generator, suppressed and secreted away somewhere within the plantation.

Back in the guard room I stretched out on a disagreeably smelling mattress and tried to sleep. As I rested, my tired brain returned to recent events.

I was now faced with having to carry the burden of knowing what I did but without being allowed to talk about it. I had been told, in effect, that Malaya would probably be attacked quite soon, and I had reason to think that the early hours of Monday, 8 December, would be the likely time. Right now it was Saturday. If I tried to tell my colleagues and friends that I was convinced that the camp would come under air attack on Monday morning, I would as like as not be reported either for spreading damaging rumors or for displaying signs of anxiety neurosis, both to the detriment of morale generally.

My head was awhirl with unanswered questions. For instance, there had been Jan and the Hudson. Was it possible to believe all Jan had said about himself and his connections? There had also been the two Frenchmen in Cambodia, French Indo-China. About them I had been told virtually nothing. And then there was the strange matter of the Hudson, a civilian plane, coming into Sungei Patani and using the facilities as it were. Then there had been the very odd squadron leader who had suddenly appeared on the camp, in time, as it happened, for the Hudson's arrival. No one to whom I had spoken knew his name with certainty, and then, after the interrogation at Kuala Lumpur, he had donned civilian clothing and flown off with the two other civilians. Who was he? To which branch of the RAF was he attached? How was it that the squadron leader managed to have the two of us flown down to Kuala Lumpur at such short notice? Who were the two civilian men whom we had met there? I had not even been told their names, let alone the name of the department they represented. Why was it that, apart from the squadron leader, no one on the camp had spoken to me about the affair? And why had it been necessary for the squadron leader to so forcibly impress on me that I must not speak to anyone about any part of the operation? Such were the questions that plagued me. Eventually, even these nagging uncertainties failed to stop me sleeping.

I was awakened at 4:00 A.M. It was time for me to commence my second spell of guard duty.

My Indian colleague joined me once more and we stumbled our way down through the trees to the airfield, which was now covered by ground mist a couple of feet deep. It occurred to me that, if there were any Japanese infiltrators around intent on wrecking or seizing the airfield, my soldier colleague and I would be little more than useless in trying to stop them. I imagined the dark shape of a figure rising up, only ten or fifteen feet away, from out of the mist. Then I imagined myself shouting, "Halt—who goes there?" And then I imagined a brief bright spurt of orange flame and a sudden devastating blow to my chest. I imagined myself sinking down into the layer of mist and the few seconds of indescribable pain, the pungent fear, the feeling of faintness, and then the slipping away from the strange dreamlike world in which I now found myself.

The plain fact was that I had good reason to think that the camp might come under attack at any moment. If an all-out assault on Malaya was planned to start on Monday, 8 December, was it not reasonable to think that a certain amount of infiltration and sabotage might take place during the few preceding days? To say that I had become acutely aware of being surrounded by danger would have been putting it mildly. I was acutely aware of the peril that might even now be lying in wait, and my whole body responded accordingly. When my mouth became so dry that I could hardly swallow, and my heart rate increased to something around the 120 mark, I knew it was time to follow my instincts and forget that which I had been instructed to do by the guard-room sergeant. He had told me to walk up and down, regardless of the state of visibility, something which, in the present circumstances, I saw as stupid and potentially lethal. I decided to minimize the risk of our being surprised and took my totally clueless fellow guard right across the eastern perimeter of the airfield to the edge of the rubber-tree plantation on the south side. There I led him back into the trees for fifty yards or so, where the darkness was intense. I had reasoned to myself that any attackers or other intruders would infiltrate from either the north or the east sides of the airfield, that is, from largely wild and undeveloped terrain, distant from the camp buildings and its sleeping personnel. Thus we spent well over the last hour of our duty concealed within the plantation, bored out of our minds, but in the knowledge that any lurking person would be unable to move more than a couple of steps without inadvertently causing various items of tree debris to crackle.

When at last we emerged there was, on the eastern horizon, the merest faint suggestion of the sunrise to come, which would be in about another hour's time. Mist, now at its thickest, swirled around our legs as we walked back toward the control tower area. The Indian, relieved that he was about to go off duty, suddenly leaned his rifle up against an oil drum and with his hands started to beat a light rhythm on the thing while at the same time producing a little number from his nasal repertoire. At that, I lost all interest in him and simply pushed off back toward the guard room while he trailed six paces behind, dragging his heels and intoning maddeningly in a falsetto wail. Although I could not yet have known it for sure, the poor chap was going to learn a lot, and swiftly, within a matter of days.

I washed, changed, and had an early breakfast, by this time in dire need of several hours sleep. It was Saturday, 6 December. My leg was still painful and I went to the medical room where a medical orderly bathed it with saline solution and applied a new dressing.

"Any chance of my having an excused-duties chit?" I asked.

"Not a chance," came the reply. "You can report sick through the usual channels if you like, but I'm telling you the medical officer will turn you away. Anyway, your leg doesn't look too bad; it's clean and free from infection—look in again at 2:00 P.M. so we can check it."

I stopped at the orderly room on the way back to my hut. I wanted to have a word with the sergeant who had called me from the mess hut and taken me to see the none-too-kosher squadron leader.

"I'm looking for the sergeant who was on duty here on Wednesday evening—is he around, please?" I asked the two clerks.

I got nowhere with either of them. One had no knowledge of him while the other said the sergeant had been on camp for only three days and had then been unexpectedly transferred to another camp. I was not going to find out anything about the squadron leader via that route.

"What about Squadron Leader Pattison?" I asked the one who struck me as being the brightest.

"Who?"

"Squadron Leader Pattison, though it could have been Battison, or, perhaps, Mattison—a name like that," I said.

"Never heard of anyone with that name."

"No, never heard of anyone with that name," added his colleague.

"But he was knocking around the camp for a couple of days recently," I explained.

"Never heard of him," reiterated the helpful one. "Why?"

"Oh, nothing really. Someone said he was something to do with interviewing chaps for air-crew training." I had made this one up on the spur of the moment. "I'm already down for pilot training—I just thought. . . ." I bit off my words at this point, not wishing to stir up his interest any further. "Thanks anyway."

So my quest to find out more about both the squadron leader and the sergeant had come to nothing. While I found this irksome and curious, I was in no mood, nor had I either the physical or nervous energy, to devote further time to the mystery.

The first rays of morning sunshine glinted through the trees as I walked back to my hut. Patches of ground mist still hung around here and there. They would soon evaporate under the new day's sun.

11

The Final Two Days

Saturday, 6 December (Malaya time)

At 8:00 A.M. I found myself back in the pen, having been told that even though today was Saturday the order had been given for us to continue working on the Blenheim until such time as it was in all respects serviceable.

Half a dozen of us continued work on the plane throughout the day. In the evening at dinner one of the sergeant fitters came into the mess looking for us. When he had located our group of six, he approached and treated us to an apologetic smile.

"Sorry, you chaps," he said. "You've got to keep on working until you've finished the job." By this we correctly inferred that we were required to bring the Blenheim up to operational condition before having any extended rest break.

Someone put his oar in. "If there's a big panic on, why the hell aren't we being told what it's all about?" But the sergeant had already gone on his way.

Although I said nothing, it crossed my mind that perhaps this latest scare had something to do with the information I had given to the squadron leader and his two associates in Kuala Lumpur. And yet it was an unpleasant feeling knowing what I knew, while at the same time being unable to say anything about it.

"Best to be on the safe side, I suppose," I said, trying to make myself heard over all the noise that was going on. "It's no good having airplanes that are unserviceable if someone's about to clobber us."

"Well," another voice said, "if someone is about to clobber us, let's be knowing who it is. Why are we being kept in the dark? The powers that be never tell us anything."

We returned to the pen and the Blenheim where working under the sparse light of a few low-wattage lamps was next to impossible. Metal items became shadows and shadows assumed the appearance of solid metal. Components, screws, nuts, and the like, some virtually inaccessible or invisible at the best of times, now presented a problem of infinite difficulty.

At midnight we knocked off and got sandwiches and cocoa. We sat in a group on the warm concrete floor. Conversation was limited to a few desultory remarks. Some of the chaps had worked into the early hours of that morning and, like me, were fatigued and subdued by lack of sleep. As far as we could tell, we were the only individuals still working on the airfield. The Buffaloes, ranged up in their straight line just a few hundred yards away, at one moment hidden by darkness and the next brightly illuminated by a virtually full moon, stood quiet and deserted. It was well known that most of them remained unserviceable owing to lack of spares, yet there they were, to all appearances solid and businesslike in the warm, peaceful night, but hopelessly unready for whatever might happen.

I still retained a residual instinctive confidence that the British military high-ups, including RAF top officials, were fully aware of the present situation and would therefore not be caught napping by the Japanese. As far as Sungei Patani was concerned, plans would undoubtedly have already been drawn up for its effective defense, and for the roles its two squadrons would play in the event hostilities broke out.

The early hours brought light rain, the kind of rain that makes little noise other than an almost imperceptible hissing sound but which, being so fine, drifts around in the slightest current of air, thereby thoroughly dampening things whether under cover or not. I worked on slowly as though drugged. At one point my thoughts returned to Kuala Lumpur and the two men in white. They flitted across my memory like figures in some dream. I heard, in my reeling mind, their voices; I felt the appalling heat of that office in which I had been interrogated; I tasted the acidic lime-juice cordial; and I felt the gnawing burning ache of my shin. Muddled, disorganized thoughts surged through my brain, coming and going, flooding back and forth, but seeming always to have the one substance—the question as to who the two men were, and what action they were likely to have taken as a result of all that I had told them. Such dulled and infinitely weary deliberations lurched through my mind as the night wore on.

The two men, I thought, and perhaps also the squadron leader, were most probably attached to some official organization concerned with security matters. Thus, having received the facts as related to them by me, they would pass them up to a higher level, presumably High Command Headquarters in Singapore. In turn, the information would most probably then be passed to the War Office in London, because Singapore and Malaya would hardly be authorized to engage in either full-scale offensive or defensive military action without the sanction and blessing of the War Office. The War Office would then pass the information on to the U.S. Embassy in London, and also to the White House in Washington, D.C., on the grounds that a fleet of Japanese naval ships had been reported as probably being already well on its way toward launching an attack on Pearl Harbor. In the light of the information I had gathered, the reasoning that had been applied to the matter, and the deductions drawn from all this at the meeting in Kuala Lumpur, it seemed crucial and imperative that the United States should be informed accordingly. Even though the United States might already be at a high state of alertness, and might indeed already know of Japan's huge fleet having left Hitokappu, it would surely be a straightforward act of courtesy and friendship on the part of Great Britain to pass the word to the United States, who, although not formally involved in World War II, had already given and was continuing to give very substantial material support to Great Britain.

It was, however, unthinkable that the Japanese fleet, if in fact any such existed, would proceed all the way to Hawaii without being seen and reported either by U.S. naval ships or commercial vessels. The sight of such an immense collection of capital ships headed on an eastern course would be guaranteed to create astonishment, interest, and alarm. It would be really something to write and signal home about. Such a staggering sighting would become world news within a matter of hours once the press agencies got hold of it. The first to be told of the seaborne Japanese armada would be those U.S.

defense authorities, whose job it was to safeguard U.S. Pacific interests, and Hawaii would be included in these. Thus, even supposing that a Japanese fleet really was planning to attack Pearl Harbor at Hawaii, the appropriate U.S. defense authorities would receive sufficient warning and would therefore take the necessary steps to either frustrate or repulse such an attack.

Once the element of total surprise was lost, the prospects of a successful outcome for Japan would be severely limited. It seemed a fair bet that Japan would rely on achieving total surprise because any prior warning of the attack, whether by formal declaration of war or detection, might easily result in disaster and humiliation for the attacker—a dire calamity that could well spell out the end of Japan as a militaristic, power-seeking nation. Its days spent in dreaming of a Greater East Asia Co-Prosperity Sphere, with Imperial Japan as the big fish in the pond, would be dashed forever.

And there was another thing. If the presumed attack on Pearl Harbor were foiled, and Japan's wider military intentions thereby brought to light by simple deduction, it would render any attack on either Singapore or Malaya highly improbable. It was therefore vital for the United States to be informed about the Japanese fleet being already within aerial striking distance of Pearl Harbor, though, likely enough, well to the north of the islands where the ships would perhaps stand the best chance of being undetected.

There was, however, yet another thing worth considering; simply, if Japan did attack Pearl Harbor, the United States would without question immediately declare war on Japan, and, in accordance with the Tripartite Treaty, Germany and Italy would come to Japan's aid, and this would mean war being declared between the United States and Germany and Italy. Such a development would be of immense value to Great Britain; it could well mean the difference between a ruinous and lengthy war with Germany and Italy, possibly culminating in defeat for a struggling Great Britain on the one hand and a decisive early defeat being inflicted on Germany and Italy by Great Britain and the United States on the other. This being so, it could be argued that it would, in this sense, be against Great Britain's interests to divulge to the United States the startling facts about the Japanese fleet.

I had put it to those at the Kuala Lumpur interrogation that an attack on Pearl Harbor would be timed to take place simultaneously with attacks on Malaya and Singapore. At least this is what I had understood the Jap to have intimated to me. This made sense because for the Japanese to attack Pearl Harbor only would result in Great Britain being alerted, and if either Malaya

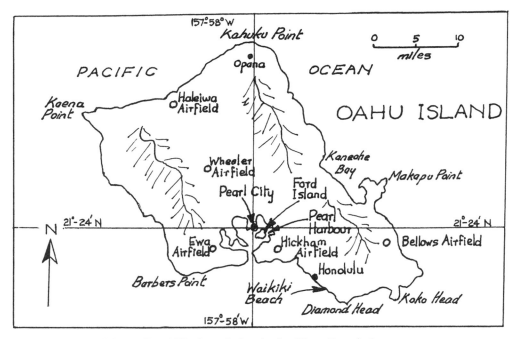

Map 4. Pearl Harbor, Oahu, in the Hawaiian chain.

or Singapore were to be attacked but without a simultaneous attack on United States being made, the United States would be similarly alerted. Hence it seemed likely that Japan would attack the three places near enough at the same time, thereby achieving the immense advantage of surprise in all cases. Once again, the timing of the attacks, as I had already suggested as being the most likely, worked out as being dawn on Sunday, 7 December (Hawaii time)—the very early hours on Monday, 8 December (Malaya time), in reality, coincident times.

More and more, however, I was coming to believe that the U.S. authorities would not receive the warning in time to stir their military high-ups into taking appropriate and meaningful defensive measures. I had, in fact, a horribly dismal feeling that the warning had somehow been allowed to get bogged down, or even peter out completely, even before reaching General Headquarters in Singapore. My earlier uncanny premonition of impending disaster, which I had put down to the monsoon climate, the gloom of the rubber trees, and the strangely unnatural atmosphere of my surroundings, was now

An aerial view of Pearl Harbor, Oahu, as it was when Japanese planes struck the U.S. Pacific Fleet here on 7 December 1941. *Associated Press Ltd.*

becoming much more than just a worrying feeling. My sense of foreboding had been replaced by a numbing fearfulness driven by my personal conviction that the camp would be attacked from the air within twenty-four hours or so.

Most days only little more than half an hour would elapse between the full darkness of night and bright daylight. On this day, owing to low cloud and a fine drizzle, dawn appeared late, and at 6:30 A.M., when we went for breakfast, it was still virtually pitch dark, the day being Sunday, 7 December (Malaya time). A sergeant tracked us down and informed us that we must carry on working until lunch time, when another team would take over from us. We were glad to hear this because there were at least another ten hours of work yet to be done on the Blenheim.

We resumed work again and in midmorning Flight Mechanic Myers turned up on his crudely repaired bicycle bearing his precious tea-urn and a load of sparking plugs. "How are all you bastards this fine Sunday morning?" he shouted out as he propped his conveyance up against one of the Blenheim's wheels.

None of us felt any urge to reply; no one spoke. He realized that we had been working throughout the night and, no doubt guessing our condition, just dispensed the tea without further yap, took the requisite payment, and shoved off to the next pen where others were now working. That was the last I ever saw of Myers and his tea-vending contraption. It is interesting that I have remembered him over the years even though he played such a small part in my Malayan experience. Perhaps it is that the tea he hawked around was, on occasion, a real morale booster. Or it may be that one feels a certain residual shame on account of having teased and provoked him so relentlessly.

At lunch I dozed over my food, only the clatter of cutlery and crockery keeping me awake. At one point my mind flashed back to Penang where I knew it would be just as it was when I had been there with George. I thought of the dancing, the Hawaiian music, and the gin and tonic. I thought about chasing those little sand crabs on the beach at Springtide. I thought of Wan and how she had kept waving as I had departed into the distance with George in that rickshaw. I thought of the cinema show in Georgetown, and I thought of the thunderstorm that had broken over us as we boarded the evening ferry to return to the mainland. Then I thought of the terrible depression that had come over me on my return to the camp at Sungei Patani, the almost palpable sense of foreboding and the feeling of unreality I had experienced.

The six of us were informed that we must carry on working on the Blenheim until it was ready to be test flown. We had expected to be replaced by another team of fitters and flight mechanics so we could return to our huts and sleep. However, the sergeant who broke the news to us told us it had proved impossible to get together a team from those not already occupied on other duties. There remained about three hours' work still to be done, but fatigue had severely reduced our rate of working and it was anyone's guess as to how long it would, in fact, take.

Thunder came at around 4:30 P.M. and stayed with us until it was time for us to go for our evening meal. At this time one of the flight mechanics packed it all in by keeling over and refusing to get to his feet. He was taken away in the camp ambulance.

In the dining hall there was the usual animated chatter, the crashing of cutlery, the overpowering heat, and the usual smoke-laden atmosphere. I ate hardly anything, for all I needed was sleep. I pushed my plate away and looked around the place, my eyelids drooping and waves of dizziness making it difficult for me to hold things in focus. Someone near me was droning on about Christmas and particularly as to what in-house arrangements should be made on camp as regards entertainment.

I quickly lost interest in the pathetic controversy that followed and promptly fell asleep with my head on my arms. I became aware of someone shaking me. On looking up I saw it was George. He was staring down at me in anxious disbelief, his face as despondent as ever and flushed with the heat. He was perspiring heavily and a lock of his prematurely greying hair was hanging limply over his forehead.

"I don't suppose you could lend me a couple of dollars, could you?" he asked, once he was sure I was more or less awake.

I remembered the money Jan had given me. I took the envelope from my overall pocket, fingered out a couple of five-dollar notes, and held them out, low down, for him to take. He got the message and continued to keep them more or less out of sight. His countenance lit up, which for George was a big thing. His eyes danced, as the saying goes, and he said, "Bloody hell!"

"Take that," I said to him. "Have a few drinks on me."

"Thanks, Peter," he said, "I'll see you tomorrow."

I did see George again, though not on the morrow, but in South Africa—eighteen months later.

Another member of our crew failed to return to the pen, having initially been unable to rise from his chair in the dining hall and then promptly slumping down again when assisted to his feet. There now remained only four of us to complete the outstanding work on the Blenheim.

Our work was not completed until a few minutes before midnight. A tractor was brought and the Blenheim was towed out onto the immediately adjacent perimeter track where the two engines were fired up and put through their paces. My last recollection of this final stage of our endeavors is that of the smell of orange-flamed, hot, petrol-rich exhaust gases and the roar of the engines in the darkness.

At 12:30 A.M. the pen lights were at last switched off. The cloud cover had broken up quite considerably, though the moon was still hidden. We struggled up the incline to our quarters, and the other three broke away toward their hut. I continued for a couple of hundred yards to the clearing at the very summit of the incline where my hut, in the light of reluctant splashes of moonlight, stood in silence with all its doorways and shutter openings in total darkness.

As good as asleep on my feet I looked back as I entered the doorway. The clearing was quiet, save for the background sound of insects in the leaves of the rubber trees and the subdued hum of the electricity generator. I turned again to enter my room and, as I did so, the full bright moon at last broke free from cloud and illuminated the hut and the clearing and, as likely as not, the entire camp.

I lowered myself onto the edge of my bed, though quietly so as not to disturb the other chap sleeping in there. I wrenched off my canvas work-boots, lowered the mosquito net and crept under it, and, still in my overalls, dirty with oil and grease and perspiration and stinking of petrol, I instantly fell into a deep sleep.

The time was 1:00 A.M., Monday, 8 December (Malaya time). Over at Kota Bharu, and three thousand miles away in the Pacific things were fast developing. Earthshaking events, evil and unspeakable, were about to erupt.[1]

12 A Personal Disaster

As I slept, the night hours passed and darkness again deepened as the hitherto brilliant full moon slowly sank below the tree line. Intensified darkness seemingly brought with it intensified silence—a silence that admitted only the smallest suggestion of sound—a falling twig or leaf; the rustle of some small nocturnal creature in the trees; the transient exploratory movement of a larger-than-usual flying insect; and, always in the background, the faint, regular, muffled throb of the generator. Quietness could hardly have been more complete. As the hours went slowly by, the usual tenuous ground mist formed, and, lulled by all this peaceful tranquillity, I continued to sleep—in unsuspecting oblivion.

An unusual, disturbing intrusion of noise brought me abruptly into half-waking consciousness. In an instant my brain became acutely perceptive. The noises, as though heard in sleep, were very different from the various noises to which I had become accustomed. They were very loud, individual detonations that carried with them the impression of violent, unleashed power. My mind, still

drugged by sleep, yet galvanized by an instinctive sense of danger, raced over the situation. In but a fraction of a second I perceived the detonations to be explosions coming from the direction of the airfield. I was, however, allowed no time to consider their possible nature, although I knew them to be imminently menacing. A series of detonations, far louder than the preceding ones, commenced in an approaching barrage, each louder and more powerful than the one before and with perhaps a half second between them. Still half asleep but in the realization that the barrage was rapidly moving in my direction, and being fearful for my safety, I leapt from my bed and wedged myself down between it and the adjacent wall. There I crouched with my head between my arms and my eyes tightly shut. The movement could have taken no more than a second or so.

The next explosion was massive and very close indeed, and I knew that if there were to be another, it would without doubt be the end of me. I waited—a wait that lasted no time at all but which was filled with all the horror, the dark, dreary despair, and the melancholy sadness of some terrible nightmare. Then, as though decreed by destiny, a monstrous explosion blasted over and around me.

I felt tired, very tired, as though I had been suddenly awakened from the deepest sleep. I felt no desire to move—not even just a little. I opened my eyes and stared up at nothing in particular; in fact, there was nothing in particular to stare at anyway. There was nothing to interest me—just a lot of early dawn sky filled with slowly drifting, dark-grey smoke. I wanted to sleep but instinctively knew this would not be a good idea. I decided I ought to move a little. I tried, but everything felt too heavy—too weak—I had not the strength. I knew I was lying flat on my back but was not sure where. My back was hurting—hurting badly. It was not an ache or a sharp localized pain, but more like an excruciating deep-seated burning and twisting pain that was becoming worse by the second.

I began to emerge from the initial numbing shock of whatever had landed me in my present predicament and realized that I was in serious trouble. Something terrible had happened—something I was still too tired to think about. I attempted to move again but without success. I tried to concentrate my mind, but overpowering weariness defeated me. Then the pain became too much to bear; I half-groaned, half-screamed, yet so weakly that no one could possibly have heard. I could vaguely recall having heard loud crashing

and banging noises, and I remembered crouching down behind my bed, and it all seemed just a fraction of a second ago. But now I was not in my room. There were no walls and there was no ceiling—there was nothing but the sky with its drifting smoke, and me lying on the ground among pieces of broken concrete. I was aware that everything was quiet. Nothing seemed to be happening. I still could not move and I was being tortured by the pain in the lower part of my back.

I called out, "Help!" It was more of a feeble and instinctive spasm born of desperation than a full-throated cry for assistance. Even to me my appeal sounded like an infinitely weak and timorous murmur. I suddenly became frightened as it was now obvious to me that I was in great difficulty. "Help," I again called out, in a voice shaking with weakness, fear, and desperation.

A young airman stepped into my line of sight. He stood, looking down at me. "There's one here!" he shouted.

A second airman appeared. I remember his face awash with perspiration and that he appeared to be terrified out of his wits. They both continued to stare down at me, neither speaking. After a few seconds they turned and disappeared from my sight. I had no idea where they went; I simply lay there, shivering with shock and trying to tense myself against the agonizing pain.

The two returned some minutes later, carrying a stretcher. One of them lifted my shoulders, the other my feet. I bent in the middle, shrieked out in torment, and immediately passed out.

This second bout of unconsciousness was of fairly short duration. I knew this because as I came to my senses the two airmen were putting me down on the wooden veranda of the sickbay, scarcely three hundred yards from my hut, where, presumably, they had found me. Once again they lifted me to take me off the stretcher, and as they did so I screamed out, "Don't—for Christ's sake!"

I was too late and the pain evoked another shriek that barely began before my brain switched off for the third time.

When I came around it was to find someone putting a lighted cigarette to my lips. I shook my head to indicate that I did not want the cigarette. It was removed from lips that I noticed felt warm and wet and swollen.

Two medical orderlies were tending an airman who was lying alongside me. He was conscious and I immediately recognized him as one of the airframe fitters. He was a lad of about twenty-one, and a decent and intelligent chap. They were doing something to one of his legs, and their actions were

frantically hurried. I looked down to where they were working. His leg finished before it reached the knee. A mess of gory flesh and bone protruded from the leg of his khaki shorts, and one of the orderlies was tightening a tourniquet around the thigh with hands that were shaking violently. I raised my head a little to look at the lad's face again. He was staring straight up, his features ashen grey and his lips trembling. Then he turned his head in my direction and, for a moment, I thought our eyes met. But there was just a faraway, mystified look in his eyes; tears were welling up and running down his cheeks. A growing pool of his brilliant red blood spread rapidly in my direction.

I was still shivering with shock, but my mind had started to clear. The terrible pain remained, but I was no longer passing out every five minutes or so. I had not yet seriously begun to consider what had happened, even though I realized that some sort of devastating violence had been involved. I was concerned to know the extent of my injuries and began examining myself as well as I was able. I was still wearing my work overalls and the front was saturated with blood. My mouth kept filling with blood and there was blood on my left arm. My bottom jaw was stiff and felt as though it was being clamped tightly in a vise. Some of my teeth had broken off. Every part of my body hurt unspeakably.

Any interest I had in examining myself quickly lapsed, such energy as I had being far better spent on trying to deal with the agonizing pain. My mind darted about feverishly, trying to recollect what I had been doing immediately before the calamity had struck.

Through the haze of distress I could recall lying on my bed, suddenly awake and hearing a deafening barrage of explosions. I remembered leaping off my bed and crouching down with my head between my arms. There had been an interval during which, strangely, I had experienced many emotions— an interval of time that must have been less than a second but in which there had been time for me to experience a kind of intense feeling of inevitability and hopelessness. Then there had been a deafening blast and I had sensed my life to be at its end. I remembered returning to consciousness and looking up at drifting smoke in the dawn sky and feeling infinitely weak and tired. Then, when the two airmen had lifted me, I had experienced a pain so awful that my mind had straightaway sought refuge in unconsciousness. It had been like some dreadful obscene nightmare—a nightmare that was still with me; a nightmare with real people, real sickly salty blood spilling from my mouth, and real pain.

I could not understand why it seemed impossible for me to remember anything further back than my waking up and hearing all those explosions. Yet I somehow realized I was at the RAF camp at Sungei Patani and that I was in Malaya. And I knew it to be Monday and even that the time was shortly after dawn. I moved my right hand to the breastpocket of my overall. I seemed to remember having put my watch in there. It was there all right, but I had neither the interest nor the energy to fish it out to look at it. My hand was covered with blood.

A tormenting, tearing, twisting pain racked my lower back, yet everything else from my waist down to my knees seemed not to exist. My buttocks felt as though they were immersed in molten steel. When I tried to move my legs to ease the frightful agony, nothing happened other than that the agony became worse.

I moved my hand over my lower abdomen, and down the front of my thighs and found nothing but numbness. I rested for a few moments, trembling with added fear. When I resumed my investigation, this time more thoroughly, my shock became even more complete for everything was quite dead to the touch.

A young chap to my immediate left, half-sitting, half-lying on the floor, started to groan. I had not paid him any attention up to this point. His upper torso was naked, and blood was running freely from a hole in his back—a hole the size of a pocket watch. His face was white and his fair hair was hanging untidily over his forehead. Although apparently undamaged in either spine or lungs, he was spilling a lot of blood and much of it was in a spreading pool that had now reached the spot where I was lying.

The sun's early rays were penetrating the trees and flooding onto the veranda, the warm, dazzling light adding yet another torment to the already nightmarish ordeal. The camp medical officer came and stooped by my side in a pool of blood. He was, I suppose, in his mid-twenties, and he seemed utterly shocked and confused. "Have you got any pain?" he asked.

"Yes," I mumbled through my bloodied mouth, "my back—terrible." And I added something else—something that struck me as being of even greater significance than the pain. "I can't feel anything down here," I mumbled, pointing toward the front of the trouser part of my overalls.

"You'll be all right after the war," he replied, a reply that to this day I recall with vivid clarity. Having given me this piece of encouragement, he left me.

I lay and suffered in the early morning sunshine on that warm wooden veranda, its floor glistening with fresh bright blood. And I watched as the youth to my left finally collapsed onto his side as an agitated orderly frenziedly packed gauze into the gaping hole in his back in a vain attempt to staunch the flow of blood. The youth was unresponsive to the pain. He just lay there, unmoving.

The medical officer reappeared a little later, by which time I was moaning and groaning and calling out to be given something to relieve the insufferable pain. Within a few minutes I received the first shot of morphine I had ever had. It was to prove one of the very many I would have over the coming weeks. I felt myself drifting off into a dreamy, comfortable state in which I lost all interest in things around me. My fears and anxieties ebbed away, and my pain became just a kind of dull aching soreness that I found, in a way, not unpleasant. Though close to oblivion, I remained vaguely conscious of the fact that horrors were going on around me and that I was very much one of them.

They moved the youth, leaving behind his pool of now-congealing blood. He was quite still, his face very white and strangely expressionless. His eyes, pale blue, took the full glare of the sun without flinching, one eye almost closed, the other wide open but unseeing.

An hour or so later I was placed in an army ambulance, which then moved off along the bumpy, winding road through the rubber trees. And so it was that I made my exit from the camp at Sungei Patani after a period there of around nine weeks. I could not have known that, when next I returned, half a century would have elapsed.

It was, I recall, about half an hour later that the lurching ambulance came to a halt. I was carried into a wooden building and there placed on a bed in a stiflingly warm room in which there were other beds. The morphine was beginning to wear off, and a range of increasing discomforts were now rushing back to plague me. I estimated the time as being about 10:00 A.M. The ward was small and white and bright, with wooden walls and ceiling. Dappled sunlight shone through open shutters. There were about ten beds in the place, each one occupied and, judging by the sounds that issued from behind screens, a good number of serious injury cases waiting for or already receiving attention. I watched as a number of white uniformed male nurses moved purposefully up and down the ward, fetching and carrying things that were of little interest to me in the state of mind I was in. The nursing staff were, for the most part, Malays, though a few Chinese and individuals of mixed race were in evidence. Two Sikh doctors were at work in the ward, each complete with heavy beard and turban.

Presently a male Malay nurse came to my bedside. I was in no condition to engage in conversation with anyone. All I wished to know was what had happened, and where I was. He smiled down at me, his brown face kindly and anxious.

"Hello," he said quietly, a little embarrassed, I thought. "You awake now. This place Bedong—it rubber estate hospital for plantation workers. You from Royal Air Force. Come from Sungei Patani. We treat you soon. You want water?"

I nodded, for my mouth was in a dreadful state, my jaw being locked solid and feeling as though it had been hit with an iron bar. The nurse had to trickle the water between my lips from the spout of a bed-beaker. When he turned to leave, I managed to utter a kind of desperate cry. He asked me what I wanted and I mumbled the barely audible words, "What happened?"

"It air raid," he explained, with an apologetic smile, as though in some way he felt himself partly to blame. "Japanese airplanes bomb airfield—not declare war." Then he left me.

His words jogged my memory. My brain began to grapple with something I could partly remember but which seemed to have taken place in a dream, and the more I struggled with the dream, the more complicated and incomprehensible it became. I kept slipping back into little patches of short but soothing sleep, but every time my consciousness returned, so did the dream, but only in snatches. And yet I knew I had lived through the dream—I had been part of it, although for the most part, it remained beyond my mental recall.

I was in horrible pain again. Then, just as it seemed to me that I would go mad if something were not done to help me, one of the Sikh doctors suddenly appeared. He said nothing, but in his hand was a small enamel dish, and in the dish was a hypodermic syringe.

This time the morphine put me completely out within five minutes. When next I surfaced I saw that my overall had been removed and that I was quite naked, under a threadbare white sheet covering the lower half of my body. My jaw had been bandaged and my bottom lip felt huge and raw. My left arm, from shoulder to wrist, was also sheathed in bandages. The base of my spine had begun to torment me again, the whole of my pelvis feeling as though it were being crushed in a hydraulic press and my buttocks again immersed in molten metal.

Using just about the only part of me that did not hurt too much, my right arm and hand, I cautiously lifted the badly worn sheet. There was terrific bruising, some areas almost black and others purple and violent indigo. From waist to well down the thighs there was virtually just one huge black and blue bruise, yet all was numb, with, here and there, hideously swollen tissue adding to the sorry picture.

My right leg seemed, in general, to be in reasonable condition, but the ankle was twice its normal size and bruised to an awesome extent. I could not move it, and every five seconds or so it was gripped by a short, exquisitely excruciating stab of pain. There was a bandage on my left shin, but this I gave only scant attention. Numerous relatively small surgical dressings were in evidence on parts of my body where, presumably, tissue had been pierced, lacerated, or otherwise abused.

But something else was troubling me. As the morphine wore off even further, it became clear to me that I needed to empty my bladder. The discomfort of a full bladder had been masked by the pain, deadening effects of the injection, but, now, I was about to experience, for the first time, the torment that accompanies a surcharged bladder. I waved my hand to attract anyone who might help me with my problem. After about ten minutes a Malay male nurse came over to me.

"You want something?" he asked, kindly enough.

I nodded and gestured to him that I wished to empty my bladder. "Okay," he said, "I get bed-bottle."

He brought a bed-bottle and helped me with it. Nothing whatsoever happened—I was unable to pass even one drop of urine.

One hour later I was still waiting, my bladder ready for bursting and driving me into a delirium of agony. I felt my lower abdomen. It was numb on the outside, yet greatly distended and as hard as a football. The nurse had been sympathetic and considerate and patient, but my urgent problem needed much more than that.

After a nightmarish period of time the Sikh doctor came and examined me, gently pressing the bladder region.

"You want to pass water?" he inquired.

"Yes, yes, yes," I mumbled desperately.

He obviously saw and judged that I was in torment for he hurried off and returned a few moments later with a brown rubber tube in a white enamel dish. I was about to be catheterized for the first time in my life. The process took ten minutes or so. As my bladder emptied, the gradual relief was indescribably wonderful, for, over those few minutes the frightful agony gradually abated until, finally, I was left sweating and trembling. I had just experienced the agony of that particular condition described, almost casually, by the clinical expression "retention of urine."

When he had restored me to relative sanity, the Sikh medic gazed at me with deep, dark brown eyes.

"Were you in the bombing?" he asked.

I nodded.

"It was the Japanese," he continued. "Very bad raid. Also Singapore bombed in the night—and Hawaii." He then turned and left me.

His words sliced through my brain, awakening memories as though relieving a pressure that had been suppressing my ability to recollect recent events. For a few seconds my mind conjured up a host of images that brought me instantly back into the world of reality. It is claimed that a single word, or a particular sound, even an odor or fragrance, can be the means of liberating locked-away memories. To those who have never experienced this remarkable phenomenon at either first- or second-hand, the claim must seem farfetched. I can, however, vouch for a certain truth in the claim. In my case a curtain rose in the very instant the Sikh doctor uttered those few words. It was for all the world as though some master switch had been thrown, thus immediately reenergizing countless memory cells in one sudden cascade of neurological energy. I could now recall events of the previous night: the Blenheim on the perimeter track; the smell of petrol and hot exhaust fumes; the toiling walk up through the trees to my hut; the last look around before I entered my room and how the moon's silvery disc had suddenly appeared and had spilled bright, revealing light over the silent, sleeping clearing. I remembered even further back: the flight to Indo-China; the Japanese engineer; the flight to Kuala Lumpur and my discussion with the two men in white and what we had talked about.

I thought of how, less than twenty-four hours ago, I had been, though physically and mentally exhausted, a fit and healthy and normal person. But now I had been transformed, as though by some bizarre evil metamorphosis, from the person I was of yesterday into another self of today. My world had changed, and, through all my pain and travail, I was filled with revulsion at the act that had been carried out by the Japanese without provocation or warning: How could they just come along and kill and mutilate their fellow men and leave innocent and unsuspecting souls to endure agonies of pain and everlasting hopelessness and misery?

And then there was the sadness that accompanied the terrible realization that life as I had known it had probably gone forever. The expectancy of good times to come, the fun and the excitement and anticipation, the planning for the future and all the things that drive a young person on. These things were now all gone—all torn away in a fraction of a second, and replaced by disability, pain, and suffering.

And from out of the sadness were burgeoning the first roots of bitterness—a bitterness that was destined to stay within me long into the future.

Afternoon came and the ward became even hotter and more humid. The continuing reek of chloroform filled the stifling atmosphere. The cries and pleadings of agonized despairing voices issued from behind those screened-off beds of misery and fear, and, through the airless sultry gloom of it all, stole the first distant rumble of thunder.

The morphine had worn off again. The pain, frightful and all-consuming, was so awful that it became impossible for me even to moan in that to do so only caused more pain. I was aware that I was awash with perspiration and that I was trembling; and I was conscious of my heart beating swiftly but weakly, my breathing rapid and shallow.

A Chinese nursing orderly offered me water, tepid and tasteless. He came again a few moments later accompanied by the Sikh doctor who lifted my eyelids, then used his stethoscope on my chest. "He is in great pain," he said.

The thunderstorm broke. Rain pounded down on the roof and cascaded past the wide-open shutters with a tremendous roar; then the Sikh came with his syringe. I felt myself sinking down into a dark, comfortable world where all sounds gradually became hushed and soothing, and my pains faded until I could no longer feel them. My eyes remained half open even though I was drifting in my own delicious haven of peace. Then I heard the Sikh's voice again—from, it seemed, a million miles away—a voice that at first I recognized but which quickly became distorted and hysterically insistent. "The Japanese bombed Singapore and Hawaii!" it shrieked.

And in my mind I heard myself shout back, "I knew they would—I warned those men in Kuala Lumpur!" I heard my words, angry, loud, bitter, and protesting. But, in reality, perhaps it was that I made no sound at all.

13

Hell Trains and Hospitals

Evening, Monday, 8 December

Long, dark shapes moved slowly back and forth against a snow-white background. I watched as they silently advanced and receded, drifting in and out of my vision but gradually becoming clearer.

Then one of the dark shapes loomed over and spoke to me. "You go on train tonight. First in ambulance—then on train. You go south, away from fighting."

The talking shape came into focus. It was the face of a Malay nursing orderly. My mind tore itself away from the comforting embrace of morphine and started to think. Reawakened awareness of my predicament brought with it a bombarding confusion of anger, bitterness, revulsion, and helplessness. Outside it had become dark and the time was, therefore, some time after 7:30 P.M.

They took me by ambulance to Sungei Patani railway station and put me aboard a train bound for I knew not where. On the train I was conscious of very little apart from there being a line of bunks along each side of a saloon coach. The coach had only a few dim lamps, owing, doubtless, to blackout restrictions. The windows were wide open.

The train pulled away from the station at around 10:00 P.M. and laboriously gathered speed with much clattering and juddering, the racket of wheel on rail adding yet another fearsome dimension to the sheer torture of it all. Nothing existed for me now but noise and pain, the jolting, the shouts and pleadings of other patients—and loathsome drifting stenches. I was deeply into a never-ending, fearsome nightmare—adrift in an eternity of baleful horrors.

The dreadful sleep of delirium began to steal over me. Visions and images drifted and darted and rushed and spun in a devastating tormenting pur-gatory to the accompaniment of horrifying, demented noises. It was during a brief period of lucidity, when the train was stationary, that I saw the face of an old Chinese woman at the open window alongside my bunk. She was wearing a battered Salvation Army bonnet and looked as old as the hills. She brought her face to within a couple of feet and looked at me for a moment or two; then she said, in perfectly understandable English, "God bless you, my son." Then she withdrew back into the shadows. The memory of that brief incident, so unexpected in the middle of the night and the prevailing cir-cumstances, has remained with me over the years.

At one time I became vaguely aware of pressure on my abdomen and I felt liquid on my lips and the pool of molten metal under my buttocks. There came a short series of blows to my arm and the sharp prick of a needle. Slowly the agonies and discomforts and delirious imaginings departed from me. And, as I lay there deeply drugged, the train continued to pick its way ever southwards down the peninsula.

Tuesday, 9 December

I came to my senses to find that the blackness of night had given way to the first translucent mistiness of early dawn. Gusts of air were still rushing over me, warm and now laden with the smell of rain and vegetation. I lay resting, relieved at being free from delirium and all the manic frightfulness that the night had brought. A person immediately opposite me had one of his legs in plaster up to the hip. Blood-soaked gauze protruded from the upper end of the plaster. He appeared to be asleep, his unshaven and incredibly gaunt face glistening with droplets of perspiration. Then I saw that his other leg was missing, there being just a heavily bandaged short stump. The cotton wool and windings of the dressing shined with fresh wet blood. Another bunk held someone whose chest, abdomen, and arms all had the appearance of blackened, glistening crust. The body lay quite still. These were just two

of those whose voices, during the long night of horrors, I had heard feverishly pleading and imploring.

The train rattled into the small station of Tanjong Malim, a small village
I had passed through on my way up north to Sungei Patani back in late
September, and jerked abruptly to a halt.

The freshness of dawn, with its agreeable smells of warmth and dampness, blended with the fragrance of flowers and fruit and woodsmoke that
I may well have found uplifting under more merciful circumstances. But I
had been totally drained of fortitude and resilience, having endured ten or
more hours in a kind of blacked-out torture chamber.

They took me off the train. I was able to reason out that it had taken around
ten hours to travel something like 160 miles. Then there was an ambulance,
one of several, and Indian army stretcher-bearers. Then a hospital, old and
grim, and they carried me onto a veranda on which there was a line of empty
beds. I was left on one of the beds, feeling horribly sick and thirsty.

The hospital appeared to be no larger than the average-sized Victorian
detached house. An hour or two passed before I was taken up a winding
staircase to a ward above. The ward had about six beds along each side of
its length. It was a small ward with high shuttered windows and a few slowly turning propeller fans high up in the ceiling. There was a lot of noise, clattering and crashing, urgent conversation, the hurried footfalls of medical
staff, and the unsettling shouts and groans of the wounded. The heavy and
sickly-sweet smell of chloroform filled the air as a couple of doctors administered this crude anesthetic to patients undergoing emergency surgery. I
could see no sign of the two casualties who had lain opposite me on the hell
train. A few days later I learned that they had both expired directly after they
had been taken from the train. It took some time for me to get it out of my
head that these two RAF airmen, injured at Alor Star airfield, twenty miles
north of Sungei Patani, had probably breathed their last while lying on the
railway station platform, in the early morning light, surrounded by the colorful brightness of hibiscus and bougainvillea.

I spent the rest of the hot morning enduring pain and in a state of bewilderment. There were moments when I remembered those sensations of profound foreboding that had often swept over me at Sungei Patani, and it seemed
to me that my present state was simply a continuation of that experience—an
experience that surely had been a kind of shadowy and melancholy fore-
warning of things shortly to happen. My vague anxieties and depressions had
been the outcome of my instinctive feelings and growing suspicion that RAF

officialdom was probably incapable of recognizing and assessing the Japanese threat or of dealing effectively with any attack that might be made by Japan. In the few days preceding Japan's attack I had, of course, been in possession of information which, naturally, had only served to heighten my anxieties, something that I had been powerless to do anything about. It all amounted to the fact that I had not only sensed but had virtually known what was about to happen; yet I had little suspected what the outcome for me would be.

They injected more morphine and I watched the revolving blades of a ceiling fan as they caught the sun and shot bright flashes of light in my direction. My discomforts faded, and I watched as hail beat on the grass of an airfield. I watched a Hudson landing amid a tremendous spray of glistening rainwater. And I watched a perspiring, strong-jawed Oriental point excitedly at a little map and then confidentially mouth the strange-sounding word, "Purhabba." The visions receded and in their place appeared nothing that I could recognize, or even wished to recognize. I just felt infinitely tired and comfortable and sleepy. I descended into yet another prolonged narcotic stupor.

Thursday, 11 December

Still in the hospital at Tanjong Malim my condition had miraculously improved to the extent that I had largely recovered from the initial shock of my injuries. The general pain associated with massive wrenching and bruising had greatly reduced. However, my back pain, although that expression hardly conveys the extent of torment involved, remained with me. I had received no medical treatment other than basic attention to my open wounds, these having been redressed from time to time. I had been catheterized according to need and the availability of a doctor, the procedure usually being carried out two or three hours after my initial call for relief. I had not yet been thoroughly examined with a view to the extent of my injuries being determined, neither had I been X-rayed. I had been informed, but only in a casual way, by one of the nursing orderlies, that I now had a bladder infection—apparently always a continuing and serious risk associated with urinary catheterization. I had eaten absolutely nothing since being injured, on account of the ongoing nausea, the pain, and the almost continual stupefying effects of morphine. But my spirit had, to a certain extent, returned, and I was now occasionally able to pay attention to things that were going on around me. At any time I expected to hear that the Japanese had been sent packing and that things were rapidly getting back to normal. It even occurred to me that perhaps my injuries might not be as serious as I had at first thought, and that, in a few weeks' time, after a period of treatment and convalescence, I would be fit enough to return to Sungei Patani and resume my life as it had been. I was not to know that destiny had already ruled this out.

I heard that during the previous day, 10 December, the two British naval ships, *Prince of Wales* and *Repulse,* had been attacked and sunk off the east coast of Malaya by Japanese torpedo planes. This had made no real impression on me on account of the effects of the morphine. The sinking of these two capital ships amounted to a major calamity—a tragedy that one reads about to this day with a mixture of poignant sadness and incredulity.[1]

There had also been talk about the attack on Hawaii where, apparently, the U.S. naval base at Pearl Harbor had been subjected to a two-hour air attack carried out by several hundred carrier-based Japanese naval aircraft. In my comatose state, the snatches I heard about Pearl Harbor became, in a way, blended with my recollections in relation to my recent flight to Indo-China and to the subsequent one to Kuala Lumpur. Thus I was not in the slightest surprised by what I heard. It was rather like listening to a story I had heard before. To me it was not news—it was more like seeing a film I had watched being made.[2]

Word had been going around about the continued bombing of RAF airfields by Japanese aircraft and of Japanese troops landing at Kota Bharu. I also learned that Japan had now formally declared war on Great Britain and the United States, and that the latter two had declared war on Japan. The news could hardly have been worse. The northern leased territories of Hong Kong had been attacked and much ground captured by the Japanese. Hong Kong Island had been subjected to frequent air attacks and shelling, though it had been virtually unable to retaliate. Several RAF airfields in northern Malaya had been completely evacuated, including Sungei Patani, Alor Star, Kota Bharu, Machang, Gong Kedah, and Kuantan.[3] The Japanese were in possession of the airfield at Kota Bharu and were already using it as a refueling station for their bombers and fighters. Japanese troops had crossed the Siamese border and were now driving southwards through inexperienced and bewildered Punjabi forces. Japan had bombed the U.S. Philippines and landed troops at strategic points there.

It all seemed incredible. Things had moved so rapidly. Yet I could not, in my mind, accept that the British would not retaliate in a really big way. What I could not know, however, was that the air defense strength of Malaya and Singapore had already been so badly crippled that it was well beyond recovery—after only slightly more than two days the combined RAF and RAAF air forces had been reduced to pathetic remnants.[4] Here there were no

Hurricanes or Spitfires, as in the Battle of Britain of 1940, to clear the skies of Japanese bombers. By comparison, the lumbering Buffalo fighters were curious, impotent relics, which even the most courageous and competent of pilots—and it turned out there were quite a few—found next to useless against Japanese fighters. And in place of the blue skies of a beautiful English summer there were, here in Malaya, towering dark thunderclouds and torrential rain through which Japanese bombers could fly for hours on end with little fear of being seen, let alone intercepted, by the struggling, wallowing, ill-armed Buffaloes.

I was awakened at 3:00 A.M. the following morning to be told that I was going to be taken, along with a few other patients, down to Johore Bahru in southern Malaya, and that the train would depart from Tanjong Malim at 7:00 A.M.

Friday, 12 December

It took seven hours for the train to travel the two hundred miles to Johore Bahru. It stopped frequently and, at Kuala Lumpur, remained stationary for upwards of an hour. Inside the coach were fellow patients, none of whom I knew. The most harrowing sights were two burn cases, neither of whom could lie on account of their horrific burns. They had each been secured, in a sitting position, with bandages tied to timber uprights wedged between floor and ceiling. All they could do was sit and loll in the position in which they had been left. Each had burns to the back and chest. One also had burns to his face, arms, and hands. He had no lips. One of his eyes was part of the overall blackened facial crust. His remaining bright blue eye stared and stared because it had no lid. Now and again, in an instinctive movement, one of his cindered hands would come up and attempt to wipe the eye. It was quite impossible to judge his age. He could have been any age, but it is likely he was in his twenties. The card around his neck gave his name and rank—Sergeant something—a Scottish name. During the journey, with the sun pouring through the windows and the whole coach like a diabolic furnace, this tortured soul sank lower and lower in his constraining bandages until, after a sudden nerve-racking shriek of agonized protest and hopelessness, he collapsed into stony silence. The passage of many long years has failed to eradicate from my memory the sight of that poor doomed creature secured to a length of timber alongside me, his exposed teeth seemingly fixed in a dreadful grin and his one poor eye occasionally looking at me with, I fancied, an expression of infinite pleading and puzzlement.

In the early afternoon I was carried into the hospital at Johore Bahru which, as I would learn a few days later, was a brand-new, substantial, red-brick, multistory affair.

14 Slipping Away in Johore Bharu

My stay at the General Hospital in Johore Bharu lasted approximately five weeks. Although the place had been built for civilian use, it had been agreed that one wing, as yet unused, should be taken over by the military.[1] Everything was new, the ward beautifully clean and bright. The two surgeons and the senior nurses were members of the Royal Army Medical Service. There were also a number of Chinese and Eurasian female nursing assistants and two or three British civilian ladies acting as voluntary general untrained helpers. I can remember only three names. Major Max Pemberton and Captain Cameron were the two surgeons. Nurse Nicholls, a delicious café-au-lait skinned beauty of about twenty, with curiously attractive protruding front teeth, was a locally born assistant nurse. Years later, I would find out that Major Pemberton was, at the time, just thirty years of age and was the senior surgeon of the Royal Army Medical Service in Malaya. He would later spend three and a half years as a prisoner of the Japanese, running makeshift hospitals on the infamous Burma Railway. I have no certain knowledge of what became of Captain Cameron, and the last time I saw

Nurse Nicholls was aboard a riverboat in Singapore docks two days before the island surrendered to the Japanese.

The day after my arrival at the hospital I was thoroughly X-rayed. The general findings were much as I had suspected. Fractures included the lower jaw, left elbow, right ankle, the pelvis and sacrum, the latter being the large triangular shaped bone at the base of the spine. It was assumed that a lot of nerve damage had been caused as a result of my having received a heavy blow to the lower spine, thus giving rise to the numbness in certain areas, my inability to pass water, and the fact that my bowels had apparently ceased to function. Such wounds that I had received were of minor importance compared with all the rest of it. I was, at last, suitably strapped up and bandaged, though nothing was done with regard to the spinal injury, which, apart from the neurological deficiencies mentioned, continued to cause me terrible pain, so much so that I was now kept more or less in a state of seminarcosis during the day and in full narcotic unconsciousness at night. Due to constant nausea, I could eat nothing and tried to drink as little as possible in an attempt to keep the need for catheterization to a minimum. The logic behind this being simply that such catheterization was always carried out far too late and that each day there would be at least two periods when, while urgently needing to be catheterized, I would be compelled to wait for hours in an excruciating agony of pain. It did not help, in a psychological sense, to know that it was merely damage to perhaps just one minutely thin nerve fiber that prevented things from functioning normally, and, instead, gave rise to intolerable anguish.

I have memories of a gramophone and of the way two records were played in preference to all others. I came to loath them because their repetitive music had the effect of intensifying my mental suffering. One of these was "Waltzing Matilda," on the other side of which was the curious song, "Waiti Poi." Both were sung by the one-time-famous baritone Peter Dawson. The other record, played around twenty times each day, was "The Last Time I Saw Paris." To this day, whenever I hear any one of those songs I am immediately spirited off to that hospital in Malaya, with all the dreary regrets and connotations that evokes.

A few days before Christmas I suffered a series of those devastating "retention of urine" agonies. Because the procedure could only be carried out by either of the two surgeons, and because they were both usually busy in the operating theater now that new patients were being brought in at an increasing rate, I was kept waiting for attention for even longer than usual.

WOUNDED IN MALAYA

The parents of Peter John Shepherd, of 15, St. Agnes Road, Doncaster, have been informed that he has been seriously wounded in Malaya while serving as an aircraftman. It was one of the early Japanese raids on Malaya. He had been there some months.

An old Doncaster Technical College boy, Peter, who is 18, joined the R.A.F. as an aircraft apprentice at the age of 15½ immediately on leaving school, and is now an AC1 fitter. For many years he was a member of the Balby St. John's Scout troop.

A clipping from the *Doncaster Chronicle* (January 1942) in which the author is reported as having been injured while serving with the RAF in Malaya.

On the final occasion I became so demented with pain that I cried out for assistance to any passing nurse—not one cry but several over the next two hours or so. When I was eventually catheterized, the urine that drained away was bright red in color, a certain indication that I was hemorrhaging from either the kidneys or the bladder owing to rupture of the tissues, itself due to an unsustainable buildup of internal pressure. In the middle of the night that followed I was taken down to the operating theater. I woke next morning, back in the ward, infinitely weak and, as usual, heavily sedated. A substantial rubber tube protruded from a hole in my lower abdomen. They rigged up a blood-transfusion drip, cutting down to a vein in my right arm in which to insert the glass canula. Then came the rigor—coldness and uncontrollable shivering—and a priest in his black and purple robe. He stayed with me for a long time. He did not speak, but merely sat, alternately looking into my face and praying with his head down. The following morning there was another transfusion, and another bout of shivering; and the priest joined me again. I was too weak even to close my eyelids. Nor could I speak.

A few days later, I think it was Boxing Day, the matron was able to get through to me that a telegram had been sent to my father in England informing him that I had been wounded. What she did not tell me was that the telegram simply stated that I had received injuries to the chin and back and that my condition was critical. My father was able to show me the telegram eighteen months later. He heard nothing more about me until I turned up in the British General Hospital in Karachi in March the following year.

During all this time, that is, from the day I received my injuries, not one representative of the RAF came to visit me. It was as though as far as the RAF was concerned I had ceased to exist. I had lost all my possessions and all my clothing; my watch had disappeared and so had that wad of hard-earned Malay five-dollar notes. I had been totally severed from my past way of life and with no official or even unofficial letter or message of goodwill or sympathy sent to me.

By the second week in January the fighting up in north Malaya was still continuing, and although I was unable to have any deep interest in the details as they became known, it was manifest that Japanese forces were progressing rapidly down the Malayan peninsula. In fact, apart from the now almost daily bombing of Singapore Island, Japanese troops and tanks had taken Ipoh, Tanjong Malim, and Kuala Lumpur. British North Borneo had been invaded and the majority of oil wells there had been captured. Japan could now replenish its oil stocks from this source and at any moment start to bomb Singapore from a secure airfield in southern Sarawak only 350 miles away.

I had recovered from the hemorrhage crisis, but I was still declining, being riddled with infection and unable to eat. I just lay, day after sweltering day, occasionally watching what went on in the ward, but mostly drifting in and out of drugged sleep, and attempting to blank out "Waltzing Matilda" whenever it became unendurable. The only antibiotic available was sulfonamide, a variant of which, sulpha-diazole, I was obliged to drink three times a day. It was, as far as I recall, of little help to me; in fact, many years later, I read that this particular drug had proved to be dangerous to some in that, used incautiously, it was prone to cause fatal kidney damage.

15 Tragedy and Exodus

Japanese troops had advanced so far down the peninsula that on or about 18 January 1942 the task of evacuating patients from the hospital began. I was taken to Singapore in an ambulance at midnight. I recall the journey very well. It took about forty-five minutes. I also remember the ambulance pulling up under the portico at the main entrance of what turned out to be Singapore General Hospital.

I was placed on a bed in a ground-floor ward adjacent to the main entrance. It was hot and smelly and filled to overflowing with wounded servicemen. Over the next three and a half weeks I continued to lie and wait. I received no remedial treatment whatsoever. Supplies of morphine had all but run out, and patients were having to make do with such things as aspirin, phenacetin, and codeine. I spent the first week coping with withdrawal symptoms in addition to my other discomforts.

The hospital was, I found out, about half a mile from Keppel Harbor and the docks, which meant that it fell within the general target area whenever the harbor was being bombed—an almost daily occurrence and frequently during the night. The main railway station was just a quarter of a mile away and lay between the hospital and the docks. Air-raid sirens sounded off at any time. In the end it was rare for the all-clear to be sounded and, in effect, the island was under continual alert. The noise of exploding bombs was daunting and terrifying. Almost as bad were the ear-splitting reports of the several 4.5-inch antiaircraft guns that were evidently positioned not very far from the hospital. It was impossible to judge whether a particular crash was an exploding bomb or a shell being blasted several thousand feet into the sky.

Civilian casualties were now being brought into the ward that had hitherto accommodated service wounded only. They were laid on mattresses set directly on the floor. It became almost impossible for staff to squeeze through the terrible collection of beds and mattresses, each with its severely injured patient. Only the worst cases were being brought into hospital, less urgent cases being accommodated in schools and other public buildings around the city.

Word went round on 2 February that all British troops had been withdrawn across the causeway from Malaya to Singapore Island. Even this news failed to frighten me because I still felt certain, rather than just hopeful, that reinforcements would arrive at any moment and that the Japanese invaders would be repulsed. Such optimism sprung, of course, from my youth but was very much ill-conceived. Within a few days it became known by all who were capable of grasping the situation that Japanese heavy guns had begun to shell the island. On 8 February Japanese troops landed on the north coast, having crossed the Johore Strait by all conceivable means (many in fact actually swam across the half-mile-wide water obstacle), the causeway, with its road and railway line having been dynamited by retreating Australian troops. The Japanese were now opposed by a massive concentration of British and Australian forces, all compressed on the relatively small island. It was difficult to imagine how the invading troops could make any further progress against this multitude of defenders. But the island's air defenses were now, to all intents and purposes, finished. Even fifty-one Hurricanes, which had arrived in crates by ship in mid-January, and which had been assembled at RAF Seletar, mainly by ex-Halton apprentices, had been decimated either through combat loss or by bombing.[1] The RAF airfield at Kallang, less than a mile from Raffles Hotel on the east side of the city, was now a favorite target for enemy bombers in that the few remaining serviceable Hurricanes mainly operated from there. Every so often I would hear the encouraging sound of a Merlin engine as a Hurricane sped over the hospital. Much of the news was beyond me at the time, although I was able to comprehend the general gist. Being still very much on the downward slope inasmuch as I was receiving nourishment in liquid form only, it was impossible for me to become too worked up about things. I felt sure that in a few days time reinforcements would arrive and push the Japanese back into Malaya. Failing that, Japanese troops would fight their way into the town and then Singapore would be entirely taken over, British resistance at an end.

The general atmosphere was something that cannot easily be imagined or described. Uncertainty and hopelessness went unsaid. Bitterness and fear showed in the faces of ward staff. Hysteria accompanied the terrified civilian visitors who now came in at virtually any time to see their friends and relatives, Malays, Chinese, and Indians, all lying on floor mattresses. There was a lot of rain and thunder, especially in the afternoons and early evenings. It was suffocatingly hot and oppressive, and a dismal and somber atmosphere gripped the overflowing ward. It was a deeply melancholy place, and would have been even without the casualties that lay in there. Heavy rain and thick cloud failed to prevent the bombing. Often, the crash of bombs and the tremendous reports of heavy antiaircraft guns would join with thunder to create a living hell. From time to time the lighting would fail and then the ward would be left in gloomy half-light for an hour or more while Japanese planes continued to bomb indiscriminately.

Wednesday, 11 February 1942

On this day an incident occurred that, I have always felt, marked for me the beginning of the final phase of events in Singapore.

At around 9:00 A.M. an Indian doctor came to my bed. He was accompanied by a Malay nurse whom I had never before seen in the ward. She was tall and wore a white nurse's smock and a white head covering low over her forehead. She was very slim and her taut features showed her tiredness and anxiety. The doctor pulled down my bedsheet, exposing my entirely naked body with its dressed wounds and the half-inch diameter drainage tube that protruded from my lower abdomen and led to a urine bottle tied to my bedside.

The doctor spoke to the nurse. "This patient has a spinal injury. This tube is a supra-pubic urine catheter. The wound is a little infected and needs irrigating. When the sister is free, you must tell her that this must be done." He turned and squeezed his way from my bed, leaving the nurse to rearrange my sheet.

She leaned over the bed to draw up the sheet, and for a brief moment I noticed her studying my face intently. Then she lifted her eyes and looked at the name card hanging at the head of the bed, as if to confirm that which she already half-suspected. I saw the sudden expression of dawning recognition on her face as she read my name, and it was in that moment that I, too, recognized *her*. She looked older, and the girlish, light-hearted joyousness that had been there when last I saw her had been displaced by an air of deep apprehension. She caught her breath, for a fraction of a second, and just the merest hint of a frightened, embarrassed smile appeared on her lips. Then her eyes filled with tears.

It is beyond my ability to describe the emotions I felt in the split second that I realized I was looking at Wan, the girl I had met in Penang. Surprise, heartfelt joy, happiness, regret, and sadness were all instantly there in a be-wildering clutter that swept over me and left me broken. Even as I said, "Hello, Wan," through my now almost-healed lips but still hurtful jaw, I saw her lips tremble.

Then she spoke; it was the first time I had heard her voice since that Sunday afternoon at Springtide many weeks earlier. "Hello, Peter." She spoke her words weakly and hesitantly as though still hardly believing it was me she was looking at. Then she asked, "What happen, Peter?" Her face was a picture of concern and heartbreak.

Over the next two or three minutes I explained as well as I could what had happened to me. I also told her why I had been unable to see her again in Penang as arranged, and how I had worried myself sick about it. I explained why I had not telephoned or sent her a letter and how angry I had felt at not being able to see her again. Then the thought occurred to me that she must have failed to recognize me straightaway on account of my present run-down appearance. I knew that I looked terrible, my hair long and unkempt, my face unshaven for more than a week, my features pale as death, gaunt and hollow-eyed. Yet after the first minute or so Wan seemed not to notice any of this. She explained to me that she and her friend had waited for me at the Springtide Hotel until, by the end of the afternoon, they had concluded that I would not be coming. She had been saddened and had briefly thought of writing to me but had lacked the courage. Also, she explained, she had not known my full name with certainty and had been unsure as to how to address the letter anyway. She had been training at this hospital for some months but had only today been transferred to this particular ward. We chatted urgently for two or three minutes, and then she had to go.

In the mid-morning Wan returned along with one of the Indian sisters. Together they did what was necessary for me. Wan tidied things up and managed to spend another couple of minutes with me before her duties called her away. During the rest of the day I could only watch as she went about her work in the ward. Frequently she waved to me and smiled joylessly and wistfully. On several occasions, when the "danger imminent" whistles were sounded, she and all other staff would leave the ward in order to take shelter.

Wan went off duty at about 10:00 P.M. but came to see me before leaving. She looked totally worn out, having been at work in the hospital since 7:00 A.M. We exchanged very few words on account of my sickly languor, her own exhaustion, and the sense of heavy apprehension and hopelessness that invaded all and everything. At one point she asked, "What we do, Peter, when Japanese in Singapore?"

"I think everything will be all right," I replied. "After a few days, if the British stop fighting, things will settle down. There'll be no more shelling and bombing. In a way things will be better than now. I don't think you need to be frightened, Wan." I had, of course, not the slightest idea what things would be like if the defending forces were to surrender Singapore to the Japanese, but I certainly never imagined that the conquering Japanese troops, if in fact it should come to that, would proceed to conduct themselves in any way other than with well-disciplined civility and courtesy, qualities for which, I had been taught at school, their race was noted. Even allowing for a bit of high-handedness and ill-mannered behavior here and there, things ought not to turn out too badly for either prisoners of war or members of the general population. At the time, of course, I had no idea of Japanese ways in the role of conqueror, nor for that matter had millions of others throughout South East Asia.

Thursday, 12 February

Wan came on duty again at 7:00 A.M. It was still dark and raining heavily. Within the ward conditions were terrible. The lying and waiting, not knowing what was going to happen next, being unable to get off the bed, or even discuss the situation in an informed way with anyone, all left me intolerably anxious and frustrated.

But, of course, I was not alone. In the ward were probably fifty other casualties, on beds, on floor mattresses, some motionless, some crying out in pain, others shouting out for attention. Throughout the entire ward were abject misery and wretchedness. I thought how unfairly the fates had treated me at this late stage; I had now been at the hospital for something like three weeks and during all this time Wan had been working in a nearby ward, yet I had not known. Whenever the opportunity arose she smiled and waved to me and, later, we were able to talk for a while when she attended to some of my surgical dressings and that of a very young Malay boy of about nine or ten, one of whose legs had been amputated a couple of days earlier. He had been a victim of bombing, yet seemed amazingly unconcerned about what had happened to him. He just lay on his floor mattress at the foot of my bed, his hugely bandaged stump propped up on a small cardboard box. I can picture his face to this day, sometimes bewildered, sometimes frightened, but on the whole remarkably nonchalant considering his predicament. He lessened his bouts of unease by consuming large quantities of star-fruit that his many relatives and friends brought in for him.

In the afternoon Wan told me she had heard that a merchant ship heavily loaded with RAF personnel had left Singapore early that morning. Eighteen months later, George, who had been with me at Sungei Patani and had joined with me in sampling the delights of Penang, told me that he had been one of those on board. The ship was the *Empire Star.*[2] It had been bombed several times shortly after leaving Singapore. The word was that there were no RAF planes left to continue the job of harassing the Japanese. From this information I assumed, with substantial accuracy as it happened, that the RAF had flown its last sortie and had departed en-block from Singapore. In reality a small number of RAF personnel found themselves, for one reason or another, left behind on the island and these unfortunates subsequently used every conceivable means to get away. Inevitably some failed in the attempt.

The noise of heavy gunfire and exploding shells confirmed that the fighting was now closer to the town. The afternoon darkened early and it rained steadily for a couple of hours. Everything fell quiet around 7:00 P.M. I had the chilling feeling that at any moment a Japanese soldier might appear at the shuttered opening alongside the head of my bed. I wondered what I should do if this were to come about.

Wan came over to my bed again before going off duty. "I see you in ten minutes, Peter," she said. Then, before I could reply, she squeezed her way through the beds to the door.

When she returned—it would by then have been 9:30 P.M.—she was dressed in an ankle-length skirt and a jacket, both of finely and intricately embroidered silk material. In the bright coloring of this attire she stood out in the drab and gloomy misery of the ward. Her head was covered by a white square. Despite her great tiredness she was almost once again the Wan I had first met at Springtide, on the island of Penang. For some reason it occurred to me that she must have brought her colorful outfit to the hospital just so that she could for the last time dress up for my benefit before the Japanese descended on us. It was a saddening thought and one that brought me even deeper heartache. She sat on the edge of the bed. "Tomorrow," she said, "I give you picture and my address. If any problem with Japanese you write me letter some time." She gazed at me with a soulful look in her eyes, then I felt her hand on mine. Without thinking, I entwined my fingers in hers and smiled what I imagine can only have been a wistful smile.

"Yes, Wan," I replied, "and you can write my home address down, too—in case I have to leave Singapore before I'm able to tell you."

"Maybe," she said, "we can meet again in Penang when you better and fighting is finished."

I could not see how that was ever likely to be possible, but nevertheless I replied, "Yes, that would be wonderful. One day, some time, I'll write to you and arrange for us to meet on the beach at Springtide. When I do, Wan, will you promise to be there? I would just want to walk along the beach and see you coming down from the hotel—rather like it was on that Sunday morning in November when we first met."

She smiled tearfully, and her lips trembled. "Okay, Peter," she breathed. "I be there—I promise. Anytime—one year—two year—many year—I promise."

"But you might be married, Wan," I ventured.

She replied in the only way it is possible for a very young girl who fancies she is in love to reply. "I not marry, Peter. I not marry until. . . ." Her voice trailed off. "I wait at Springtide for you—always."

And then it was time for her to go. She collected her few things together and gave me another of her sad smiles, but then stood as though waiting for something—reluctant to leave.

"I'll see you tomorrow morning," I said, "and please be careful."

"Yes." Wan replied, "about eight o'clock I see you."

"Goodnight, Wan."

"Goodbye, Peter"

She pushed her way toward the doorway and, among the people gathered there, she turned around and waved—an almost slow-motion wave that instantly awoke in me the memory of the wave she had given when George and I had departed from Springtide in that rickshaw almost three months ago. I waved back to her. Then she disappeared.

I slept very little, but toward dawn I fell into a worrisome and restless sleep from which I was awakened by a kind of instinctive fear. I immediately heard the sound of falling bombs. A sound that began as an almost imperceptible whistle of escaping steam that swiftly increased in intensity over three seconds or so until it took on the sound of a hurtling high-speed train. A series of terrific explosions was instantly followed by the sickening, heavy, progressive rumble of collapsing masonry—a noise that carried with it the hideous message that, almost certainly, innocent humans were being crushed and buried alive under tons of debris.

There were fifteen seconds or so of eerie silence. Then the "danger imminent" whistles began shrilling out. It must have been a full minute later that the air-raid sirens at last began sounding out their dreaded wailing alert. Then I heard the bells of approaching ambulances.

It was 7:45 A.M.—daylight, and with just the slightest movement of warm air at the shutters. There were no lights in the ward. The ceiling fans had stopped revolving.

Friday, 13 February

At about 9:00 A.M. one of the Indian doctors informed me that I was to be evacuated by sea during the morning but that first it would be necessary for me to be taken to the operating theater for my drainage tube to be changed. I would be taken straight from the theater to an ambulance that would then take me to the nearby docks.

They changed my tube while I was almost fully conscious even though I had received an injection of sodium-pentothal that presumably should have knocked me out. I found myself lying on a wheeled stretcher in a corridor. A few feet away the sun was shining dazzlingly through a wide open doorway. Two Chinese girls, nurses, ran through the doorway and into the corridor. One of them glanced at me as she passed by. She stopped and came back, clearly having recognized me.

"What you doing?" she asked breathlessly.

Still bemused by the effects of the anesthetic, I mumbled, "Leaving. Going on ship—somewhere."

"When?" she asked, and I was getting the impression that she was ill at ease.

"Now—I think—this morning," I replied drowsily. Then I thought of something. "Wan—I must see Wan—before I go. Ask her—come see me now please." I closed my eyes and drifted away in a warm, dazzling soft cloud.

Then I drifted back again and the nurse was shaking my arm. She was looking down into my face and speaking, her clipped staccato words filled with great urgency. "I know Wan your good friend. Sorry—very sorry. Wan hurt in bombing today—she hurt badly."

My brain struggled with what she had said but I was still too far gone to fully grasp her meaning.

"But Wan see me soon—tell her please," I remember saying, yet with a growing awareness that there was something horrible I was not understanding. I struggled to focus my thoughts.

The nurse looked away as though desperately seeking an excuse to leave at once. Then she burst into tears and her Chinese features crumpled up pitifully. "Wan not come anymore. She not come ever—it not possible—I very sorry." She let out an unsuppressed wail of utter anguish and, head down, ran off down the corridor. But suddenly she stopped and turned, her tearful face a picture of frantic despair. "Wan dead!" she screamed, and her voice carried in it all her terrible misery and bitterness. "Wan no come again—she dead now!"

Another anguished wail reached my ears—a wail that echoed back and forth along the length of the corridor. Then she turned again and resumed her headlong dash toward the horrors of the wards.

The sun shone mercilessly through the open doorway, bathing me with hot, brilliant light. I could still hear the nurse's final crying words, but although my mind had grasped a little of the meaning of her words, the full pungency of her stark message had not yet completely registered on my stupefied senses. I lay there, in the sunshine, on my own, still waiting but with the growing uneasy feeling that something baleful and awful had transpired—something that, for the time being, I could not bother to think about.

Two Indian army stretcher bearers put me in an ambulance. The journey to the docks, through streets piled with debris, took about ten minutes. I was removed from the ambulance without delay and was able to take reasonable stock of the scene. The sky was deep bright blue and clear of cloud, although patches of black and dark-grey smoke drifted here and there over and around the town. The blazing sun, now almost overhead, drenched the dockside with blinding light and heat. The quayside was thick with people, most of them military types, RAF, army and navy, but there were, too, dense surging groups of civilians, mainly men, in white duck suits and solar topis, clutching hand luggage and all looking as though negotiating and bargaining for a place on the diminutive paddle riverboat tied up alongside and already so deep in the water that the gangplank, instead of sloping upwards toward the boat, lay virtually horizontal. I could hear the sound of heavy gunfire coming from the north of the city. Enemy planes had the sky to themselves and every so often the crash and blast of exploding bombs broke in on the intensely urgent buzz of conversation going on all around. The whole scene, even to me in my semidrugged state, was one of hopeless desperation and pitiful sadness—for what I was witnessing was a seething mass of British subjects clamoring to get away from Singapore. After around one hundred years in the role of virtual ruler of Singapore and Malaya, the British were hastening away from these hitherto greatly prized and happy lands—in fact, they were literally being driven into the sea at the culmination of a campaign that had lasted little more than nine weeks. On this sunflooded quayside was a cross-section of members of the British military together with civilian advisors and administrators, all gathered in a baffling and lamentable display of hopeless defeat. Some would escape, but there would be many who, along with well over one hundred thousand army personnel now fighting a lost battle on the outskirts of Singapore town, would be left behind to experience the as-yet-unsuspected style of Japanese chivalry and mercy.

As I was carried across the gangway to the boat, I noticed the name displayed on its hull. It was a name that has doubtless been long remembered by many—*Wu Seuh*.[3] I also noticed a group of male civilian Europeans gathered in a tight cluster at the outboard end of the gangplank, in heated argument with members of the military police and a couple of naval officers. I especially noticed one of the civilians, for, as I was carried past him, his gaze fell on me. I had seen that gaze before, but in a different world. I had seen it in a dimly lit hut in a rubber plantation; I had seen it on a dark, water-logged airfield; I has seen it in a hothouse of an office on an aerodrome at Kuala Lumpur; and I had sensed it going straight through me as I had listened to a voice saying, "Remember, Shepherd, not a word to anyone about any of this." The pale blue eyes raked me from head to toe and finally came to rest on my face, yet not the slightest hint of recognition appeared in them—just, I fancied, the merest flicker of an eyelid as I was carried forward on to the boat.

Once on board I was placed on a makeshift bunk under an awning on the open deck. Other casualties were closely packed around me. A nurse walked by in a brilliant white uniform. I recognized the delicious Nurse Nicholls straightaway. She had been the one who had helped to nurse me at the hospital in Johore Bahru—the nurse with the interesting café-au-lait skin color and the curiously beguiling protruding front teeth that had the effect of bestowing on her a captivatingly coy and innocent appearance. She looked at me as she approached but went past without recognizing me. I was too weak even to raise an arm to attract her attention. It was the last time I ever saw her, but there was something else about her sudden surprise presence on the *Wu Seuh* that I have never forgotten. Though she had looked tired and harassed, her unaffected, almost childlike allure remained intact—but it was not even *that* which has remained in my memory. It was the fact that she was carrying a box of Cadbury's Milk Tray chocolates, the familiar and homely design and purple color of which seemed strangely incongruous under the bizarre circumstances. She was offering them around to any patient who appeared half-able to appreciate one. As it happened I could not have eaten one—being fully occupied with another attack of nausea. I have often wondered how she had come by those chocolates, and, for that matter, why they had not melted in the fierce heat long before she began offering them around. I shall never know.

In the late morning the boat slipped away from the docks and maneuvered slowly toward the open sea. As it churned away from Singapore Island, I looked back at the scene I was leaving. I saw huge silver oil tanks along the western shoreline; I saw rising land to the northwest of the city—land covered with the brightest of green vegetation; I saw the somewhat futuristic tower of the Cathay Cinema where five months before I had watched a film entitled *Blood and Sand* featuring Rita Hayworth and Anthony Quinn. I saw the spire of St. Andrews Cathedral and I saw the mouth of Singapore

River with its untidy swarms of junks and its rows of ruined and smoking go-downs. A pall of smoke drifted slowly eastward over the besieged and stricken city. I saw ships and boats massed in the wide harbor, many of them in various stages of haste, threading their way out to sea. As did the little *Wu Seuh,* a few would miraculously complete the perilous journey to Batavia, some seven hundred miles away to the south. Over to the northeast I saw the low outline of buildings fronting Kallang airfield from which the ill-fated Hurricanes and Buffalo fighters had recently flown, but which was now simply a forlorn, abandoned place with only the burnt-out wreckage of planes to indicate what it had once been.

The residual effects of my earlier anesthetic finally wore off when we were well out to sea, still surrounded by a motley collection of small struggling craft all heading in the same general direction, some overtaking us, some falling behind. It was then that I began to think of Wan.

I thought of her for a long time, and it was in fact late afternoon with the sun just starting to dip below the western horizon and the bow of the crowded flat-bottomed boat pointed on a southerly course across the gently heaving Java Sea before my mind at last came to terms with the fact that Wan was gone and that for me she would forevermore be just a poignant memory—a memory that might, perhaps, fade with the passage of time. I remember weeping helplessly as the dying red ball of the sun at last slipped below the horizon and brisk rain began to fall over the grey, darkening sea, its disorganized collection of fleeing vessels now stretched out over the miles ahead and astern. Then, suddenly, my devastating grief and pity changed into seething anger and bitterness, but about which, of course, I was powerless to do even the slightest little thing.

Sunday, 15 February

Wu Seuh had been at sea for two days when just after sundown the news went around that Singapore had finally fallen to the Japanese.[4]

Sunday, 1 March

On this day I reached Karachi on the hospital ship *Karapara,* having been transferred from the heroic little riverboat *Wu Seuh* at Batavia, Java. Years later I discovered that the escape from Singapore had been the riverboat's one and only deep-sea passage, it not having been constructed for such service.

By midday I had been admitted to the British General Hospital where I was put in a small ward on my own. Medical notes written on this day, relating to my condition and treatment on admission, include the following: "Operation carried out to insert supra-pubic catheter in bladder through an existing sinus from which urine and pus is leaking. The patient's general condition is weak and wasted. He has a deep raw bedsore about two-and-a-half inches in diameter."

I was not allowed to sit or stand at any time during the following ten weeks. During all this period I remained flat on the bed, never once leaving my room. I received no physiotherapy whatsoever, nor was I given any treatment other than that the supra-pubic catheter was changed under general anesthetic once a fortnight, this procedure being carried out in my room. A few days after being allowed out of bed, and when I had just reached my nineteenth birthday, I was weighed for the first time since before having been injured. I tipped the scales at 102 pounds, a figure that pointed to a weight loss of no less than 60 pounds over a period of five months. More than twelve months would pass before I would be sufficiently recovered to enable me to be discharged from hospital for transfer to a convalescent unit.

Epilogue

The following condensed notes may be of interest to certain readers, though principally to those curious to know how anyone could possibly have been taken into the RAF while still little more than fifteen years of age.

I did, in fact, enter the RAF in January 1939, at fifteen and a half, under the terms of a solemnly sworn and legally binding contract under which I would undergo a three-year technical apprenticeship and then serve for a further twelve years as a fully trained aero-engine fitter (Aircraftsman Fitter IIE). My father had been required to give his written consent to my signing the contract document. Such RAF aircraft apprenticeship training had been in existence since the year 1922 and the course duration had always been three years or more.

The days I spent at the Aircraft Apprentices' Schools of Technical Training at RAF Halton and RAF Cosford were enormously challenging and, on the whole, thoroughly enjoyable. I had found life at RAF Halton and RAF Cosford exacting but immensely satisfying. Indeed, despite that my subsequent life in the RAF proved nothing short of calamitous, I still look back on my RAF apprenticeship days with genuine nostalgia. To this day a rather special camaraderie exists among ex-RAF apprentices regardless of age and station in life.

When Great Britain declared war on Germany in September 1939, conditions changed for some apprentices. The contracts of certain apprentices were, in effect, disregarded by the Air Ministry/RAF even though such had been understood by the apprentices and their parents to be legally binding.

In my case, the effect of the Air Ministry/RAF having disregarded the terms of my contract was that my three years' apprenticeship was reduced to just twenty months! At the end of this period I was posted to No. 15 Flying Training School at RAF Kidlington where, undertrained and underage, I worked on North American Harvard and Airspeed Oxford aircraft.

A few days before my eighteenth birthday I was informed that I had been selected for overseas posting (even though the minimum age for conscription was eighteen and a half). My troopship departed Glasgow on 1 June 1941 and arrived in Singapore on 8 August 1941.

In early December 1941, when, had the Air Ministry/RAF not changed the duration of my apprenticeship I would still have been at RAF Halton in the final month of my apprenticeship, I was seriously injured in a Japanese air attack on RAF Sungei Patani in northern Malaya close to the border with Siam (now Thailand). As a result of my injuries I spent almost two years in various hospitals. From the day I was injured to the day I was discharged from my final place of convalescence I received not one official word of commiseration or guidance, either by mouth or in writing, from any officer of the RAF. I had spent two years in various military hospitals under the care of army medical staff and it seemed, to all intents and purposes, that I had ceased to exist as far as the RAF was concerned.

I was invalided out of the RAF in March 1944 due to my disablement and was awarded a disablement pension of twelve shillings and sixpence per week. On discharge I received no official word by way of good wishes for my future or in appreciation of my services, nor did I receive any counseling or advice or assistance in any form from the Air Ministry/RAF authorities. A few months later, however, I received through the post a zinc buttonhole badge bearing the words "For Loyal Service." There was no covering message— just the badge. Much later I received four war service medals including the Pacific Star—but, again, no message.

This, then, is the abbreviated account of my enthusiastic entry into the peacetime RAF and my subsequent devastating experience therein.

Mulling It Over: A Consideration of Pivotal Events

I have failed to unearth any official records concerning the more singular events related in this book, and I have only my own observations and feelings to guide me with regard to the characters and circumstances connected with my flight to Indo-China and my later interrogation at Kuala Lumpur. My past inquiries have been directed at the Foreign Office (Historical Services Branch), the Ministry of Defence (Air Historical Branch), and the Public Records Office—all to no avail.

This may simply mean that, in the heat of the moment, crucial records either were not made or were lost at the fall of Malaya and Singapore. It has been suggested that if such information did at some point find its way into official files in London, then such may subsequently have been deliberately "lost" on the grounds that it would not necessarily have been in the best interests of Great Britain to retain it. In the past I tried to make contact with the then–Station Commander of RAF Sungei Patani, Sqn. Ldr. Rupert Cuthbert Fowle, and his then–Adjutant, Pilot Officer P. Swaby, in the hopes that they might have been able to help my research. However, official sources informed me that they were deceased.

Whenever I mull over my recollections I unfailingly reach the conclusion I have always reached. This conclusion is, I feel, in all likelihood and in all major respects accurate. It is formulated by my following beliefs:

a. I have always taken the view that the squadron leader (Mattison?) was a member of an organization such as the Special Operations Executive (SOE) in which role he would have been afforded the full, unquestioning cooperation of the RAF. Such would have accounted for his offbeat demeanor and unconventional manner of dress.

   The SOE operated in Malaya and Singapore under various guises, although few at the time knew this. Thus the Far East Combined Bureau (Military Intelligence) and the Oriental Mission of the Ministry of Economic Warfare (Singapore Branch of SOE) were both active in a half-hearted sort of way. Sadly, the Public Records Office in London has virtually nothing of documentary interest concerning military intelligence matters (with respect to the Japanese threat) covering the period mid-1941 to the fall of Singapore.

b. It is clear, for want of a more certain reason, that Jan had been in the business of regularly flying contraband goods out of French Indo-China into Sumatra. Such could have been opium-based drugs but far more likely were precious stones or other material. The British had noticed some of his "over-flying" and had alerted the Dutch authorities, who had then uncovered the activity of the people for whom he acted as courier. The Dutch authorities had, on pressure from the British, allowed Jan to make one last flight to French Indo-China on the understanding that he would bring a certain British man back with him and drop him off in Malaya. The RAF would not have risked sending one of its own planes to do this because the Japanese may have spotted it and used its presence over French Indo-China as an excuse to commence hostilities against Great Britain, and London had given most strict instructions that the Japanese must not be provoked. Jan's outfit already had the full facilities in place to carry out such a mission. I speculate that the British man to be brought out of French Indo-China was either a discredited diplomat to whom the Japanese felt some rancor or someone connected with intelligence gathering who had been dropped in French Indo-China and who had now to get out in a hurry.

c. The regular Dutch observer/technician/handyman had apparently been taken off the flight due to his sudden indisposition. The Hudson, of course, had to land at Sungei Patani anyway, so that the squadron leader could give Jan the necessary last-minute instructions in regard to picking up the British man in French Indo-China. This, at least, is as I worked it out and have remembered it. A stand-in second man had to be found for Jan and I fit the job description reasonably well, that is, I was a trained aero-technician, I had undertaken a short theoretical course on the Lockheed Hudson aircraft, I was keen to fly and was, in fact, waiting to be called for pilot training. I was very young and enthusiastic and unlikely to ask too many awkward questions. Moreover I was fit, ambitious, and anxious to please my superiors.

d. The two British men by whom I was interrogated at Kuala Lumpur were civilians connected with some official intelligence department—possibly one of those mentioned in *a*.

e. It is my unshakeable view that no then-serving member of the RAF was in any way responsible for encouraging me to fly to Indo-China with the Dutchman whom I knew as Jan. Furthermore I am also of the view that, whatever incidental involvement RAF personnel may have had in the flight, such involvement must have been in some singular way entered into on a "no questions asked" basis as a result of pressure having been brought to bear by some high-level non-RAF department or other in liaison with the Dutch authorities. The rather odd individual, Mattison or Battinson or whatever his claimed name had been, and who had worn squadron-leader epaulette stripes in a haphazard sort of way and on an occasional basis at that, never struck me as being a genuine RAF officer.

Going Home and Getting on with Life

My career with the Royal Air Force had been effectively brought to an abrupt end by the Japanese attack on Sungei Patani,[1] but it was some time before I was returned to the United Kingdom.

The riverboat on which I had escaped from Singapore took me to Batavia, Java. There I was carried aboard the hospital ship *Karapara,* which a few weeks later landed me at Karachi. On Christmas Day 1943, I was again put aboard *Karapara* but now as a walking patient. A few days later I was transferred to *Talamba* and headed for Durban, South Africa. There followed a couple of months in hospital at Pietermaritzburg, then a sea passage round the Cape to Capetown where, in a huge holding camp at a place named Retreat, several thousand British troops awaited repatriation. I was returned to the United Kingdom aboard *Queen Mary* along with eight thousand Allied troops and a similar number of Italian prisoners of war. I finished up in hospital in Oxford—St. Hugh's College, which had been temporarily converted into a head and spinal injuries unit. I saw 1943 out at a convalescent camp a few miles away in the country at Middleton Stoney.

I was invalided out of the RAF in early 1944 and set my sights on a career in engineering, obtaining my first appointment as a draftsman with the Fairey Aviation Company, Lancashire. In the evenings I studied engineering at Manchester College of Technology.

The end of World War II brought widespread redundancies and I found myself on the job market during the exceptionally hard winter of 1947, when deep, dislocating snow lay over the entire country until mid-March.

In late spring I was taken on by the National Gas and Oil Engine Company as a design draftsman and spent a few months in an oven of a drawing office sweating over the mysteries of torsional vibration in the crankshafts of heavy marine engines. I moved to Yorkshire and took my studies with me to Doncaster Technical College where I had been taught as a boy. Eventually my studies brought their reward and a few years later I became a chartered engineer and was accepted by the Institution of Mechanical Engineers as an associate member. For the next forty-one years I remained in continuous employment in various branches of engineering—coal mining with the National Coal Board, the manufacture of agricultural machinery with International Harvester, armaments production with the Royal Ordnance Factories, nylon spinning with British Nylon Spinners, and, for the last twenty-two years, Director of Works and Consultant Engineer with the University of East Anglia in Norfolk.

When I retired at sixty-five my wife, Diana, said to me, "Now you can get rid of all those boring old engineering books." She had, of course, her eye on the space such would create.

"No way," I replied, "they stay." It would have been like betraying and discarding old friends. Those books, each of which I had studied and referred to a thousand times, had become an important part of my life—they were definitely not going to be discarded like so much rubbish.

The effects of my injuries have stayed with me and have not improved. A number of surgical incursions and interventions have been necessary. However, despite that my career linked to flying had been so drastically terminated, I spent a considerable amount of time clocking up hours as a private pilot. My operating area was mostly Norfolk and Suffolk, but it eventually dawned on me, after a number of near misses and far worse, that this was no place in which to be tempting providence in a Cessna 150. It so happened that the entire region was officially designated as an area of high-density, high-speed, low-level military air traffic, there being numerous RAF and U.S. airbases within sixty miles or so from Norwich airport out of which I flew. "Air traffic" meant F1-11s, A-10s, Phantoms, Tornadoes, Jaguars, and the like, while "low level" meant anything down to fifty feet. One could not relax. When things became too ridiculous I quit.

I miss the exhilaration and the sense of freedom and isolation that solo flying brings. There have been times when it would have taken little to persuade me to acquire for myself, say, a restored PBY Catalina flying boat. I fancy I would have ventured out in it to the Far East and there alighted on the glittering waters that surround Penang and also, I am sure, a dozen other mystical beckoning places along the siren shores of Malaysia.

Fifty Years On—Walking in the Past with Ghosts

In December 1991 I returned to Malaya (now Malaysia). I had, of course, often contemplated going back but for many reasons had never undertaken the journey. At last, realizing that time was rushing on, I put my doubts to one side and booked a flight to Kuala Lumpur.

I stepped from the Malaysian Airline 747 on 6 December 1991, just as dusk was turning into night and into an atmosphere I had left behind fifty years ago—hot, unbelievably humid, and still laced with the faint evocative smells of woodsmoke and damp vegetation. I was back in Malaya, in an atmosphere that my senses immediately recognized, and my mind responded to it. Strangely, I suddenly felt much younger. My mind felt as though it had regressed to the days when I was an eighteen-year-old in the Malaya of 1941. All the knowledge I had gained and all my experience of the past half century seemed to fade and assume a curious dreamlike quality and insignificance. I was back in Malaya and the impression I was getting was almost that of actually being in the Malaya I had known all those long years ago, and as the person I had then been. This curious state of awareness worried me over the next few days—I had never before experienced anything like that. I cannot truthfully say that this condition of mind diminished, but rather that I came to accept it.

I was back in the air by 7:00 A.M. the following morning. On the airport bus from the departure lounge to the Boeing 737 I saw, in the grey light of dawn, nothing that looked even remotely like the grass airfield of 1941 where here at Kuala Lumpur I had sweated in a hut while being questioned about certain things I had learned while in French Indo-China. Then, as the aircraft accelerated along the runway, I noticed a long line of palm trees extending along its boundary. Something vaguely familiar about them fleetingly reminded me of a sun-scorched airfield from another age.

I was on my way to Penang. I had chosen to go to the island because there was something there I wished to see; also, it was reasonably close to my old airfield at Sungei Patani. The flight took no more than 45 minutes and when, almost suddenly the island came into view, I was again thrown back into the past. I vividly recalled what had turned out to be my last glimpse of Penang when I had flown over it in a Blenheim fifty years ago. Little had I then imagined that it would be half a century before I saw the place again.

The next day was 8 December—a date that had remained indelibly in my mind. I had deliberately arranged my itinerary this way. It was early morning and still dark when my taxi left the hotel on the island of Penang, and it was no lighter when the ferry set out to cross over to the mainland.

The return (December 1991): The author standing on the site of the 1941 RAF airfield at Sungei Patani, Malaysia.

By 6:45 A.M. the taxi was within ten miles of Sungei Patani. The Chinese driver drove unhurriedly with the windows down, and warm morning air, moist and filled with smells evocative of past days, drifted into the taxi. The sky had turned to a light blue-grey. From behind mountains far to the east the first tentative golden fingers of sunrise were emerging. It would not be broad daylight for another twenty minutes or so.

The taxi passed interminable paddy fields, flooded because this was the season of the northeast monsoon. It passed through oil-palm and rubber-tree plantations and little groups of Malay houses set by the roadside under the shelter and shade of tall coconut palms. The terrain was almost dead flat, but as the light increased, a dark mass appeared ahead and a little toward the left. I knew what it was. I had lived with it next to me all those years ago. I had long forgotten the shape of its outline against the northwestern sky, but now it came back to me as though I had never been away. We crossed a small metal girder bridge over Sungei Muda, a narrow river running into the sea just five miles away. We reached Sungei Patani with, at its far end and set in the middle of the road, the somewhat incongruous very British clock tower that had been erected in 1936—the kind of thing one would be less surprised to find in the center of somewhere like Chesterfield back in England.

It was 7:30 A.M. when the taxi passed through the gates of my old RAF camp. I had previously arranged to be allowed into the camp at this precise time and on this date, the place now being home to the 6th Brigade of the Malaysian Army. I was received by a captain who, for the next hour or so, drove me around the camp in his new Proton. The endless lines of rubber trees were gone, replaced now by a few trial areas of oil palm and a lot of wild shrub turning to jungle. The depressing gloom that had once pervaded the entire camp was also gone. But many of the huts that had been there when I was a youth were still standing. One would have thought that the heat, the dampness, and the constant exposure to the activities of tropical wood-boring termites would, long ago, have turned these wooden buildings into ravaged relics. Thus, rows of living quarter huts were not only still standing, but were actually in use. In my curiosity I checked on something. The ablutions, toilets, washrooms or what you will, still had in them their original WC pans and handbasins. I knew this as fact because of their 1930s design, which I recognized and also because the maker's name, "Twyfords," was fired into the glaze of each item. Some, naturally, exhibited the multiple scars of half a century of use, but these blemishes only went to confirm my belief that this was original equipment.

The Malay captain drove me down to the airfield, used now apparently only by the occasional helicopter. The grass field looked very much smaller—though it had looked small enough back in 1941. I guessed that the surrounding scrub and jungle had been allowed to creep in on the field. Gone were the massive petrol tanks—they had been blown apart exactly fifty years ago to the day! (See chapter 11, note 1.) For today was, of course, the fiftieth anniversary of the Japanese air attack on the camp. Gone, also, were the pens in which we had repaired the Blenheims. Gone, too, were the control tower and the operations room, and a little workshop that had been used, I remembered, by a chap named Myers who had spent his days doing little but cleaning sparking-plugs and brewing the most awful tea one can imagine. Gone were the Blenheims and gone were the woefully inadequate Buffalo fighters. I had to stand and concentrate hard in order to convince myself that this was the very place where I had lived and worked so long ago. There were no young airmen about to bring it back to its original life, each going about his business in khaki overalls and pith-helmet; and there were no young Australians moaning on about the shortage of spares for their ailing Buffalo fighters. But one thing still remained, and the morning sun was already bringing out the colors of the thick, wild vegetation that covered its eastern slopes. Mount Kedah, Kedah Peak, or Gunung Jerai—whichever name one applied to it—stood there looking no different from how it had always looked.

In my mind there were visions: a group of airmen toiling away on a Blenheim but so infinitely tired that they could barely move, let alone work; Myers cycling along the perimeter track with his mixed load of sparking plugs and revolting tea. It almost seemed that these things could have transpired this very morning. As I stared out across the neglected shrunken airfield, I fancied I heard the approaching throaty roar of aero-engines; and I had a vision of a Lockheed Hudson rushing over at near zero feet, then banking sharply to go round again. Then, in my mind's eye, darkness fell and the airfield, deathly silent, now lay under a covering of mist three feet deep and I saw two figures, on guard duty, walking dejectedly through the dark swirling vapors, their heads and shoulders illuminated now and again by a fickle moon.

We drove up through the scrub a little way and came to a bare patch of concrete, mostly broken up and in randomly piled fragments with scrub bushes growing through. I knew this was where I had lain on my bed in the darkly depressing afternoons while thunder crashed all around, and where, on a half-hourly basis, a beat-up gramophone had wistfully played "Among My Souvenirs." This was the place where, exactly fifty years ago, as dawn broke, my life had been abruptly and savagely changed by a Japanese bomb. I experienced a surge of renewed anger and bitterness, mixed with a kind of inexplicable sadness that had little to do with my own misfortune. I was thinking how very different things may have turned out had a certain warning been heeded!

It was hot now and the sun was well up. I had a last look around the site on which my hut had once stood but which was now just a ruined raft of shattered concrete, abandoned to struggling jungle growth.

I stepped into the shade of the captain's car, and he drove back toward the main gates. The complete absence of rubber trees seemed somehow to have changed the layout of various buildings. Some minutes later we drove past a wooden building marked "KLINIK," and it dawned on me that this must be the old medical room and sickbay—the place to which I had first been taken on being injured. I asked the captain to stop the car and I stepped out. The appearance of the place had not changed in the slightest over fifty years. I walked onto the veranda where I had lain among the shocked, the injured, and the dying—where bright, glistening red blood had spilled over floorboards bathed by the dazzling rays of the early morning sun. And I walked up an incline on which young oil palms were growing. A couple of hundred yards on I came across the traces of an old pathway which, for a few minutes, I followed. Then there was nothing to guide me further except more broken concrete almost totally overgrown by dank ferns in which moved huge black leeches. This is where the orderly room had been and where I had first met a man whose gaze was strangely penetrating and whom I had taken to be a squadron leader. It was the place where I had met a Dutchman by the name of Jan, who had flown me off to French Indo-China against my wishes and better judgment. And this was where, I had much later been informed, the duty telephone operator had been killed on the morning of the first Japanese attack. Sungei Patani camp was, for me, now a place of ghosts—a place of joyless memories. Yet, curiously, in spite of this, and perhaps even because of this, it had an aura that pulled at me like a powerful magnet. For this was where for a short time I had lived as a fit and healthy young person, but who had, in an instant, been changed into someone quite different. I had left my youth behind at this very place, and it was as though the essence of that youth still lurked here, like some ethereal lost spirit, captured among the aging wooden huts, the countless rotting stumps of rubber trees, and the wild tropical scrub—and all the time under the watchful eye of the impassive mountain.

It was with a saddened heart that I departed from the camp to commence my journey back to Penang. I was reluctant to leave this special part of Malaya. In Sungei Patani town I asked the driver to stop at its only hotel. Inside, I found a kind of pre-lunch party warming up, although it was still only midmorning. There were about a couple of dozen Malay, Indian, and Chinese characters, all of them male and perhaps members of the local version of the Chamber of Commerce and already well into their fruit juices and stronger beverages. Being in no mood to get involved, I naturally stayed clear of the activity, but, after a stiff, ice-cold Johnny Collins, I infiltrated their ranks and pretty soon found myself being introduced around as though I were some important guest of honor who had managed to make it at the last moment. It seemed not to matter that none of them knew me, and no one was rude or tactless enough to ask. I finished up having lunch with them. There was a lot of almost childlike jollity, spurred on by the fact that Christmas decorations were already in place. When at last I went out to rejoin my taxi I felt in decidedly better spirits—as though, for the present, I had come to terms with myself about something important. I was not exactly drunk, but, as the saying goes, I'd "had a few." The entire gathering came out onto the road to see me off with good-natured salutes and waves and rows of laughing white teeth. To this day I have absolutely no idea what the party was all about.

I hung around Penang for a few days but quickly grew tired of the tourist attractions and the tourist hotels. Indeed, I grew tired of the tourists themselves, their mission being very different from mine. I left my pilgrimage to Springtide until the end of my visit. I had already been to the old Windsor Cinema, now the Capitol, and had, for five minutes between shows, stood in the circle remembering George and the Gary Cooper film. And I had found the services club in which George and I had swigged bottles of Anchor Beer and played "Singing in the Rain" and "Ramona" on an elegant 1920s wind-up gramophone. The place was now derelict, vandalized, and clearly unsafe to enter. I pushed a tall, weedy palm aside to peer through the decaying slats of a window shutter into the room where we had spent that Saturday afternoon at a time when the vast majority of the people presently on the island had not yet been born. There was now nothing in there but flaking plaster and rotting floor boards.

I went to Springtide on a Sunday morning, just as I had done a couple of generations ago. The taxi stopped close to the sea, alongside a patch of land covered with building debris, discarded soft-drink cans, and other trash through which grew a profusion of wild flowering hibiscus bushes. Behind this and parallel with the sea was a line of coconut palms and then a width of sandy beach sloping gently down to the calm sea.

I looked at the Madrassi taxi driver. He said, "Springtide," and nodded in the direction of the beach.

"Hotel?" I asked, puzzled. But even as the word came out I sensed what his reply would be.

"Hotel—it finished—no more—long time."

"Ah, yes," I murmured. "It's been demolished."

I was disappointed that the hotel had, along with the past, ceased to exist. I was pretty certain that the spot on which I was standing must have been the place where Wan and her friend had stood as they waved George and I good-bye on that unforgettable Sunday afternoon in 1941. I recollected how, even when we had been almost out of sight, Wan had continued waving, slowly and regretfully, as though somehow sensing that we might never see each other again.

The beach had changed but little. Even tiny sand crabs, identical to those that George and I had chased all that long time ago, were still in residence, practically invisible and always careful enough to keep within rapid scuttling distance of their minuscule funnel holes in the sand.

I looked out to sea while lazy, half-hearted waves spilled softly onto the sand. In the far distance, over on the mainland, Kedah Peak rose above the skyline. In my mind, the mountain marked, as a kind of monument, the place where my past existence in Malaya had suddenly ceased and, instead, I had been propelled into a nightmare of horrors.

Turning around, I looked at the sad and disordered patch of land on which the hotel had once stood, and in my imagination I captured a vision of two young Malay girls standing by the veranda and then venturing down to the beach. One of them was tall and slim and beautiful. For a minute or so I allowed my imagination to retain the image of Wan, knowing that once I let her go, the magic would probably be gone forever. I watched her as she paddled into the sea—then she turned around as in slow motion and smiled. I felt myself being compelled to walk toward her, and, as in a dream, I took two or three tentative steps in her direction.

Then I was visited by a foolish wave of emotion and my eyes misted over. When they cleared, nothing remained save the empty beach, the waves gently lapping on the shore, and the timeless smell of the sea.

I retraced my steps toward the taxi to be driven away from this place of memories. The scenery had been changed—that was all. This Sunday was really no different from that other Sunday. In my mind I felt no different; the sand was the same, and the sea and the sky were the same. The sun and the heat were the same, and it seemed there could be no reason at all why Wan should not once again appear just as on that other occasion. But of course she could not do that and it would have been immature and pointless even to entertain the heartfelt wish that fifty years had not passed—that time had stayed still. The taxi returned me to Georgetown and my hotel. Downhearted, I went into the bar and stayed there for some time. Then, on impulse, I packed my things, asked reception to book me a flight on the afternoon plane to Johore Bharu, then took a taxi to the airport.

As the Boeing 737 climbed away from the island, I felt I was leaving part of myself there—something that would forever remain. The plane climbed swiftly and steeply and, as it turned to head south, the beach at Springtide, the streets and buildings of Georgetown, and the distant shadowy mass of Mount Kedah all finally slipped out of my line of vision.

At Johore Bharu I spent most of the evening poring over a map of Singapore and the next morning I motored westerly along the coast road to the Sultana Aminah Hospital. I could hardly have expected to recognize the building, for although I had spent many days there during December 1941 and January 1942, I had stayed in one ward throughout—for most of the time struggling to keep my maker at a respectable distance.

A sympathetic and understanding Indian superintending sister accompanied me to my old ward up on the fifth floor. I remembered it had been on that floor on the west side of the building. Nothing much appeared to have changed in the ward apart from that things had aged, including the bedframes, which originally had been finished in pristine white enamel. But now the enamel was yellowed and marked by the ravages of long, hard use. The beds were even arranged in the same manner as when the ward had first been taken into use in December 1941. The pantry at one end was still exactly that. The walk-in drug cupboard was still precisely where it had been.

I walked over to where my bed had stood and, for a short time, attempted to recall the sickeningly sweet smell of ether and the stench of burned and putrescent flesh. I tried to remember the fearful anguished cries of shocked and bewildered young men, the sound of surgical instruments in stainless-steel dishes; and then I heard, without even having consciously thought about it, the sound of the opening bars of "Waltzing Matilda" being played on a cheap wind-up gramophone. And then, suddenly, I felt myself being enveloped and taken up into the atmosphere of the ward as it had been. I had let my imagination off the leash. I had concentrated too hard and had stepped into a daydream that was more a product of self-hypnosis than mere simple reflection.

"Mr. Shepherd, I've brought some of the girls to meet you." It was the voice of the sister at my elbow. She had with her half a dozen young Chinese nurses—all eager and interested, with bright-eyed smiles, wonderful teeth, and spotless white uniforms.

Her voice snapped me out of my trauma-like reverie, and in an instant the past retreated back to where it belonged. I was left standing with the sister and the nurses and with twenty or so female patients eyeing me with curiosity—the ward now apparently being used mainly for problem maternity cases. Much genuine interest was shown when I explained that I had been one of the first patients to be admitted to this ward on the very day it had been hurriedly opened and when I was still only eighteen. Most of the girls had only the vaguest notion of the role played by Great Britain in the history of Malaya and Singapore—and even less about the three and a half years of Japanese occupation. My fifteen minutes with them was not all serious. They laughed very easily and were fascinatingly respectful and polite.

I crossed over the causeway to Singapore Island and during the next four days visited places that were of interest. I visited the place that once had been RAF Seletar where I had worked on the Catalina flying boats. I visited the old part of Singapore town but found most of it gone and replaced by office blocks and hotels—resulting in a good 90 percent of the Old World mystery and charm having been wiped out by property tycoons. I found the Cathay Cinema without difficulty, but somehow its tower looked less impressive than in earlier times. I was driven along the Orchard Road, once a magnet to the lower orders of the military services, but recognized next to nothing. I visited the site of the old transit camp where I had spent my first few weeks before being sent up-country to Sungei Patani. Nothing remained of it. The whole area, once a shady rubber plantation with a few huts for RAF personnel and Indian Army troops, was now taken up by high-density, high-rise, concrete condominiums. I had a look at Singapore Railway Station from which I had started out one midnight for northern Malaya and my destiny. I tried to find the quayside from which a little riverboat by the name of *Wu Sueh* with me aboard had set off for Batavia. But there had been changes— big changes. The old docks, along with much land reclaimed from the sea, had been redeveloped and was now a vast area filled with row upon row of boring, highly stacked shipping containers.

I went to the official War Graves site at Kranji on the north side of the island and there walked under the fierce sun among the thousands of stark, silent headstones and read on the sculpted Roll of Honour the names of the RAF youths I had known and who had died out there in 1941–42 and had, in a sense, never grown older.

On the morning of my last day in Singapore I undertook my final pilgrimage. I asked the taxi driver to take me to the old Singapore General Hospital in which I had spent several dreadful weeks. The driver took me to a large and impressive new hospital which he told me had been built on the site of the old building. I was bitterly disappointed and, because the new building held no memories for me, I asked to be taken back to my hotel. But as we were leaving the site, I happened to glimpse the portico of a tired-looking stone building. My heart leapt because I realized that the planners must have retained the main entrance of the old hospital as a kind of memorial to what had been the principal hospital of Singapore for perhaps ninety or so years. We drove under the portico and I stepped out of the taxi. I well remembered having been brought here during the night in January 1942 and recalled at that time having briefly caught sight of these pillars in the meager blackout lighting. And then they had carried me inside and placed me in the first ward on the left, given me a warm milk drink that tasted like no other drink I had ever tasted, and then informed me that their stock of morphine had run out.

I walked into the building just as the heavens opened and rain began deluging down. The place was busy with lots of mothers and children, all in their various native attire. When I looked into the ward on the left, I saw that I was in a school of dentistry. In fact, apart from the main entrance and reception area in the hall, the ward was the only remaining part of the building. There were rows and rows of dentists' chairs, each more or less with its own patient, demonstrating dentist, and two or three attentive students.

Gone were the gaunt, tortured faces and the nauseating smells of long ago; gone, too, were the crowded beds and floor mattresses; gone were the unnerving shrieks of pain and terror, and that somber, depressing lighting and the suffocating, unrelieved heat. But, despite this, I knew this to be my ward.

I walked, unchecked and unquestioned, into the wide open doorway of the ward, then stopped and gazed at the scene before me: the tall shuttered windows, admitting light and fresh air and everyday sounds from the world outside; the busy overhead fans, modern and suspended from a spotless, shiny, cream-colored ceiling. I saw the normality and hygienic cleanliness of it all.

But my attention was drawn to the place where my bed had been, against a wall and alongside one of the shuttered windows. I thought, deliberately, of a particular occasion, and presently I saw myself lying on a bed, bandaged and tubed and infinitely miserable amid other beds with their equally miserable burdens. And I saw a Malay girl, her beautiful features dulled by weariness and anxiety, sitting on the edge of my bed and looking down into my face. She was dressed in a bright and colorful *baju kebaya*,[2] her hair covered by a silk scarf in Muslim fashion. I saw her hand gently take hold of mine, and I heard her telling me that she would come to see me on the following morning. Then, as I watched, she looked deep into my eyes, smiled sadly, and rose from the bed. She began picking her way through the beds toward the doorway where I was standing and, as she approached, I saw tears of despair and hopelessness flooding down her cheeks. I willed our eyes to meet and involuntarily lifted an arm to stay her. But Wan continued toward me, unseeing; and as she brushed past me, I fancied I felt the touch of her headscarf on my bare arm. I turned at once, half expecting to see her moving on toward the main entrance, but she had vanished, and out beyond the portico there was only the rain and the low rumble of thunder.

I stood there, empty and dispirited, unable for a time to drag myself back into reality. No one paid me any attention. It was for all the world as though I was not there at all, and, for all that those around me could possibly have known, never had been.

A Courtesy Withheld

Over the years I have repeatedly pressed the Japanese government for an apology in respect of the injuries inflicted on me by Japanese bombs before any formal declaration of war against Great Britain had been made. My early approaches were totally ignored, but in 1995 I received a letter from the Embassy of Japan in London enclosing a blanket apology (". . . to the people of many countries") issued by Prime Minister Tomiichi Murayama on the occasion of the fiftieth anniversary of the end of the war in the Pacific and Far East.

I cannot accept the apology as being a sincere and meaningful apology to me personally. Having ensured that the Japanese government is in possession of the full, officially verified facts of my particular case, I can see no sound reason why a simple courteous apology should continue to be withheld. Such an apology would cost Japan very little—indeed, in comparison with the distress I have had to endure through life as a result of Japan's past treachery, the cost would surely be regarded as negligible.

In seeking an apology from the Japanese government, I do not forget the plight of others who suffered as a result of Japan's barbarous acts of December 1941. I especially refer to those civilian and military unfortunates who fell victim to Japan's acts of surprise aggression before its government made any formal declaration of war against either the United States of America or

Great Britain; nor do I forget the anguish of those who were captured by the Japanese and forced to work as slaves for years on end under wretched and humiliating conditions. It is just that it would be of some satisfaction to me to be officially acknowledged by Japan as one who, without any provocation, was deliberately and criminally abused by that nation's military machine prior to any formal declaration of war against Great Britain, my country, having been made.

Notes

Chapter 1. Malaya 1941
1. Sir Andrew Gilchrist, *Malaya 1941* (London: Robert Hale, 1992), 44–46, 73–75.

Chapter 2. Arrival in the Far East
1. Maj. Gen. Woodburn S. Kirby, *The Loss of Singapore,* vol. 1 of *The War Against Japan* (London: HMSO, 1957), 44, 63, 69.

Chapter 3. RAF Sungei Patani
1. Changi jail—a daunting military prison reserved for serious offenders and situated on the southeast coast of Singapore Island.

Chapter 4. Tension and a Surprise Summons
1. Gilchrist, *Malaya 1941,* 87; Kirby, *The War Against Japan,* 171; Lt. Gen. A. E. Percival, *London Gazette,* 20 February 1948, 1265.

Chapter 5. Night Flight to the North
1. Gilchrist, *Malaya 1941,* 169–72.
2. Ibid., 89–90.

Chapter 8. Return Flight to Malaya
1. Christopher Shores and Brian Cull, with Yasuho Izawa, *Bloody Shambles* (London: Grub Street, 1992), 76, 77: A 205 Squadron Catalina flying boat took off from Seletar, Singapore, at 2:00 A.M. on Sunday, 7 December, briefed to search the Gulf of Siam for the large convoy of Japanese naval and merchant vessels that had earlier been reported. At 8:30 A.M. a Japanese naval plane spotted the Catalina in the vicinity of Phu Quoc Island and, coming up behind the flying boat, attacked with a burst of gunfire.

Thirty minutes later a patrol of five Japanese fighters also spotted the troubled Catalina. They immediately attacked and within a few moments the Catalina exploded and hurtled into the sea. There were no survivors from the eight-man crew. No signal had been received from the Catalina by Air Headquarters, Singapore. The facts of this criminal attack became known, from Japanese records, only after Japan had been defeated by Great Britain and the United States three and a half years later.

Chapter 11. The Final Two Days

1. **Japanese naval and troop-transport vessels move into the Gulf of Siam:**

On 4 December 1941 eighteen Japanese troop-transport vessels departed from Hainan Island off southern China. The convoy sailed due south, then southwest toward the Gulf of Siam. These ships were accompanied by two cruisers and twelve destroyers. An additional four cruisers and three destroyers followed not far away. One battleship, two cruisers, and ten destroyers were being held ready to provide further support.

On 5 December the convoy was joined by another fleet of ships from Saigon: seven troop transporters, one cruiser, and one destroyer. A total of around thirty thousand Japanese troops were now at sea.

At midday on 6 December sections of the combined Japanese fleet of ships were spotted by Hudsons of the RAAF from Kota Bharu. The sightings were radioed to GHQ at Singapore. GHQ could only speculate as to the Japanese intentions. The fleet was now positioned about 160 miles northeast of Kota Bharu and therefore posed an obvious threat to Malaya. The British took no action.

A Catalina took off from Seletar, Singapore, at 6:30 P.M. to continue the search. It, too, failed to find the convoy owing to darkness and cloud. The fate of a second Catalina, which took off from Seletar at 2:00 A.M. the next morning, is briefly related (see chapter 8, note 1).

On Sunday, 7 December, around 9:00 A.M. the Japanese convoy, now positioned in the center of the Gulf of Siam, split up, one group heading due southwest toward Singora, on the coast of Siam, the other due south toward Kota Bharu, Malaya. (Gilchrist, *Malaya 1941,* 99; Kirby, *The War Against Japan,* 180)

While GHQ staff at Singapore agitatedly chewed their nails and quaked and quivered with uncertainty, the Japanese continued to bear down on Malaya.

The policy of GHQ remained "wait and see," even though a Catalina had mysteriously gone missing and it was also known that Japanese ships were lurking in strength within an hour or so of the Malayan coast. The time for active defensive measures to be taken was glaringly obvious. Time was fast running out and, besides, had not a *certain warning* already been given?

The Japanese landing at Kota Bharu, 8 December 1941 (Malaya time):

At midnight 7/8 December three Japanese troop transport vessels anchored offshore at Kota Bharu. Aboard the ships were 5,500 troops. Protecting this invasion force were four destroyers and two cruisers. The night was further darkened by heavy low cloud which had descended over the area an hour or so earlier. The troops began disembarking into landing boats, which then set out for the Malayan shore.

About thirty minutes later a barrage of shells fell on such coastal defenses as there were. News quickly reached the nearby Kota Bharu airfield that Japanese troops were landing on the beaches. Immediately six RAAF Hudsons took off to attack the invasion ships.

By 6:30 A.M. the three transporters and their naval escort had withdrawn to the northwest, one of the transporters burning furiously. But the Japanese troops were on Malayan soil, pushing through the Indian defense lines and now within striking distance of the airfield. Two Hudsons had been shot down and several others badly damaged (Kirby, *The War Against Japan*, 182).

Had the RAF tried harder to locate the initial Japanese armada of troop carriers and its escorting naval vessels, and had RAF aircraft attacked and possibly thereby balked the intention of this force, the landing at Kota Bharu may never have come about. Neither perhaps may have the crucial landing at Singora where, within twenty-four hours, substantial quantities of tanks, heavy weapons, and troops had been put ashore by the Japanese invader. GHQ and the RAF could not have known with certainty the intentions of the Japanese, but, under the circumstances then prevailing, the pressure of doubt and suspicion, together with a notion of the probable consequences of a Japanese assault on Malaya and Siam, ought to have resulted in the RAF locating and attacking all vessels reasonably judged a threat. Such vessels would, obviously, have been those likely to be carrying troops, that is, transport vessels, for naval ships alone could hardly have posed a landing threat.

Such action would have introduced another dramatic and providential element into the whole matter—one that may well have resulted in the RAF ultimately being viewed as the force that foiled Japan's grand strategy to colonize Southeast Asia and much of the Pacific area instead of going down in history, even though perhaps unfairly, as the force that failed to save Malaya and Singapore. It can be said that all chance of saving Malaya was lost on 7 December 1941 (Malaya time), lost even before the fighting started. Moreover, on that day the fate of Pearl Harbor was sealed. If Great Britain had attacked the Japanese ships believing them to be an imminent threat the United States would have given its support because, in effect, an existing agreement already provided for such. London has already given Singapore GHQ the all-clear to attack Japanese forces in the event of a perceived Japanese intention to land on Siamese soil. Thus the United States would have been bound to join in with Great Britain in curbing Japan by military means. Pearl Harbor defense organizations would have been brought to a higher state of alertness than ever before, and its reconnaissance Cataliners, of which there were many, may well have spotted the approaching Japanese armada, which at midday Sunday, 7 December (Malaya time), was little more than two hundred miles north of Oahu, Hawaii, and could therefore have easily been spotted by U.S. long-range flying boats operating from Pearl Harbor.

The bombing of Singapore, 8 December 1941 (Malaya time):

Just before midnight on Sunday, 7 December, thirty-one Mitsubishi twin-engined bombers took off from an airfield near Saigon, French Indo-China. Their mission was to bomb Singapore some 650 miles away. Only seventeen completed the trip to Singapore, the remaining fourteen having been forced, on account of technical problems, to return to Saigon.

The approaching planes were detected by radar when 140 miles from the island, and antiaircraft units were put on instant alert. The air-raid precaution organization could not be alerted for the simple reason that its headquarters was not manned. From the first sighting on radar to the arrival of the formation over Singapore at 4:10 A.M., Monday, 8 December (Malaya time), some thirty-five minutes had elapsed.

The bombers experienced no difficulty in finding Singapore. There was a bright full moon and the island remained fully illuminated. The main targets were the RAF airfields at Seletar and Tengah, and Keppel Harbor, although it was later estimated that most of the bombs had been dropped on the city. Antiaircraft fire was ineffective even though the guns of both *Prince of Wales* and *Repulse* joined in the action. None of the Japanese planes were shot down, and all droned away from the island at around 4:25 A.M.

In this criminal surprise air raid, perpetrated by Japan prior to any declaration of war against Great Britain, sixty-one civilians were killed—mainly Chinese and Indians. At Seletar three RAF airmen were killed (Kirby, *The War Against Japan,* 183; Shores and Cull, *Bloody Shambles,* 85–87).

The bombing of Sungei Patani, 8 December 1941 (Malaya time):

During the early hours of Monday, 8 December, the Operations Room at Sungei Patani had been notified of the Japanese landing at Kota Bharu and had been ordered by Singapore Air Headquarters to send Blenheim fighter-bombers off at first light to attack the invaders. Eight Blenheims took off from the airfield as dawn was breaking at 6:45 A.M.

Fifteen minutes later the airfield was notified of two unidentified planes approaching from the west. Four RAAF Buffalo fighters were placed on immediate readiness. A short time later five twin-engined bombers were spotted approaching the airfield at around twelve thousand feet. This would have been the time for air-raid sirens and "danger imminent" whistles to have been sounded, but there were none at Sungei Patani. The station commander, Sq. Ldr. Rupert Cuthbert Fowle (who was also No. 27 Squadron's commanding officer), ordered the pilots to do nothing. Within seconds bombs began to rain down on the airfield and the camp buildings.

Two Buffaloes roared off through the exploding bombs and chased the departing Japanese aircraft. When at last they had climbed up to and overtaken the enemy planes, both pilots found their guns inoperable!

The bombs caused considerable damage, loss of life, and injury, the author being one of those seriously injured (see chapter 12). Three of the four remaining Blenheims were badly damaged and the last of the four, on attempting takeoff, was struck by a bomb blast, its pilot and air gunner mortally wounded.

Four Buffaloes were destroyed and great damage was done to ground technical installations. The camp headquarters was hit along with the orderly room where the duty telephonist and another airman were killed. Five other airmen were killed on the airfield, and in the plantation coolie lines sixteen women laborers died.

The airfield had been seriously cratered. An emergency strip was hurriedly marked out for the eight Blenheims still winging their way to Kota Bharu. On returning to Sungei Patani, having failed to locate any of the invasion forces, they found the camp a very changed place.

Much later in the morning the camp was bombed by twenty-four Japanese planes, Squadron Leader Fowle having again withheld permission for the Buffaloes to scramble to engage the enemy whose bombers were barely at 1,500 feet. In this raid the ridiculously conspicuous two hundred thousand-gallon petrol dump was hit and went up in flames. A few hours later the camp was abandoned (Shores and Cull, *Bloody Shambles*, 87–89; David J. Innes, *Beaufighters over Burma No. 27 Squadron, RAF, 1942–45* [Poole, England: Blandford Press, 1985], 27).

Japan's attack on Pearl Harbor, Sunday, 7 December 1941 (Pearl Harbor time):

Japan's fleet of ships had begun to assemble in northern Japan at forlorn Hitokappu Bay in mid November 1941, the decision to attack the U.S. naval base at Pearl Harbor having been made in October 1941. Records suggest that Japan's Emperor Hirohito understood that the massive air attack would be carried out at the very moment the United States was being informed, by a written statement, that Japan could see no possibility of reaching agreement through further negotiations (on the subject of negotiations see chapter 2). Hirohito, "Prince of Enlightened Peace," finally gave his sanction to the attack on 3 December 1941, when the Japanese fleet was already well on its way to Hawaii and Pearl Harbor.

Japan's statement to the United States, formally worded and presented, did not amount to a formal declaration of war and was presented fifty-five minutes *after* Japan's attack on Pearl Harbor had commenced.

Hitokappu Bay, some six miles wide and biting deep into the coastline of the island of Etorofu, provided an amazingly effective place of concealment for the fleet in which to assemble. At the extreme north of Japan's main islands, in a remarkably remote position, the terrain of Etorofu was bleak and uninviting. The bay's beaches were largely strewn with boulders and shingle, though its eastern coast was bounded by high cliffs. A few miserable houses, sheds, and the usual trappings of a fishing village on hard times were collected at the northern end of the bay. At this time of the year, November, snow regularly fell and more or less covered the entire island. This year had been no exception. The whole place was shrouded in mist, when it was not covered by dense, freezing fog. Altogether Hitokappu Bay was a gem of a hideaway for a naval task force wishing to escape from the prying eyes of the outside world.

By late afternoon on 25 November the last ship had arrived in the bay. At 6:00 A.M. the following morning, 26 November, the entire fleet of ships weighed anchor. The sky was a daunting dark grey and the sea like hammered lead as, one by one, the ships slipped away from the sanctuary of the bay. There were flurries of snow in the blustery chill wind as, over the next hour, thirty or so ships moved cautiously out into the open, inhospitable northern Pacific Ocean. Only the top officers of the big capital ships knew their ultimate objective, but a lot of accurate speculating went on among the lower ranks.

The attack on Pearl Harbor was intended to be delivered by stealth, that is to say, the Americans were not to suspect it was about to happen—in fact, they were not to get even a whiff of imminent war until after thousands of U.S. military youngsters had been blown to kingdom come.

By mid-afternoon on their first day at sea, the various Japanese ships had taken up the positions they would more or less keep throughout the long passage to Hawaii. First went a line of destroyers, three miles apart. Behind these were two parallel lines of aircraft carriers, six in total. Then came two cruisers, followed by two mighty battleships. At the rear were the vital supply ships and the tankers. Protecting the flanks of the fleet were yet more destroyers and submarines. Radio silence was to be maintained and transmission totally barred, although incoming radio messages could be received—indeed, such signals were crucially important to keep the fleet informed of such things as the latest position in regard to the Japan/U.S. diplomatic negotiations still continuing in Washington, and the current disposition of U.S. naval ships at Pearl Harbor. Many Japanese nationals lived and worked in Hawaii and especially so on Oahu. The Japanese therefore knew, almost from one moment to the next, which ships were at Pearl Harbor; Tokyo was kept fully informed, via diplomatic channels and in code, as to the current position.

A problem to be faced was that of essential refueling at sea. The sheer distance to be traveled, from Japan to Hawaii and back, a matter of around eight thousand miles, meant that most ships would have to be refueled several times.

As the fleet moved steadily eastward, the chances of detection increased, even though the part of the ocean it was traversing was known as "The Vacant Sea" because very few ships used it. If the fleet were to be detected, it would spell the failure of the whole operation—the armada would, as was the agreed strategy, turn about and return to Japan as though it had merely been on some kind of routine exercise.

The days passed. No other ships were seen and the weather remained exceptionally favorable. The fleet, with all the incredible and monstrous luck of the devil, butted on through the seemingly limitless windswept ocean. Shortly, the whole world would be awakened to Japan's power and heroic capability. Such thought must have entered the heads of those who had helped to plan the mission and who would shortly give the word for the execution of the final act.

At 5:30 A.M., Sunday, 7 December (Pearl Harbor time, which was 11:30 P.M., Sunday, 7 December, Malaya time), the Japanese fleet was two hundred miles north of Oahu, the position from which the attack would be launched.

A brisk easterly wind carried a driving, biting spray over the decks of the six blacked-out carriers. In the lead of Japan's ignoble procession of heaving ships was the cruiser *Abukuma,* behind which tore four destroyers. Three miles astern thundered the two battleships *Kirishima* and *Hiei*. Four miles to port sped the cruiser *Chikumo,* and, to starboard the cruiser *Tone*. Behind the battleships the carriers cleaved confidently through the dark, tempestuous sea, *Soryu, Hiryu, Shokoko, Akagi, Kaga,* and *Zuikaka*. More destroyers covered the fleet from the sides and rear. Sleeking through the water behind this throbbing assembly of shadowy objects of death and destruction rushed three submarines, each more than capable of keeping up with the now-racing fleet.

Signals from Tokyo were now coming in virtually nonstop, though no acknowledgment could be transmitted back. One of these signals informed Vice Adm. Chuichi Nagumo, Commander in Chief First Air Fleet, aboard *Akagi,* that as at 6 December (Tokyo time) U.S. naval ships at Pearl Harbor included nine battleships, three cruisers, and two destroyers. The two U.S. carriers, normally based at Pearl Harbor, *Lexington* and *Enterprise,* were absent, and it was therefore assumed that these vessels must be out on exercises. Another signal confirmed the absence of barrage balloons and antitorpedo netting.

On the carriers some members of the flying crew listened to wireless music being broadcast by Radio Hawaii, station KGMB. Strangely enough, others were tuned into this station, namely thirteen U.S. B-17 bombers being flown to Hawaii from California who were using the station as a homing beacon. It was also the case that, as long as station KGMB kept broadcasting dance music, it remained certain that the Japanese fleet had not been detected.

At 5:50 A.M., still about two hundred miles north of Oahu, the six carriers turned into a fierce east wind. The waves were high and it was only after half an hour or so that the first fighter roared off from *Akagi* into the darkness, to be quickly followed by fighters from the other five carriers. Within fifteen minutes 183 planes were airborne—forty-three fighters, forty-nine high-level bombers, fifty-one dive-bombers, and forty torpedo planes. The planes assembled over the task force and then set out for Oahu. At 6:20 A.M. the first pale light of dawn became visible.

On the carriers there was no time for relaxation. A second wave of fighters and bombers had now to be prepared for takeoff in one hour's time.

Flying time to Oahu was estimated at one hour and twenty minutes. There was a lot of cloud at five thousand feet as Japan's lead plane homed in on KGMB, just as the thirteen B-17s now 350 miles northeast of Oahu were doing. At 7:30 A.M. the cloud cover broke up and sunlight shone down on the sea. Straight ahead lay the dark outline of Oahu.

At 7:38 A.M. Oahu was spread out below the attacking planes, the bombers and torpedo planes at ten thousand feet and the fighters four thousand feet above. The U.S. ships were positioned precisely as had been reported. There was no antiaircraft fire and the sky was clear of intercepting fighters.

At precisely 7:40 A.M. the dive bombers hurtled down on the airbases at Ford Island and nearby Hickham Field. Seconds later bombs were exploding on the two airfields and their buildings. Guns strafed parked aircraft. Bullets tore into hangars and airfield equipment.

At 7:53 A.M. the leader of this first wave broke the news to the task force that complete surprise had been achieved and that the attack had commenced. The torpedo planes sped down and, unimpeded, began slamming their specially modified torpedoes into carefully selected target ships. The torpedoes, released from as low as fifty feet, wreaked havoc on the battleships and cruisers. The air over the harbor filled with thick ballooning black smoke as the stricken vessels began burning furiously, some exploding in great flashes of flame and eruptions of disintegrating metal. On the ships, young men were being blasted to pieces and hurled high into the air—their bloodied and burned remains showering down onto nearby ships and into the water.

Then it was the high-level bombers' turn to add to the terrible carnage. Each carried one 800-kilogram armor-piercing bomb fashioned from a 16-inch naval shell. Despite the drifting smoke, the bombs were aimed at the U.S. ships with dreadful accuracy. The dive-bombers turned their attention to three other airfields, Wheeler, Haleiwa, and Ewa, all of which were heavily riddled with machine-gun fire.

At about this time the thirteen B-17s arrived over Hickham Field at the end of their fourteen-hour flight from California. Their reception was very different from that which had been expected.

By 8:30 A.M. the entire first wave was on its way back to the Japanese carriers two hundred miles away. Ten minutes later a second wave arrived, 167 planes intent on pounding Pearl Harbor into oblivion with torpedoes and those special bombs.

The Japanese planes finally departed at 10:00 A.M., leaving the ravaged ships, the harbor installations, and the protective airfields in a state of terrible ruin.

Japan's air losses amounted to thirty-nine planes, most of which had fallen victim to antiaircraft fire, while its naval losses included one heavy and five midget submarines. U.S. losses, on the other hand, were horrifying: 2,335 servicemen and sixty-eight civilians killed, 1,143 servicemen and thirty-five civilians seriously wounded. Eight battleships, three cruisers, and three destroyers were sunk, capsized, or heavily damaged; the battleships being *Arizona, Tennessee, Maryland, Nevada, West Virginia, Oklahoma, California,* and *Pennsylvania*. The U.S. Naval Air Force lost 80 planes and the Hawaiian Army Air Force lost 202 planes, mostly as a result of strafing action.

The Japanese task force, having recovered its two waves of planes, immediately set course for Japan. (Gordon W. Prange, *At Dawn We Slept* [New York: Viking Penguin, 1991], 499–550).

How was the attack on Pearl Harbor allowed to happen? How did Japan's task force manage to reach Hawaii without being detected? The armada was at sea for twelve days apparently without being suspected, let alone detected, and all the time occupying around one hundred square miles of ocean! Surely some hint of what was afoot must have been stumbled upon or elicited at some stage by someone, and, if so, why was this astounding knowledge not acted upon? This point and the question it raises are obviously of special interest to the author, for, as related herein, the cold fact of the matter is that he himself had indeed stumbled across far more than just a mere hint of what lay in store for Pearl Harbor and Malaya and had passed on, to presumed higher authority, all he had heard.

The fact remains that on that pleasant Sunday morning in Hawaii, Pearl Harbor and its unsuspecting servicemen and civilians paid the monstrous and unforgettable price for a lamentable lack of both vigilance and perceptive imagination.

Chapter 13. Hell Trains and Hospitals

1. **The sinking of Prince of Wales and Repulse, 10 December 1941:**

The battleship *Prince of Wales* and the battlecruiser *Repulse* arrived in Singapore on 2 December 1941, having been sent out on account of the mounting tension with Japan. Adm. Sir Thomas Phillips, Commander in Chief Eastern Fleet, along with Capt. J. C. Leach, flew his flag on *Prince of Wales* and in the late afternoon on 8 December took the two ships and an escort of four destroyers northwards up the east coast of Malaya, his idea being to strike at the Japanese transport ships known to be unloading troops at Singora on the southeastern coast of Siam. Admiral Phillips had already received information that the Japanese landings were being protected by at least one battleship, five cruisers, twenty destroyers, and a host of submarines. He had also been told that he could not rely on any air cover by RAF planes.

Late in the afternoon of 9 December, Japanese aircraft were sighted shadowing Admiral Phillips's ships. All chance of surprising the Japanese had clearly been lost, and Phillips turned back toward Singapore. The fleet had also been sighted by a Japanese submarine and torpedo-bombers were sent out from Saigon to attack but, failing to find the ships, returned to Saigon around midnight.

When the fleet was about three hundred miles from Singapore, it was sighted by Japanese search aircraft, which alerted the air-strike force already in the air consequent upon the receipt of signals sent from the Japanese submarine. Early in the morning of 10 December this strike force of thirty-five high-level bombers and fifty-one torpedo planes departed Saigon to attack Admiral Phillips's ships.

At 10:30 A.M. *Repulse*'s radar detected enemy planes approaching from the southwest and at 11:00 A.M. aircraft were seen coming in. The ships were relentlessly attacked with torpedoes and bombs, and by 1:20 P.M. both had gone down. Forty-nine officers, including Admiral Phillips and Captain Leach, and 893 ratings perished.

The two ships sank in relatively shallow water about twenty miles due east of Kuantan. It is said that, on calm days, they can easily be seen from the air—sad shadows lying there in the depths.

In this infinitely pitiable action, pathetic and memorable because of the virtual certainty of its outcome from the very start, the Japanese lost only three aircraft and their crews of about nine in total.

Deprived of air support, *Prince of Wales* and *Repulse* stood no chance whatsoever against Japan's torpedo planes, which, it should be pointed out, had flown almost seven hundred miles to attack the ships. (Kirby, *The War Against Japan,* 195–99; Vice Adm. Sir Geoffrey Layton, *London Gazette,* 26 February 1948, 1237–44.)

2. See chapter 11, note 1, "Japan's attack on Pearl Harbor."

3. Kirby, *The War Against Japan,* 201.

4. Ibid., 353.

Chapter 14. Slipping Away in Johore Bharu

1. Percival, *London Gazette,* 1295.

Chapter 15. Tragedy and Exodus

1. Kirby, *The War Against Japan,* 341, 375, 387.

2. Ibid., 398.

3. Percival, *London Gazette,* 1295.

4. The Japanese invaded Singapore Island in the late evening of 8 February 1942. Over the four days that followed, the Japanese advanced south and west in the face of fierce British and Australian opposition, the Australians especially putting up heroic resistance. Allied troop strength, under Lt. Gen. A. E. Percival, stood at well over one hundred thousand, while the Japanese strength was estimated at thirty thousand. It still seemed more than possible, therefore, for the defenders to counterattack and drive the enemy back into the Straits of Johore. But exhausted Allied troops, many lacking in training and fighting experience and unused to the intensely hot and humid weather conditions, gradually fell back in the direction of Singapore town.

   Gen. Archibald Wavell, Supreme Commander Far East and South West Pacific, flew by Catalina from his headquarters in Java to issue his strict order, which included, "The battle must be fought to the bitter end." General Percival, before passing this latter order to his own commanders, added the words, "It will be a lasting disgrace if we are defeated by an army of clever gangsters, many times inferior in numbers to our own."

   By the afternoon of 13 February, however, Singapore was in its death throes. General Percival ordered his commanders to continue the fight, although by this time it should have been obvious that there was nothing left to fight for. During the night a flotilla of small ships slipped away from the docks carrying three thousand selected military and civil government personnel. The rout was now on and very few of those left would succeed in getting away.

   On 14 February Percival received a message from the director general of civil defence stating that complete failure of the city's water supply was imminent. The governor of Singapore, Sir Shenton Thomas, explained that the danger of a disease epidemic, due to water shortage, was very real. Percival again demanded that his commanders continue the fight.

   At 4:00 P.M. Japanese tanks penetrated the west line of defense and drove to within one mile of the docks and Keppel Harbor. Prolonged air raids on the city in the late afternoon resulted in heavy civilian casualties. All civilian labor disappeared. The dead could not be buried; roads could not be cleared of debris; hospitals were full; and hotels were being used as first-aid posts.

At 9:30 A.M. on 15 February, Percival decided he had two choices. He could either counterattack or capitulate. His commanders unanimously supported the latter and, having received General Wavell's permission to use his discretion to discontinue resistance if he felt all was lost, he sent a joint military and civilian deputation to meet the Japanese at Bukit Timah.

At 1:00 P.M. the deputation returned to Singapore bearing instructions that General Percival should go to the Ford Factory at Bukit Timah to meet the Japanese. At 5:15 P.M. Percival was received by the commander of the Japanese 25th Army, Gen. Tomoyuki Yamashita, who demanded unconditional surrender of the British garrison. After almost one hour of turbulent discussion, Percival signed the terms of surrender at 6:10 P.M. (Kirby, *The War Against Japan,* 414–15.)

On his return to Singapore town Percival issued the orders required to implement the terms of surrender—in effect, that all resistance must cease at 8:30 P.M. The next day Japanese forces marched into the city.

In the defense of Singapore and Malaya almost 10,000 British and Allied troops lost their lives and 130,000 were taken prisoner. Civilian deaths were estimated at 5,000.

Thus ended the battle for Singapore and Malaya, a major battle that need never have been started had a *certain warning* been heeded by the British—and if Japanese troop transport ships had been driven away from the Malayan coast during the day of Sunday, 7 December 1941 (Malaya time), thus alerting and involving the United States. Japan would not only have withdrawn from its plan to invade Malaya but would almost certainly have shrunk from attacking Pearl Harbor. Japan's leaders were like a thug who aims to knife someone in the back: they were depending absolutely on total surprise. But, incredible as it may seem, that *certain warning,* somehow, somewhere, had been allowed to fall on stony ground.

Epilogue

1. See chapter 11, note 1, "The bombing of Sungei Patani."
2. *Baju kebaya*—a Malaysian traditional and attractive style of dress occasionally worn by younger women. It is usually colorful, figure-hugging, of ankle length, often having a high neckline and tight full-length sleeves.

Sources

Sources

In writing *Three Days to Pearl* I have endeavored to engage, inform, and intrigue a wide range of readers rather than present a detailed collection of facts and opinions such as would evoke interest, more or less exclusively, in the domain of assiduous historians of military history. Hence I have restricted the following list of sources to a relatively few publications in which readers will find information concerning the events and circumstances mentioned in this book. For the same reason I have deemed it inappropriate to include an extensive bibliography.

Published Works

Gilchrist, Sir Andrew. *Malaya 1941*. London: Robert Hale, 1992.

Innes, David J. *Beaufighters over Burma No. 27 Squadron, RAF, 1942–45*. Poole, England: Blandford Press, 1985.

Kirby, Maj. Gen. Woodburn S. *The Loss of Singapore*. Vol. 1 of *The War Against Japan*. London: HMSO, 1957.

Layton, Vice Adm. Sir Geoffrey. "Loss of H.M. Ships *Prince of Wales* and *Repulse*," *London Gazette*, 26 February 1948.

Percival, Lt. Gen. A. E. "Operations of Malaya Command, 8 Dec. 41–15 Feb. 42," *London Gazette*, 20 February 1948.

Prange, Gordon W. *At Dawn We Slept*. New York: Viking Penguin, 1991.

Shores, Christopher, and Brian Cull, with Yasuho Izawa. *Bloody Shambles*. London: Grub Street, 1992.

About the Author

Peter John Shepherd was born at Doncaster, England, in 1923. He received his early education at Doncaster Technical College and at the age of fifteen entered the Royal Air Force as an aircraft apprentice. His apprenticeship was shortened to just twenty months upon the outbreak of World War II. At eighteen he was transferred from Singapore to a night fighter squadron in Sungei Patani, Malaysia, where he sustained serious injuries during a Japanese bombing attack on the same morning as the attack on Pearl Harbor. After two years in the hospital, Mr. Shepherd was invalided out of the Royal Air Force in 1944.

Following these events, Mr. Shepherd pursued an engineering career at Manchester College of Technology while working as a draftsman for the Fairey Aviation Company. He gained recognition as a chartered engineer upon his election to membership of The Institution of Mechanical Engineers and followed his engineering career through to his retirement in 1988. Mr. Shepherd's interests include recreational flying, ultra high-speed boat design, and screenplay writing for cinema.